Plays from Contemporary Hungary

Plays from Contemporary Hungary: 'Difficult Women' and Resistant Dramatic Voices

Prah
Prime Location
Sunday Lunch
The Dead Man
The Bat

Edited by
SZILVI NARAY

LONDON • NEW YORK • OXFORD • NEW DELHI • SYDNEY

METHUEN DRAMA
Bloomsbury Publishing Plc
50 Bedford Square, London, WC1B 3DP, UK
1385 Broadway, New York, NY 10018, USA
29 Earlsfort Terrace, Dublin 2, Ireland

BLOOMSBURY, METHUEN DRAMA and the Methuen Drama logo are trademarks of
Bloomsbury Publishing Plc

First published in Great Britain 2024

Copyright © Szilvi Naray, 2024
Prah © György Spiró, 2004, translation © Szilvi Naray, 2024
Prime Location © György Spiró, 2011, translation © Szilvi Naray, 2024
Sunday Lunch © János Háy, 2010, translation © Szilvi Naray, 2024
The Dead Man © János Háy, 2016, translation © Szilvi Naray, 2024
The Bat © Krisztina Tóth, 2020, translation © Szilvi Naray, 2024

Szilvi Naray has asserted her right under the Copyright, Designs and Patents Act, 1988,
to be identified as editor and translator of this work.

Cover design by Ian Scullion

All rights reserved. No part of this publication may be reproduced or transmitted in any form or by any means, electronic or mechanical, including photocopying, recording, or any information storage or retrieval system, without prior permission in writing from the publishers.

Bloomsbury Publishing Plc does not have any control over, or responsibility for, any third-party websites referred to or in this book. All internet addresses given in this book were correct at the time of going to press. The author and publisher regret any inconvenience caused if addresses have changed or sites have ceased to exist, but can accept no responsibility for any such changes.

No rights in incidental music or songs contained in the work are hereby granted and performance rights for any performance/presentation whatsoever must be obtained from the respective copyright owners.

All rights whatsoever in this play are strictly reserved and application for performance etc. should be made before rehearsals by professionals and by amateurs to Casarotto Ramsay & Associates Ltd, 3rd Floor, 7 Savoy Court, London WC2R 0EX. Mail to: agents@casarotto.co.uk. No performance may be given unless a licence has been obtained.

A catalogue record for this book is available from the British Library.

A catalog record for this record is available from the Library of Congress.

ISBN: HB: 978-1-3503-7073-9
PB: 978-1-3503-7072-2
ePDF: 978-1-3503-7075-3
eBook: 978-1-3503-7074-6

Series: Methuen Drama Play Collections

Typeset by RefineCatch Limited, Bungay, Suffolk
Printed and bound in Great Britain

To find out more about our authors and books visit
www.bloomsbury.com and sign up for our newsletters.

To Leo and Melody

Contents

Introduction: 'Difficult Women' and Resistance 1
Playwrights' Biographies 7
The Plays 10
Prah by György Spiró 21
Prime Location by György Spiró 65
Sunday Lunch by János Háy 119
The Dead Man by János Háy 181
The Bat by Krisztina Tóth 213

Author Biography

Szilvi Naray (PhD) is a university lecturer, translator and theatre director.

She lectures in drama and translation studies at the University of Salford, England. She is the founder and artistic director of Ignition Stage, a Manchester-based theatre company which specializes in pioneering Eastern European plays in English translation. She publishes in the fields of literary translation with a special interest in feminist translation and has been critically acclaimed for her English world premiere productions of her translations. Her publication 'Goulash Socialism vs. Feminism? Beauvoir in Hungary' in *Translating Simone de Beauvoir's The Second Sex* is published in 2023.

Acknowledgements

I would like to thank Prof. Alan Williams, Prof. Ursula Hurley, Dr Helen Pleasance for their professional guidance and encouragement throughout this process as well as my graduate students Jessica Bradshaw and Charlie Hinkley for their script editing skills and enthusiastic support of the project. I would like to take this opportunity to thank all the 'difficult women', friends and colleagues who have inspired the angle on this book. Special acknowledgement goes to my daughter, Melody Davey, whose astute observations on drama and deep insights into 'difficult womanhood' have shaped my work.

Introduction: 'Difficult Women' and Resistance
By the editor/translator Szilvi Naray

The common thread that binds these five Hungarian contemporary plays together is that they all share a female protagonist who expresses her resistance through anti-social and destructive behaviour. Anti-social is to put it mildly as, out of the five leading female characters, two commit murder, another one is accused of attempted manslaughter, the fourth quasi-abandons her eldest child who gets in the way of her social climbing via a new marriage, and the fifth one demands that her husband burns his winning lottery ticket and therefore throws away the opportunity for her family to climb out of poverty. What also unites these mothers, carers and wives is that we meet them at their breaking point. In all five plays the women are faced with questions such as: success but at what cost? Or, what is the real cost of having an emancipated voice?

As a translator and theatre maker, what attracted me to translating and introducing these plays to the English-speaking world is precisely the fact that they all have 'difficult women' as protagonists. It is beyond the scope of this introduction to go into detail and into the genesis of the culturally accepted misogynistic term, so let it suffice to say that the leading female characters in this collection all challenge the status quo, make themselves heard, do not back down, are difficult to please and headstrong – to use vocabulary under a patriarchal lens. Yet, the semantic equivalent to describe a male would be the positive traits of ambitious, driven and discerning, perhaps. For the sake of this analysis, I will engage with and embrace Cheryl Strayed's definition, that saying difficult woman is 'really another way of saying female and brave enough to express the full range of one's humanity' (Karbo 2018).

I would suggest that this concept needs to be seen as a spectrum. These women all express or embody a different form of resistance and, hence, express rather differently the full range of their humanity in varied contexts. Jane Goodall's famous, 'It doesn't take much to be considered a difficult woman. That's why there are so many of us', is a sober reminder of how being on the full spectrum of humanity is still a threat to the patriarchal status quo.

So, indeed, they can be viewed as 'difficult' as they all refuse to conform – albeit to a different degree, but all actively resist and push back against the status quo, resisting victimhood to the best of their abilities and asserting their individualism through their often-anti-social actions.

Yet, the women and their actions are not judged, which is not the case for the women of today's Hungary. These female characters were born out of a society that often judges women; we only need to look at Hungary's family policies, which are built on traditional Christian values, to see that they only reward women who stick to their prescribed gender roles. The self-proclaimed non-liberal democracy's government policies have encouraged an atmosphere of judgement towards women who choose not to conform. Refreshingly the plays do not judge them: their environment does. All these female protagonists express their resistance through destructive behaviour. We happen to meet them when they crack, at a time when they express their different levels of resistance, albeit via destruction. This makes for good drama.

Another uber theme that engaged my interest in pioneering these plays is that they are all set in the dramatic milieu of the family. As such, I will show that the family unit in these plays can be seen as a microcosm for Hungarian contemporary society. Each play examines, albeit through different configurations, the idealized or archetypal family, and as a collection they offer various permutations of it. This is of particular interest because, as the title of this book tells us, I have chosen to represent works of playwrights who are also resisting today's anti liberal government, led by Viktor Orbán. I was drawn to these plays as their protagonists, like their creators, resist their environment, the status quo and, via their actions, question the established way of how things are. These playwrights have often been vilified by the Hungarian press as being part of the left-wing intelligentsia. They are demonised by the 90 per cent-government-owned media. These plays highlight the tension between the individual and the community in two ways. The women protagonists either embody an extreme form of capitalism or they actively resist these capitalist tropes and favour the values of Hungarian 'Goulash Socialism'. The 'difficult women' in these plays, in their various ways, resist the leading traditional heteronormative nuclear family structure, which in Hungary still encourages and casts women (whether child-free or not) in the roles of servile carers. These female protagonists either have been actively victimized by the patriarchy or have internalized its misogyny. All five plays have tragic endings often centred around a woman whose tragic blind spot leads her to these tragic endings.

A note on the Hungarian language

Hungarian is a 'hopelessly isolated language in the centre of a continent and hardly penetrable for anyone not born Hungarian' (Nagy 2000: 153).

Hungarian, being a non-Indo-European language and a Uralic language, has neutral pronouns so 'he' and 'she' are the same word. This degenderization creates a fascinating effect for Hungarian speakers as both genders are referred to by the same one word. Decoding the gender is dependent upon paying attention to the context. The very fact that the translator of Hungarian into English must clarify gender is an act of interpretation. Another linguistic challenge for the Hungarian to English translator is the moderate lack of specificity of time in Hungarian. Hungarian does not differentiate between the three different past tenses as English does (I did, I have been doing, I had been doing). Being an agglutinative language, Hungarian does not have prepositions; instead, all personal pronouns and conjugation suffixes come attached to the word, making the language a very efficient and powerfully blunt tool for dialogue-writing. Register is another challenge as Hungarian language does not contain the same class distinctions as English.

Before introducing the authors and their plays I believe that it is essential to gain a basic understanding of the overall political climate under which most of the plays were born, as this will shed light onto the nature of these resistant dramatic voices.

Political and historical context of the plays: the family as political weapon

Hungary has a history of politicizing and weaponizing families. Current and past governments have politicized the family by attempting to control women's reproductive functions. It may be of interest to know that, contrary to expectations, the socialist and the now reigning anti-liberal democracy share a common gender-centred ideology in which, under the false promise of equality, the state's 'generous childcare system and pronatalist financial incentives' are in fact capitalizing on women's reproductive labour.

Pronatalist family policies, even though often linked to right-wing politics due to their link with patriotism, believe in the narrative that having children is the natural duty of women and that motherhood is a patriotic obligation. Yet, during Hungary's dark-state socialist era, between 1953–6 there was an infamous ban on abortion. The Orbán government, in power since 2010, in return questioned the 'superiority of Western democratic models and envisioned a bright national future while criticizing the EU and the UN for their migration policies' (Bajnay 2022: 10). This administration has been advocating domestic population growth as the desirable alternative to immigration. 'Population growth has been connected to traditional gender roles and what Orbán calls "gender ideology" soon became public enemy No 1' (Bajnay 2022). Eva Fodor indeed confirms in her outstanding book, *The Gender Regime of Anti-Liberal Hungary*, that, 'The need for women's paid work has a long history in Hungary, as does the unequal division of household labour. Communist parties proclaimed their intention to socialize child and elderly care as well as domestic work' (Fodor 2022: 22). I would like to acknowledge that, unlike their Western counterparts, Hungarian mothers were not treated as a problematic workforce when they went on maternity leave as we know that, 'In Hungary, new mothers (and mothers only) could withdraw from paid work for up to three years upon childbirth and were guaranteed their jobs back upon return' (Ghodsee 2005 in Fodor 2022: 22). This is now oddly echoed by the Orbán regime's family protection laws, which actively encourage married and working couples to have more children. Parents with one or more children receive tax relief which increases with the number of children. The family housing system is the current government's star policy, as families can apply for the equivalent of EUR 2,400 in grants which do not need to be repaid if they spend it on a house and agree to have children. Another blatant incentive to benefit from women's labour in both senses of the word is personal income tax exemption for women with at least four children. 'This policy encourages women to take on roles as a parent and in their careers as it is only provided to women in formal labour, which does not change the wage gap between women and men which is still an issue in Hungary, as it has the fifth biggest wage gap amongst EU countries' (Bajnay 2022: 3).

Non-liberal democracy

Hungary's right-wing prime minister held a referendum on anti-LGBT law in 2021. This was in the wake of the Budapest Pride march held on 24 July 2021. A cursory internet search reveals a plethora of articles with titles such as 'EU urged to suspend funds to Hungary over "grave breaches of the rule of law"' 'Hungary fines bookshop chain over picture book depicting LGBT families' and 'EU launches legal action over LGBTQ+ rights in Hungary'. Andrea Pető, a professor in the department of gender studies at Budapest's Central European University, has said: 'While others have progressed [with women's representation in politics], Hungary has stayed in the same place or even got worse since 1990.' She adds that 'the country has ranked among the worst in a list of twenty-eight EU nations when it comes to gender equality'. Two years previously, Hungarian education came under attack as gender studies departments were forced to close in Hungarian universities. Maya Oppenheim, the women's correspondent from the *Independent* newspaper, a leading UK liberal daily publication, says 'Hungary's far-right prime minister has banned gender studies programmes at universities – with his deputy arguing the area of study is an ideology rather than a science' (Oppenheim 2018). This idea that gender studies is an ideology and therefore needs removing without any consultation from the universities is a threat to free speech and liberalism and may explain why de Beauvoir's *Second Sex* is out of print in Hungary.

Given Orbán's myopic and binary view of society, with his homophobic, transphobic and misogynistic policies, I believe it is more important than ever to translate plays that bring attention to women, their surroundings and their experience. These plays, analysed together, can offer a microcosmic view of today's Hungary. Given the reigning myopia regarding *otherness* it is in my interest to translate the works of resisting playwrights. Both these men, Spiró and Hày, have told me in an informal interview setting that they prefer to write female characters as they are both interested in 'The Other', in their case, 'The Female'. Overall, Hungary's literature scene is gender-divided, as drama seems to be dominated by men whereas poetry and prose by women.

Rationale

I wanted to choose plays that had entered the Hungarian dramatic canon as I hoped to represent the zeitgeist of modern Hungary. These plays were all written between 2004 and 2021 and have enjoyed some notoriety. The playwright trio, Spiró (born in 1946), Hày (born in 1960) and Tóth (born in 1967), are part of the Hungarian intelligentsia and have responded dramatically, often controversially, to the fragile new Hungarian democracy. These playwrights have clearly declared or stated to me that they are not being political, yet their astutely observed characterizations, set in a Hungarian domestic setting, cannot totally be seen as divorced from their modern Hungarian socio-political context. They are by their very existence critics of Hungarian society, which has been battling with serious social problems since the end of the Cold War. They all engage with Hungary's communist regime (1945–89). Andràs Forgàch rightly quotes Spiró's unapologetic view that theatre of that period in Eastern Europe became, 'to some extent, a cultic site, a veritable church in which one could procure symbolically packaged and emotionally unfalsified truths and, all being well, take part in a ceremony of purgation and purification' (Forgàch 2000: 12). Theatre practitioners, like other artists, will react to their environment via their creative practice. Hungarian theatre has been no exception by using metaphorical language to communicate to its audiences. The shared fate and restricted freedom of expressions that Hungarians have experienced has created a fertile ground for the emergence of subtext-heavy drama. As a result, a certain camaraderie – a wink to the audience – has evolved between Hungarian theatregoers and Hungarian contemporary playwrights. 'In the 1950's and the 1960's a complete system of political restrictions and ideological expectations was consolidated under the name "theatre coordination". Some artists, however, found an antidote to this. A kind of conspiracy developed between the performers on stage and their audience, a mutual understanding as a form of public protests against the ruling regime' (Szabó 2004: 13). Clearly, Hungarian audiences have been sensitized to read between the lines and to rightly see theatre as a place of reflection and not solely entertainment. Post-1989 theatre is still not free from political censorship: it is less overt, and also appears to involve a degree of self-censorship. Interestingly, since the end of the communist dictatorship state, funding has not ceased and 'despite several changes in financing methods, the state remains the single most dominant sponsor' (Szabó 2004: 14). The state funding and subsidies that keep the theatre companies afloat are not free of political involvement, of course. The governing party will indirectly but ultimately control which playwrights are produced. In this sense, I was particularly interested in Spiró's work as he is often seen as a controversial figure. He had to wait sixteen years before having his plays produced and his no-nonsense depiction of Hungarian lives has offended in the past, as Hungarian critical tradition is to interpret many texts politically. This has resulted in good writing being judged by political and not artistic criteria – which still prevails. He is often attacked by the Orbán government, and the right-wing press has always marginalized him. Spiró explains the trend in Hungary in his article 'Rettegés a drámától' ('A Shaking Fear from Drama'): 'It has become a widespread assumption in our country that the writer is not driven by the desire to characterize humanity but rather by his desire to develop and promote his/her own political ideology' (Spiró 2001 [my translation]). This is not surprising as Spiró is uncompromised; he is not in bed with/doesn't have allegiance to any political party. He told me in one of our interviews that two of his recent plays (*Prime Location*, trans. Naray-Davey (2012) and *Elsötétedés* (2002) (*Blackout*)) have attracted controversy. Spiró is, without doubt, a controversial literary figure. He started writing plays in 1962 but only started to be produced in 1978. A few of his plays were banned in the 1980s, namely *Hannibal* and *Balassi Menyhárt*. His play *Kálmár Béla*, which he also directed in the spring of 1980, was banned by the autumn. Another play, called *Árpádháza*, which he wrote after the changes in 1993, is not produced by the bigger theatres. Overall, many of his older plays are not played any more, according to Spiró, 'because producers don't dare to'. His big success *Csirkefej* (*Chickenhead*) 'is only produced outside of Hungary', he tells me. The two plays in this volume by Spiró have received much-polarized critical receptions. *Prah* (2004) became a commercial and critical success while *Prime Location* (2012) enjoyed a polemical three-week run and received damning reviews. Spiró tells me in our meeting that the reviews he receives for his writing vary in venom and in praise depending on who is in the government at that given time. The current trend seems to be to accuse him of being a 'traitor', accusing him of painting an unrealistically dark view of Hungary.

There is a new kind of censorship at work under the Orbán government. This has meant that new theatre companies are being formed by dissatisfied actors and directors wishing not to adhere to the government's idea of what people should see. The situation was dire in 2012 when, following the election of the right-wing Fidesz party, the mayor of Budapest sacked the director of Új Színház (the New Theatre), and appointed actor György Dörner in his place. Dörner supports the anti-Roma, anti-gay and antisemitic political party, Jobbik.

Jobbik and other extreme-right groups are campaigning and demonstrating against the Hungarian National Theatre, calling its work 'obscene, pornographic, gay, anti-national and anti-Hungarian'. The campaign against a liberal Hungarian theatre, open to the world, is part of a move in Hungary towards intolerance and democracy (http://www.theguardian.com/world/2012/jan/26/liberal-theatre-under-firehungary).

According to Spiró and Háy (source: informal conversation), state-funded theatre companies will be discouraged from producing playwrights whose stories and characters illuminate Hungary's severe social and economic problems. It is a strange situation: Orbán's strategy of attacking not only political opposition but also cultural opposition is frightening. The new media laws mean that insulting the 'spirit of the Hungarian nation' is now a crime. For theatre-makers this means making controversial work will become more and more difficult. Government funding has shifted to effectively cut out the avant-garde, but it was only just over twenty years ago when all the radical art was amateur anyway, with the communist state only funding what they liked. This is not surprising as Orbán, from Hungary's Fidesz party, has 'faced constant accusations of undemocratic tendencies throughout his term. Fidesz rewrote the constitution without consultation and has already amended it five times. The opposition say Fidesz have turned state media into government mouthpieces' (Jones 2014: 1).

Both Spiró and Háy told me in an interview context that their job was to observe. The observer who is a dramatist notices and then dramatizes his observations: 'I live in Hungary so my starting point of observation will be Hungary and its people', Hày tells me in an interview in 2013. These three authors create drama from what they know and can observe. These plays are not didactic as they do not preach or offer solutions. They act as mirrors, reflecting our humanities back to us, and hence possess a universal dramatic and humanist message that would contradict any didactic element. These authors were clear in emphasizing their non-didactic and non-political involvement as they are keenly aware that Hungarian theatre has a long history of being a platform for political debate. This, of course, has arisen from censorship during communism.

I have chosen to translate the plays of György Spiró, Jànos Hày and Krisztina Tóth as they all voice resistance via their dramatic voices, albeit very differently. Even though communism is gone, social problems are enormous in Hungary and Spiró's characters' dilemmas echo the real social problems of his country. The starting point for these playwrights is the family unit, which is a well-established dramatic setting, to explore the individual versus society themes. Whether they're represented by a nursery, a village, or an old people's care home, they are microcosmic of the greater contemporary Hungarian society from which they were born. Spiró's plays clearly remind us of Lukàcs's view that drama is conflict: 'Drama is the dialectic of colliding wills' (Lukàcs cited in Muller 2004: 5). Hày's characters often resist their environment, which is often the family unit, and he puts his overwhelmingly female protagonists in extreme situations where he explores the individual society paradigm with a particular talent in characterizing people living in bad faith. Tóth's resistance is a refusal to bow down to the binaries that her environment encourages her to do. Her astute characterization of bourgeois hypocrisies and sexist behaviours are developed through a feminist/feminine lens.

Playwrights' Biographies

György Spiró (b. 1946) is an eminent and prolific award-winning Hungarian novelist, playwright, essayist and translator with twenty-eight awards so far, including the prestigious Kossuth award in 2006 as well as the Hungarian Republic's special achievement award (2005) for his internationally recognized literary career. Most recently, in 2021, he was awarded the Hungarian Contemporary Dramatist award. His plays have been set texts in Hungary's high school literature curriculum. He has become one of the most prominent contemporary Hungarian literary figures, yet he has often been vilified by the right-wing Hungarian press as the '*artiste maudit*' of his native Hungary, due to his nonpartisan involvement with Hungarian politics. His plays are known for their straight-talking, harsh language, depicting the lives of ordinary Hungarians. His brutal depiction of disenfranchised youths in his play *Chickenhead* (1987) brought him recognition as a dramatist; dramaturg Zsuzsa Radnòti has described him as the Hungarian Edward Bond. His play *Blackout* (2005) deals with the dark theme of Hungary's antisemitic laws between the wars and has only recently been produced in a non-government-funded, independent small theatre in Budapest, creating controversy whilst winning a major award. *Prah* (2004) is one of his most frequently produced plays, having been translated and produced by other Central and Eastern European nations. Spiró's work, with the exception of a few plays and his colossal historical novel *Captivity* (2005), translated by Tim Wilkinson, has not been translated into English.

János Háy (b. 1960) is a popular novelist, short-story writer, poet, essayist and playwright. He is Hungary's leading commercially successful contemporary author, who is also critically acclaimed. *The Dead Man* (2016) won the Prize of the Theater Playwrights Guild in 2017. Its first performance was at the Szkéné Theater, directed by László Bérczes. He has many awards to his name including the Best Hungarian Drama award in 2002 and the Màrai Sándor award in 2009, the Gold Medal prize in 2013 and the Heidelberg Drama Festival Audience's award in 2005. It was the publication of *Gézagyerek* in 2004 that brought him notoriety as a dramatist. The collection contains four dramas and a short story. His latest novels (*Mélygarázs A Cégvezető, Házasságon Innen és Túl*) topped the bestseller list. It is hard to keep up with his publications as he is incredibly prolific and publishes about two books a year on average. Hày has had to overcome die-hard prejudice from his bourgeois and urban Budapest colleagues as he is from a rural background, born into a peasant family. He started out as a Russian teacher and faced many failed attempts to gain entry to university. Háy's literary career started in 1989, the year that Hungary broke with communism. His voice is fresh, dynamic and occasionally experimental. Hày's dramatic language is very particular as its playful exploitation of the Hungarian language brings a harshness to the dialogue, making it a challenge to reproduce in English and a challenging task for the translator. He achieved critical success with *A Gyerek*. His work to me is a mixture of Beckettian minimalism and circularity with a mixture of kitchen-sink realism. Hày, himself, describes his style as 'not writing from above but writing in parallel' (interview 2015). This, to Hày, translates as 'writing with love' for his characters. He describes his language as a 'special language that is very familiar and domestic in style while simultaneously nursing depth of meaning'. Hày, too, has not escaped some unfounded accusations from the right-wing conservative press. Just recently he received very harsh criticism for his novel *Mamika*, which was written from the point of view of a Roma older woman. Hày was accused of being racist as he wrote the whole novel in the Romani vernacular. The attacks were politically motivated – as all attacks on the liberal intelligentsia are politically motivated in Hungary. Hày's riposte was that he simply wrote a character, a fragment of his imagination; that he was interested in exploring this otherness.

Krisztina Tóth (b. 1967) is one of the most important voices in Hungary today. She began a brilliant literary career very early, and was first recognized as a poet when she was just twenty. She is the recipient of numerous awards. She studied sculpting and literature in Budapest and spent two years in Paris during her university years.

Krisztina Tóth has published almost forty books of prose, poetry, drama and children's stories. Her children's books treat topics that are considered unusual, even taboo, for example, or: *Mum had an Operation*, a story about cancer, and *Pig and Goose*, a successful series of children's tales. *The Girl Who Wouldn't Talk* was inspired by the story of her own adopted daughter. In 2015, her novel *Aquarium* featured on the shortlist of the German Internationale Literaturpreis. Her works have been translated into twenty languages and can be read in Arabic, Czech, English, Finnish, French, German, Polish, Spanish and Swedish, amongst others. In her review of *Pixel*, entitled 'The Hungarian Author who Foresaw the Future of Nationalism', Stephanie Newman writes, 'Tóth muses that generations of humans, like bobbing needles, are "seaming together the fraying layers of the past and the present". Their countries of origin don't matter; neither do their religions, genders, or ethnicities. What Tóth creates in *Pixel* is emblematic of Europe as she sees it: a place in which "everything is sewn together while the thread itself is invisible"' (Newman 2019: 1). Difficult relationships, manipulative characters, uncertainties, and life's harsh realities and strange twists of fates are common themes that Tóth has developed in her writing, whether expressed in poetry ('Whale Song'), drama (*Pokémon, The Bat*) or prose (*Pixel, Barcode*). Her latest novel, *The Monkey's Eyes*, was Hungary's best-selling work of fiction in 2022 and has rapidly become an indispensable work of contemporary literature. No stranger to controversy, Krisztina Tóth does not shy away from bringing to light the hypocrisies, mind games and the injustices she perceives in her society whilst painting grotesque portraits of her Central European homeland with a tinge of the region's dark and absurdist humour.

Attacks on Tóth

Following her remarks about a novel by Mór Jókai, Tóth was the target of numerous attacks, particularly from media close to the government of Viktor Orbán. Asked by a journalist to give her opinion on the list of compulsory readings for school curricula, Krisztina Tóth suggested that, if a book had to be removed from the school curricula, it would be *The Golden Man* (1872) by Mór Jókai because she was of the view that he depicted women characters as servile and docile, subjected to silent men who lead double lives. Krisztina Tóth expressed her view that this is an image contrary to that of the twenty-first century and that new more contemporary and relevant works should be added to the curriculum as these novels perpetuate gender stereotyping and offer a chauvinistic world view. This comment unleashed what can only be called a witch hunt against Tóth, who was brutally shamed on national television and received misogynistic and ageist abuse on live television – especially from a politician presenter who asked his audience why should they listen to an 'ageing saggy-breasted stupid woman about what we should read'. This was in parallel to an outpouring of hatred via social media and from people on the street.

The outpouring of hatred came from social networks as well as from members of the public on the streets of Budapest. Her mailbox was filled with dog faeces. The Hungarian press, which does not shine in its plurality and diversity, has accompanied this surge. In a government-owned TV station news programme, *Sajto klub*, four middle-aged men – pro-government journalists – shamelessly engaged in Krisztina's sexist and misogynistic character defamation. They systematically called her a 'misguided crazy woman', mocked her and aimed to convince their viewers that her motivation to speak her views was solely to get her fifteen minutes of fame. Their behaviour was patronizing with full intent to vilify her. They concluded their demonization by saying that she was not the only one with these ludicrous gender ideas and ended up talking about how women can absolutely serve hot soup to their husbands and have a career at the same time. From a liberal gaze, this retrograde, right-wing, openly chauvinistic, non-liberal and Christian rhetoric was offensive. Their final thought, after calling her names, was that she should just go back to writing and not express her stupid opinions on books. I must stress that we are talking about one of Hungary's most read and critically acclaimed authors, who has been translated into many languages. Krisztina Tóth explained to me that this is not just a unique and personal case, but rather a general position of the Hungarian press towards a certain type of intellectual and writer. Right-wing trolls even threatened her life and her daughter's to the extent that she had to move house and move her child to another school. In 2021 she had to go into exile to France for six months as l'École Supérieure de Lyon reacted swiftly by offering her accommodation and some work. This is deeply shocking as it highlights the cost of freedom of speech in today's Hungary. This censorship has led to a kind of self-censorship that is reminiscent of the communist regime.

Incidentally, Ms Tóth told me in an informal conversation that a prominent theatre director said that he would only produce/direct *The Bat* if she changed the ending and gave a concrete and neat ending. He wanted the audience to know whether our protagonist, our 'difficult woman', was guilty of pushing that child in front of the car or not. He did not like the author's ambiguous ending; he claimed that audiences needed the certainty. Tóth was not willing to compromise, and the play will not be produced by this theatre company now. She is the ultimate resisting voice. Due to this resistance she will no doubt be thought of as being a 'difficult woman'.

The Plays

The following plot-revealing introductions to these plays are written with a feminist lens. In this case, this will mean that I will primarily be paying attention and notice to the female characters' behaviours, and their consequences. I will notice when women act or don't, or when they speak and when they don't and how, by looking at the conflicts within the family unit in which these plays are set, we can gain insights into Hungarian contemporary society.

Prah by György Spiró

An impoverished and politically disillusioned couple from a small Hungarian town have a winning lottery ticket. The play dramatizes what the cost of winning will be. The couple conclude that this winning is problematic as the money has come too late for them and too early for their kids. Through a mixture of tragi-comedic scenes, the wife falls out with her husband as she realizes that his hypothetical spending spree has unveiled his real personality, by which she is disgusted. She fell in love with a poor man, she says. She is so appalled by how he will spend the money and how it will impact her family that she decides she wants none of it; she breaks up with him and lets him keep the lottery ticket. He realizes that he wants her and what they had and that the only way to get it back is to . . . yes . . . burn the winning lottery ticket! The winning forces them to ask themselves troubling questions about what they want and who they are. The narrative in *Prah* has often been interpreted as a metaphor that chronicles Hungary's communist past and the transition to capitalism with all its growing pains. Although I do agree with this microcosmic interpretation, I would like to bring attention to the female protagonist: a mother, a wife, a carer who can be seen as a 'difficult woman' as she is not afraid of expressing views that contradict the status quo and the traditional maternal instinct of providing. Her strong unwavering voice leads the play as it is her actions that are responsible for the cathartic ending. She is certainly brave enough to inhabit the full spectrum of her humanity.

She, in her long panic-stricken and humorous speeches, shares her fears to her husband about how this money 'came too early for the kids and too late for us', echoing some Hungarians' reluctance to embrace the new world order and free-market economy. In a tragi-comic rant she extrapolates on her conviction that this money will corrupt her teenage kids as they will become drug addicts and pimps, who will want to accumulate things without limits which will lead to their catastrophic downfall.

She is concerned that her husband will turn into a horrible person. Her line 'I fell in love with a poor man' may hit multiple nerves with Hungarian audiences as it, I would argue, is microcosmic of the generation that was already middle-aged when the regime changed.

The threat that this unearned money represents seems to echo a distrust of capitalist self-motivated gain. She sees the destruction of the lottery ticket as a valid choice in saving her family from the inevitable destruction that capitalist greed will engender.

The Woman, who is a wife, a former carer for her elderly father and a mother, basically feels lacking in agency, having had to compromise due to family duties and the regime difficulties. Yet this, on the surface, senseless act of destruction is the self-destructive action of the scared. The Woman in *Prah* is scared by the freedom that money would bring. She is very much like a caged animal who, when released from captivity, willingly goes back to its cage as the free world is too terrifying. The Woman sabotages her freedom in the same way: she goes back to the confinement of the kitchen walls as that is what she knows and has been conditioned to feel safe in. She wants them to burn the ticket as it is a vessel for a world that she does not see herself in. Her identity is so deeply rooted in her servile roles that she cannot conceive of a self that is not about serving others. The first things she wants to buy with the winnings are curtains and beds for her children, wanting to enhance her domestic environment. Her husband, on the other hand, talks about spending the money on cars and private jets, all thrilling experiences for himself, situated outside the home and benefiting only him. So, what we have here is possibly microcosmic of a segment of Hungarian society in the early 2000s as the Woman's action to turn her back on this non-honourably-earned money represents a rejection of profit money, the foundation of capitalism. The family is radicalized in a way as it turns itself against the status quo and, in the absurd act of burning money, the family rejects the values of its nation; the final dramatic tour de force of the burning lottery ticket on the dark stage could be interpreted as an idealization of poverty and/or a pessimistic view of Hungary's place, as the family is paralyzed by fear and inaction, in a free-market capitalist European Union.

The Woman's individualist choices are in resisting the state of affairs. She chooses to 'other' herself. It is as if the idea of compromising is out of the question for her. She can only conceive of what she knows, and that is her tragedy: that she fell in love with a poor man. The Woman keeps her nuclear family at the cost of economic gain which, ironically, would have saved her from servitude. If she had allowed her husband to cash in the winning lottery ticket, she would have had to engage with change which is clearly challenging. She would no longer have to clean for the rich Austrians, and she would be able to get help with her own household. She chooses poverty and that is her act of defiance. This time it is not inflicted on her; she is not occupying the victim status. This female protagonist has been brave enough to engage with the full spectrum of her humanity.

Prime Location by György Spiró

This play dramatizes a series of strange and uncomfortable events that are taking place in a care centre for the elderly. The dramatic force of the play is that we, the audience, are as incredulous as the characters but, unlike them, we see the tragedy unfold in the perfect location of 'The Woodland of Peace', as we witness the shocking scene of the elderly residents in their wheelchairs, manically trying to wheel themselves away from gunfire. Yes: they are being hunted. The puzzle is slowly put together by us, the audience, while the other characters are blind to the fact that the care centre is, in fact, killing off their residents to create places for the new arrivals. If it sounds brutal, it is; yet the play is also very humorous and hence its success. We are trapped into laughing at the absurdity of the characters' choices and actions. The characters are deprived of heroic status as they leave the stage unchanged; we the audience are faced with pondering why they did not see the signs of impending evil. Or, rather, did they choose not to see it as collaboration was easier? Are the elderly ... a burden? The play encourages us to reflect on the ethics of how society deals with the obsolete and non-profit making: the elderly.

Prime Location can be seen as the opposite side of the same coin as *Prah* as it dramatizes, via absurdist tropes, an extreme engagement with profit making. Our 'difficult woman' in this play is Miss Judith, who has embraced capitalism to its extreme and sees nothing wrong with playing with its rules despite its criminal and immoral outcome. She runs a care home, 'Prime Location', and provides a very sought-after service: the outsourcing of care for the elderly. Indeed, she gets rid of what capitalist society finds encumbering: the non-productive, the commercially obsolete: the elderly. Her individualism could be seen as the opposite of the Woman in *Prah* as she has actively freed herself from familial servile duties, playing against the caring roles women are prescribed. She is not maternal, she is not caring; she wants to be successful and plays the capitalist game to its extreme. She goes to the absurdist extreme and, under her management, the 'sweet oldies' who are wheeled out to the Woodland of Peace for fresh air never return. The useless, the obsolete, the non-productive must be recycled into the system. She feels no remorse; she is representative of an extreme form of brutal individualism. The dramatic setting of the elite care home, which is attached to a hotel that provides hunting holidays for wealthy foreigners, attracts the adult children of their elderly parents who hope to skip the waiting list and secure a place in this hyped-up care home with a surprisingly quick turnaround. The irony is that here the family is painted as a flawed, unloving and toxic institution where the elderly parents are burdening the productivity of their children. Miss Judith is a resistant dramatic voice as she is acting against the nurturing expectation of her sex. She is emblematic of the survivor who must adapt the best to survive. She is the future; she will survive because she can prioritize her interest over the interest of the community. This could also be interpreted as Hungary trying to survive at any rate and compete with the top dogs of the European Union. Her right-hand man and partner in crime is Mr Sneak, the voice of the old socialist regime, who reminisces in his speeches about how cleverly he was able to play that system, almost gloating about his adaptability. He worships Miss Judith and is learning from her about the new capitalist way (the free-market economy way). Miss Judith, herself, is very authoritarian and is a feared character. Dramatically, she is used as an omnipresent figure as other characters talk about her, show reverence to her and wait for her to show up throughout the first act. She would fit the 'difficult woman' label because she is unwavering in her voice and has no problem with forceful leadership, and for not apologizing for her success. On the 'difficult woman' spectrum, she is up there, because being a murderer is part of her humanity. A possible way to interpret *Prime Location* is to see it as an allegory for Nazi Hungary. The disappearance and eventual murder of old people uncomfortably resonates with the disappearance and mass murdering of Hungarian Jews. The Hungarian collaborators, without whom the tragedy could not have happened, are echoed by Mr Sneak, who does not ask questions but only follows orders.

Sunday Lunch by János Háy

This play follows the life of a family whose members live in a state of Sartrean bad faith. The artifice of the Sunday lunch ritual is what apparently holds them together. This is clearly expressed by the recurring 'powdered cream of parsnip sachet soup' motif that the mother serves every Sunday lunch, adding a bit of 'sour cream' to it. The bourgeois pretences and forced civility finally give way to the main character's realization of her flaws. The anti-heroine finally cracks at the family Christmas lunch: in a moment of lucidity and pain, she realizes that she has practically sacrificed her relationship with her now estranged adult son from her first marriage to remarry and move up the socio-economic ladder. In this case the difficult woman is paired with the bad mother trope. Our protagonist is resisting her role as a good girl and her values are set against her parents, who have chosen to live inauthentically and have stayed together for the sake of the family even though they clearly hate each other. The daughter refuses to adhere to the prescribed family unit if it does not serve her. She simply changes husband and does not dwell on the consequences of this new union with relation to her first-born son by her first husband. She is in pursuit of material gain but, in her case, this comes with sacrificing her relationship with her son. She denies her maternal instinct in order to climb the socio-economic ladder. She is an individualist in the sense that she chooses her actions for herself over the collective which, in this case, would be represented by the extended, reconstituted family that she does not allow to flourish. She marches to the sound of her own drum.

If the 'difficult woman' is a spectrum scale, then the protagonist named 'The Girl' of *Sunday Lunch* may sit in the middle of that scale. She is certainly brave enough not to be easily pleased, and will not accept her marginalized status as a divorced single mother – however short in duration. She swiftly remedies her 'divorced single mother' status by hiring the no-nonsense, practical-minded Matchmaker character who sets her up with her next husband. In her case, the expression of her humanity is also the expression of her tragic flaw, as her pursuit of the perfect family unit at any cost will result in a tragedy of her own making. Her tragic flaw, the playwright told me in an interview (April 2023), is that she suffers from an emotional deficit and is unable to relate to the world emotionally. Due to this lack of emotional approach, she instead fills that void with societal expectations which sublimely whisper to her that she mustn't be seen as difficult, that she isn't allowed to be seen as a person engaging with the full range of humanity because she is a mother, a wife and a daughter. Following societal expectations gives her a fake sense of connection to her world, an artificial sense of belonging. So, what motivates her is what conventions tell her she should do. She accepts and adheres to the expectation that, for a woman to be happy, she must have children and a successful husband: this is what she will want. To be a divorced single mother is not a traditionally societally advantageous position and so she needs to get to a position that is more acceptable to her society. The play is very much a critique of the capitalist market economy, which succeeds through creating desire for more new things. Materialistic culture can cleverly manipulate us by creating a false desire for things: we did not need a product until brilliant advertising created a desire in us for that product. This is what is echoed in The Girl's actions. Her desire, her goal, is to be married and start a new family – with a better husband this time around. This desire was artificially created and is shown through her interactions with her parents who shame her for being single. She has been brainwashed into thinking that this is the way to happiness: a better husband, a better house in a better location. She wants the construct, the unit, but she is not emotionally connected to that desire. As her relationships are not built on emotional connection but on cerebral decision-making towards a goal, she is able to make calculated decisions that will have serious repercussions for others, but mainly for her son. The play's dénouement and tragic ending is that she realizes too late that her life cannot be fulfilled without emotional connections and investments. Her breaking point is her own realization of her tragic flaw, which is that her life has been an emotional desert. We witness her cracking when she ragefully turns her inner anger onto the innocent and well-meaning unmarried uncle by accusing him of taking her son's seat at the Christmas table. It is easier to scapegoat him than face her own mistakes. This makes her live in bad faith and make decisions that lead to the loss of her relationship with her son who rejects her at Christmas. The bad mother is also a trope here, which makes this an uncomfortable play as the other main female character, her mother, has played along with what is expected of mothers: to stay married in an unhappy marriage for the sake of the child, so as not to disrupt the family unit. The play highlights that both women end up compromised as they cannot win in a patriarchal system that favours men. The Girl's mother, called The Mother, holds the family together every Sunday lunch and the powdered soup sachet is a brilliant metaphor for the artifice that acts as a social glue to keep the family together. Both generations of women are financially dependent on their husbands, as they seem to be unable to survive financially on their own, and the fear of the divorced label makes them stay and seek the safety net of the nuclear family and therefore accept their dependency. The men in the play are not trouble-free either as they also seem unable to escape living up to the societal expectations asking them to be the provider, the safety nets.

The Dead Man by János Háy

The Dead Man is a powerful wartime story about grief, absence and reinvention. Originally set in rural Hungary, the universality of the themes permits geographic relocation without affecting context (with the playwright's blessing). Annuska's husband, Jànos, has been captured and held as a prisoner of war in a foreign land. Annuska and her daughter, Anna, nervously await his return. However, when he returns in a coffin, life inevitably changes. Annuska is forced into a world of independence, becoming a landowner and managing the family farm alone. She strives to overcome the resistance of the village people who struggle to accept a woman in a position of power. Battling for acceptance, she discovers true emancipation as she moves into this new phase of her life. She no longer needs a man to feel complete and puts a close to the place in her heart where her husband once lived. She accepts that her old life is no more and chooses to live and thrive in the present. However, Anna lives in tormented denial, believing wholeheartedly that Jànos her daddy would not have died without telling her. She clings to the hope that he will return: the discordance from Annuska's perspective develops into a great source of tension between them. The two women represent two different ways of dealing with grief. Nonetheless, life goes on, and

Annuska thrives while Anna lingers in the past. The second half sees Annuska's newfound freedom challenged when a stranger is spotted in the village. Rumour rapidly spreads that it's Annuska's husband – they buried the wrong man. The rumours reach Annuska and Anna: Annuska is horrified; Anna elated. It is indeed Jànos, who has returned as a skeleton from being a prisoner of war – most likely with post-traumatic stress disorder. He moves back into the family home, expecting that nothing has changed and that they can return to family life. He expects sexual intimacy from his wife; it is the thought of her soft warm body that kept him alive after all. However, everything has changed for Annuska, and she struggles to return to her subservient former role. Going back to being a wife represents a huge step backwards for Annuska – for her, Jànos is still dead; he died for her, and she refuses to go back in time. Jànos, on the other hand, simply believes that they can go back to how they were. Anna, of course, is thrilled to have her family back. With growing tensions and nightly non-consensual sex, Annuska finds herself pushed closer and closer to the edge. She hides a carving knife underneath her pillow, intending to use it if Jànos once more forces himself on her during the night. That night, Jànos forces Annuska into sex but, pushed too far, she eventually reaches for the knife, repeatedly stabbing him to death.

By losing her husband, Annuska gains her freedom and realizes that she does not need a man to survive. She can work the land by herself and has enough support from a sorority of women. She creates a successful life without being subjugated.

Annuska in *The Dead Man* is further on the difficult woman scale than the 'Girl' as she fully pushes back the status quo by destroying the unit that her society values the most: the patriarch of the family. She kills her husband and deprives her daughter of her father. The tragedy is that Annuska does not tell her husband how she feels. She does not take the opportunity to communicate with him. She bottles it all and cracks. Once again, we meet the protagonist under huge pressure. She is part of that silent generation of women who were conditioned not to speak. She does not use her words and does not actually tell him that she does not want sex with him. She thinks she has no choice but to accept that it is her duty as a wife to have sex with her husband. We can ask ourselves the question whether it even occurs to her that she has agency, that she can speak and object to the nightly intercourse with the man who, for her, has died years ago. It seems that it cannot occur to her that she can express her own volition. There has been no precedent. Women have no voices and very few choices. She sees herself as her society sees her: as a wife, a second-rate citizen, and that role entraps her even more following her experience of emancipation and life without a husband. The village she lives in operates on that level. It functions well if everybody sticks to their roles, and they do but mostly live in bad faith. The priest is corrupt and a rapist; the men drink and cheat. The women silently accept their lot. Annuska chooses to kill her husband in a very violent and premeditated act. She could have, albeit with great difficulty, chosen to leave the marriage, but she chose to murder him as if to kill the part of her subservient self. She is responding to violence by violence. The nightly unwanted sex is obviously an act of aggression but so is her society's silencing of women. This murder can be seen as an act of rebellion at the institution of marriage as such, which I have mentioned is a revered institution in today's Hungary. Her only way not to be a subservient docile wife is to be a widow, which gives her freedom and emancipation. With her husband not coming back, she is unable to be anybody's wife. She can just be Annuska and not be defined by the patriarchal conjugal coupledom. She will not be confined to that narrow life engendered in 1940s rural Hungary. To murder her husband is to murder the chance of the reconciliation of the nuclear family unit. She has chosen to kill him as he was already dead for her. Janos Hày tells us in his notes to the play that this story is a metaphor for dead relationships.

'When I was writing, I thought of all the grief that comes from when a woman loses the person she had planned her life with because he either abandons her, comes home every six months or because he dies, and she has to adapt to the absence, and I thought of all the men who wanted to return from this abandonment and return to past reality as if no time had elapsed. I have thought of all the men and women who think they can just seamlessly re-enter another person's present and, like pigs before Christmas fasting, they will most likely be slaughtered down, unnoticed' (my translation).

This murder is an act of self-sabotage with devastating consequences for her daughter who will be orphaned as such. Annuska's actions make sense as she knows that, as a woman in 1940s Hungary, she will have no voice. Her ultimate act of destruction is perhaps a brave act as she refuses to be a victim any longer by ending the suffering herself; she takes control over her own fate. The story is symbolic on many levels, but the village is a symbol for community, and so a powerful theme is the individual versus community. Annuska is a 'difficult woman' in the sense that she expresses the full range of humanity by opting out on her own terms, by her own hand, and therefore escaping the victim narrative for herself. The stage directions after the murder scene tell us that the curtain rises to reveal a law court. The playwright told me it was not a necessary scene; however, it certainly echoes the inevitable judgement Annuska would have faced.

The family, like the village, is most likely a microcosmic representation of the wider Hungarian society: the village being patriarchal and hierarchical, functioning with strict, socially prescribed roles with no chance of social mobility. It is not dissimilar to a caste system where existence is predestined; there is no possibility of self-transformation for most, but for women even less. The killing is no doubt a futile act but is nevertheless authentic for Annuska. It is perhaps emblematic of the tragedy that can happen to the desperate generation of silent women who cannot articulate their trauma.

This play is undoubtedly a tragedy and my directorial eye was attracted to the symbolic representation of grief and how the mother and the daughter, a difficult woman in her embryonic stage, represent different ways of dealing with loss. As the work's creator told me, these two different ways can co-exist together in the same person. Beyond the attraction to her archetypal story, I was taken by the lack of sentimentality of the writing – which is very much the playwright's signature style.

The Bat by **Krisztina Tóth**

A rubber bat disappears from the school nursery, and this unleashes hate, blame and suspicion, and eventually leads to tragedy. Each apparently mundane domestic scene tackles with dark humour and absurdity the sexist attacks and demonization of the heroine, who is a working mother: an actress. We follow her descent into hell as she becomes obsessed with blaming a nouveau riche family for the toy's disappearance. The play is a grotesque portrayal of the traps that the Buda Hill bourgeoisie sets itself.

The 'difficult woman' in *The Bat* is accused of the serious crime of premeditated attempted manslaughter. We follow the downfall of another protagonist, The Mother, who is a well-known actress, a mother to a preschool-aged boy and who has recently separated from the boy's father, a barrister.

The play is trying to shed light onto how many roles women must compete in and the prejudices they must face and fight if they are successful or well known. The nursery stands as a microcosm for Hungarian society, as Krisztina herself told me: narrow-mindedness, envy, racism, class war and divisions. We end up not knowing whether The Mother is guilty or not; we remain in limbo. The Mother's own mother (The Voice) puts everything into perspective and never acknowledges her daughter's reality. When the daughter says that the nursery teacher is mean, her mother (The Voice) replies by saying that she, the teacher, is very nice to her. When the daughter is upset about not being cast, her mother calls her a forty-year-old when in fact she is thirty-eight. Whilst trying to soothe her daughter she is also guilty of minimizing everything and seems to represent an unchallenged bourgeois morality that does not question her unexamined gender roles, nor does it want to be engaged in progress. Her reluctance to not use the video Skype properly is emblematic of favouring the old ways by refusing to learn new ways of communicating. Her *raison d'être* seems to be to care for others and this revolves around cooking and feeding. The women in the play all act individually without any sorority between them. I would argue that is partly why The Mother loses herself in her paranoid fabrications. If she chose to communicate with, and even befriend, the nouveau riche, pink-jacketed mother from the school gate, instead of seeing her as the enemy, fuelling her snobbism and her blatant classist views, she would not end up in the vortex she creates for herself. Women do not help other women in this play and the consequences are tragic. We could almost borrow Middleton's *Women Beware Women* as a subtitle for this play. The Mother's only confidante is her own mother who represents aspects of her own self, of her internalized judgements. One could see this as her own voice attacking her and, dramatically speaking, it is rather uncanny that The Voice, that of her own mother's voice, is played by the same actor playing the protagonist – as well as the nursery teacher and the psychologist. Her own worse sides, her own internalized misogyny, racism, ageism and short-sightedness are given voice in 'The Voice'. The nursery teacher is a bully to the boy and is actively uncaring. As the nursery is microcosmic of wider Hungarian society, the uncaring nursery teacher is an interesting trope. The message perhaps communicated is: do not trust someone because their role seems trustworthy. As an interesting plot twist, we find out that the bully teacher is the sole carer for a seriously disabled son: she too is at breaking point. The council has not put a ramp in, so she has no other option but to carry her son to the metro. The psychologist, seemingly a healing trusted professional, isn't all that she appears to be either as she seems to engage with her duties as an apparatchik – yet paradoxically also flirts with The Father. She creates binaries and shames the parents for not living together. She, like the nursery teacher, is a female authoritative and judging figure and the voice of anti-liberalism. The unbroken nuclear family is also a theme as the protagonist and the father of her child are separated, which is shown to be a threat to society. The nursery teacher's snide remarks also represent society's views of a career-driven mother who is not tied to a man, yet we find out she is single too. The teacher is a very good example of internalized misogyny as she attributes the 'difficult women' characteristics to our protagonist and shames her for having a career and for being driven and self-assured. The irony here is that The Mother needs to outsource childcare to other women who are lower in the food chain as such. Class judgements and misogyny go both ways and the working-class characters are not exempt from it either; this constant like of solidarity, and attack on each other, symbolizes the grotesque Hungarian dog-eat-dog society Tóth is painting. The judgement that The Mother must deal with echoes what the author has had to contend with, as she too has been viciously shamed and attacked on numerous occasions for no other reason than for having a voice and using it. Our 'difficult woman' here, like the playwright, is ambitious, driven and challenges the status quo. The environment around The Mother is judgemental and punitive. A successful woman in a creative industry must prove herself more as she is not allowed to exist and embody the full range of her humanity. The Mother bravely pushes back and dares to express the full range of her humanity, but the cost is huge stress, emotional instability and obsessive behaviours.

At the end of the play, the audience find themselves in the same state of uncertainty and stress as the protagonist, The Mother. The audience, like the characters in the play, have lost their points of reference. Krisztina Tóth told me that she believes this happens when an authoritarian system promotes absurd values and makes them the norm, messing with people's inner compasses and leading to uncertainties and confusion. Who is guilty and who is the victim? Is the father without guilt? And are the others completely innocent? These are the questions we are left with.

The author's notes on multi-roling are of importance as it is a device to express the theme of the play which is that women multi-task and multi-role. The two mothers and the nursery teacher are all trying to stay afloat and make sense of their servile roles. The Mother is the only one questioning this servitude, but it comes at huge cost. The psychologist perhaps represents The Mother's guilt about breaking the nuclear family structure. The child psychologist is a reminder that the innocent child is the victim of the breakup. The clinical tone and judgement echo the teacher's and The Voice's (the protagonist's mother) views as they all stand in judgement of the broken family. The appointments are a painful reminder that, if the unit is broken, outsiders will need to be brought in to fix the damage, discouraging individualistic choices such as leaving the safe, nuclear family, bourgeois comforts that coupledom brings. Our protagonist, The Mother, is the only one actively resisting her gendered duty. Her self-fulfilment is not just linked to her being a mother; she actively seeks self-fulfilment through her creative professional role. The irony is that she can only do that by outsourcing childcare to either her own mother or the nursery teacher. She is an actress and that is another metaphor for women having to play roles, for having to embody artifice. The scene where she breaks down, as she was not cast as any of the *Three Sisters*, is a clear nod to the double standard that women are faced with regarding society's acceptance of the aged female body. When she finds out that she was not cast due to her age, it unravels her and the quasi breakdown that follows is a cry for help, a symbol of the unheard cry of all women victims of agism and therefore injustice.

I hope that this introduction has created an appetite for these plays. I have translated them with a performability criteria above all but have not wished to erase the foreignness of the text and have therefore engaged with a foreignizing translation strategy as well.

This has meant that the translations do not pretend to have been written in English; they are translations and, as such, they too offer a resistance to the domesticating trend that prevails, which can sometimes lead to the ethnic violation of the text (Venuti 1995) by erasing its foreignness in order to make it more digestible to the receiving culture. So, if we agree that translating equates to translating cultures (Nord 1997) then I hope I will have done justice to both source and target cultures.

References

Bánhegyi, M. (2012), 'Translation Shifts and Translator Strategies in the Hungarian Translation of Alice Munro's "Boys and Girls"', in *The Central European Journal of Canadian Studies*, vol. 8, 1, 89–102. Available online fhttp://hdl.handle.net/ 11222.digilib/125687 (accessed January 13 January 2022).

Fodor, E. (2022), *The Gender Regime of Anti-Liberal Hungary*, London: Palgrave Pivot. Available online: file:///C:/Users./end%20user/Documents/The%20Gender%20Regime%20of%20Anti%20-Liberal%20Hungary.pdf

Forgách, A. and Wilkinson, T. (trans.) (2004), 'Breaking Out', in P. Muller (ed.), *Collision*, 9–28, Budapest: Hungarian Theatre Museum and Institute.

Jones, T. (2014), 'Hungary's Political Theatre: New Government Targets Artists', *International State Crime Initiative*. Available online http://statecrime.org/hungarys-new-right-wing-government-targets-artists (accessed 17 May 2016).

Lukács, G. (1965), *The Sociology of Modern Drama*, Vermont: Green Mountain Editions.

Müller, P. (2004), 'Preface', in P. Müller (ed.), *Collision*, 5–6, Budapest: The Hungarian Theatre Museum and Institute.

Nagy, A. (2000), 'A Samovar is a Samovar: Hopes and Failures of the Author as the Object and Subject of Translation', in C. Upton (ed.), *Moving Target: Theatre Translation and Cultural Relocation*, 151–8, Manchester: St Jerome Publishing.

Newman, S. (2019), 'The Hungarian Author who Foresaw the Future of Nationalism', *Lithub. com*, 17 October. Available online: https://lithub.com/the-hungarian-author-who-foresaw-the-future-of-nationalism/ (accessed 13 April 2022).

Nord, C. (1997), *Translating as Purposeful Activity: Functionalist Approaches Explained*, Manchester: St Jerome.

Oppenheim, M. (2018), 'Hungarian Prime Minister Bans Gender Studies Programmes', *Independent*, 25 October. Available online: https://www.independent.co.uk/news/world/europe/hungary-bans-gender-studies-programmes-viktor-orban-central-european-university-budapest-a8 (accessed 13 March 2021).

Pető, Andrea (2019), 'Attack on Freedom of Education in Hungary: The Case of Gender Studies', *Engenderings* LSE Blog, 24 September 2019. Available online: http://blogs.lse.ac.uk/gender/2018/09/24/attack-on-freedom-of-education-in-hungary-thecase-of-gender-studies/

Radnóti, Z. and Rado, J. (trans.) (2004), 'Chronicler of Times: György Spiró', in P. Müller (ed.), *Collision*, 55–74, Budapest: Hungarian Theatre Museum and Institute.

Spiró, G. (2001), 'Rettegés a Drámától', *Spirogyorgy.lap.hu*. Available online: http://spirogyorgy.lap.hu/ (accessed 20 January 2022).

Szabó, I. (2004), 'How the System Works', in P. Fábri (ed.), *A Shabby Paradise: Contemporary Hungarian Theatre*, 13–16, Budapest: Hungarian Centre of the International Theatre Institute.

Tisdall, S. (2011), 'The EU's Hungary Headache and a Whiff of Double Standards', *Guardian*, 20 January. Available online: http://www.theguardian.com/commentisfree/2011/jan/20/hungary-eu-media-law (accessed 17 May 2016).

Venuti, L. (1995), *The Translator's Invisibility: A History of Translation* (2nd edn), Abingdon: Routledge.

Prah
A Comedy by György Spiró (2004)

Translated from the Hungarian by Szilvi Naray

Characters

One **Woman**
One **Man**

Hungarian Premiere, April 2007, Radnóti Theatre, Budapest

Day.

*A middle-aged **Woman** wearing a housedress is peeling potatoes at the kitchen table. She throws the peeled potatoes into a pot full of water. From stage right, coming from the garden's side, a middle-aged **Man** enters carrying a plastic bag.*

Man   Hi . . .

Woman (*looking up*)   What time is it?

Man   Around two, maybe half past.

Puts the plastic bag on the armchair, sits down onto the other kitchen stool, huffs.

Woman   I thought I got the time wrong . . . What's the matter, are you sick?

Man   No.

Woman   Did you get fired?

Man   No.

Woman   Did the company go out of business?

Man   No.

Woman   What then?

Man   Nothing . . . I just thought, I've done enough for the day . . .

Beat.

Woman   What do you mean 'enough'?

Man   Just enough of everything.

*The **Woman** gets up, fills a pot with water at the water fountain, and puts it on the stove.*

Woman (*standing*)   There aren't buses at this time. How did you get home? Did you get on the freight train?

Man   They got rid of them things again, takes the corner so slowly it almost stops . . .

Woman   How many times have I begged you not to do that!

Man   Alright, I don't usually, I only did it today . . .

Woman   What sort of example is that to show the kids?

Man   They won't find out . . . Nobody saw me. Do we have anything to drink?

Woman   Like what?

Man   I don't know, wine, beer, brandy . . .

Woman   We don't, no. What's wrong with you?

Man   Nothing.

Gets up, drinks from the tap

Woman (*not liking it*)   We do have glasses, you know!

Man (*sits back down*)   Look, . . . I need to talk about something . . . Sit down.

Woman   So, there is something wrong. (*Sits down.*)

Man (*voice trembling*)   Well the thing is I – I've been playing the lottery.

Woman   What?

Man   Well I get a ticket, tickets . . . and I fill them out . . .

Woman   Why?

Man   I don't know . . . just came up with the idea. I thought you can win tons of money.

Beat.

Woman   When did you start playing?

Man   Since the repayments . . .

Woman   For three years?!

Man   Well . . .

Woman   You've gone mad, must have caught rabies?

Man   Why, did you actually notice? Was there any less money for food? I've been living on bread and dripping for years.

Woman   With your cholesterol?

Man   I eat cholesterol-free dripping! Alright?!

Beat.

Woman   I'm speechless!

Man   Okay. It doesn't matter anymore, it's over now . . .

Woman   You take expensive pills, but you eat dripping.

Man   I'm telling you it's over! I'll never eat dripping again!

Woman   How much did you waste each month?

Man   Not much. Five or six thousand, but I saved it on my belly!

Woman   Why do I bother budgeting and being careful when you just –

Man   Okay, it doesn't matter now, I'll never do it again . . .

Woman   They should publicly display you somewhere.

Man   We, we won! We've hit the jackpot!

Beat.

All five numbers!

The **Man** *starts to cry. The* **Woman** *is staring.*

Beat.

The **Man** *sniffles, grins, jumps up, walks around.*

The draw is on Saturdays, it's on TV, too, but I never watched it. Wouldn't have been possible, the kids watch other things, and you too. Anyway it would have been suspicious . . . I usually check it on Mondays in town. I don't buy the newspaper, really, I just flick through it at the stand and give it back . . . they're used to it . . . But today I forgot, didn't realize it was Monday . . . because I was on my shift yesterday. Only realized at noon, and as today's paper was just lying about on the table, in front of the loo, next to the ashtray . . . I looked and . . . oh my God!

Beat.

Woman How much?

Man More than six hundred million forints!

Beat.

Woman It's usually double that.

Man Only if it rolls over! A while back someone won two billion . . . Isn't six hundred million enough?

Beat.

Woman Six hundred million!

Beat.

Show me!

Man I didn't bring it with me. I just saw the front page . . .

Woman The lottery ticket!

Man Oh, that!

Takes his wallet out from the inside pocket of his suit.

I've put it in the inside pocket here . . . I buttoned it up just in case . . . the other button is missing, just noticed. I've been holding to it so tightly my left arm's gone numb . . . even on the train with them smelly sacks . . .

Sniffs his suit, shakes his head, takes out the ticket from his wallet, puts it on the table, and flattens it out.

Woman Let me see it . . .

Man Not with wet hands!

She jumps up, dries her hand with a tea towel, looks for glasses, puts them on, sits back down, carefully holds the ticket, looks at it.

Woman   They give you six hundred million in exchange for this?

Man   Six hundred million, three hundred and forty thousand!

Woman   This shitty little thing is worth that much?

Man   Yep!

Woman   It's incredible . . .

Man   Why, money's also just paper, isn't it?

Woman   That's different, that's money.

Man   This is money, too.

Woman   Who's going to believe this is money?

Man   The bank people, them who hand it over . . .

The **Woman** *jumps up, sits down, and plays with her hair.*

I had just locked myself in the loo. They fixed the lock last week. I took out the ticket . . . I usually play the same numbers, on one of them I'd put down our birthdates, yours, mine, and the kids', and my father's . . . and it was the winning one . . . On this one!

Woman   Alright, don't get worked up. Not with your blood pressure!

Man (*huffs*)   And I felt dizzy suddenly, I was scared I might flush the ticket down the loo. . . . I put it in me wallet . . . lucky I bought this wallet . . .

Woman   A leather one.

Man   Yeah, leather! It's easier to fish out if I drop it in. I was standing in the cubicle, sweat dripping off me, my heart was thumping. Because if I drop it in, the writing rubs off and they don't accept it . . . I was laughing to myself: Is this really the moment to kick the bucket? A total heart attack, that's what I was feeling like . . . I put the seat down, I sat there for a while, taking deep breaths. I was afraid I wouldn't be able to unlock the toilet door and that no one would come for me, the space is too small up there, I won't be able to climb out, I'll die of hunger.

Beat.

I came out of the toilet, but I had to run back with a bout of diarrhoea . . . I then managed to sort meself out somehow. They saw I wasn't going to be doing any packing. They said go home, that I'll be able to do overtime. I was petrified the whole time that they would nick it out of me pocket . . . Now, of all times! I saw thieves everywhere. They must have thought I was drunk, swaying like that. You don't know what I went through!

Woman   Give money away in exchange for this piece of paper!

Man   We have to hide it . . . It would be shite luck if we got robbed just now . . . Where should I put it? Got to put it somewhere they won't find, where it won't burn if there's a fire . . . Bloody hell . . . I can't think straight . . .

Woman In the sugar pot, we never use it, it's empty . . .

Man It's no good, no. Someone could knock it down and the ticket'll get damaged.

Woman We'll wrap in cling film and hide it in the coffee box . . . We don't use it anyway, it's empty.

Man Okay, but we mustn't forget it's there . . .

The **Woman** *tears off some cling film and carefully wraps the ticket up. She gets the coffee box from the bottom drawer, opens it, smells it, puts the ticket in it, and puts it up on the shelf.*

Man Put it higher . . .

Woman Why?

Man Why not . . .

Short pause. The **Woman** *places it onto a higher shelf.*

Woman This alright for you?

Man That'll do.

Woman The kids'll notice it's somewhere else . . .

Man They don't drink coffee, why would they notice?

The **Woman** *sits back down, watches the coffee box in silence.*

It's good it looks so used. Where's it from?

Woman Poor Dad got it from Yugoslavia. In the seventies when he went there for a week with mum . . . It used to have cocoa in it . . . This is what he brought me back . . . I was the only one allowed to have some . . . It says cocoa on it, and Prah too . . . I asked him what Prah meant, but Daddy didn't know . . . Maybe cocoa powder? I've got rid of lots of stuff but not this, this . . .

Beat.

If they break in, they start with boxes like these . . .

Man No one ever breaks in here. Break in here! What would they find here?! Take the stove with the gas cylinder?

Beat.

Woman Are you sure you looked at it properly? Are they the right numbers?

Man I've checked them twenty times!

Woman They are this week's, right?

Man Nothing to do with weeks. It's the five-number lottery draw. We've got all the right numbers on that!

Woman No, I didn't mean that . . .

Man It is this week's! Look for yourself if you don't believe me!

*The **Woman** gets up and goes towards the shelf.*

Man   Check it on the telly. The numbers are listed on teletext, page eight hundred and seventy and eight hundred and seventy one . . .

Woman   Have you already looked?

Man   When could I have looked? I saw it in the newspaper . . .

*The **Woman** runs out of the kitchen stage left. Short pause.*

Woman   How do you turn this thing on?

*The **Man** gets up, exits stage left.*

Woman's Voice   What's going on, then?

Man's Voice   Wait, I'm turning the pages, this crap always goes back to the beginning . . . Not long now . . . Here it is . . .

Woman's Voice   Here are the numbers! Bring it here, bring it here!

Man's Voice   It's in the coffee box, we've just put it in there! Write down the numbers for yourself if you don't believe it. But I'm telling you – there are our birth dates . . .

Woman's Voice   Where are my glasses?

Man's Voice   You left them in the kitchen. Shall I get them?

Woman's Voice   No need . . .

*The **Woman** runs into the kitchen, takes the coffee box down, and carefully takes out the wrapped ticket. She unwraps it and looks at it.*

Woman   Oh God! It's true . . . !

Man (*comes into the kitchen*)   I'll put it back . . .

*The **Man** wraps up the ticket, puts it into the coffee box, closes the lid, puts it up onto the top shelf.*

Beat.

Woman (*sits down*)   We'll get new curtains.

Man   Why? There's nothing wrong with these.

Woman   And I'm getting rid of the bunk bed from the kids' room. Their feet have been hanging off it for years . . .

Man (*fidgets, runs with his feet*)   Hooray! Hooray!

Woman   You're going to break the lamp!

Man   I'm going to buy a hundred lamps, thousands, millions. I'm losing my mind. Lost my mind!

He is out of breath, sits back down.

Woman We'll go on holiday together!

Man What for?

Woman We've never been on holiday since having kids . . .

Man They went to summer camp.

Woman But never as a family. I went on holiday with my parents!

Man Because it used to be free, the co-operatives paid.

Woman It's been a big deal for me! We could never afford to go on holiday with the kids!

Man They went to summer camps . . .

Woman But never us together!

Man We will now.

Woman They're not small anymore! You can't bring that time back! That life!

Man We won't go then—

Woman Yes, we are going! You can take unpaid leave and we'll go for the whole summer!

Man There is no such thing as unpaid leave.

Woman Then you can resign.

Man Really? (*Beat. A little less enthusiastically.*) Yeah, I could resign.

Beat.

Woman We'll buy a villa on the Yugoslavian coast!

Man Yugoslavia doesn't even exist anymore!

Woman Never mind that! It will exist just for us! Under, what's his name, under Tito. Richard Burton and Elizabeth Taylor were given an island as a gift! On the Adriatic coast! From Tito! They got an entire island . . . We'll buy that island!

Man What island?

Woman Theirs! It was in one of those Yugoslavian war movies, fantastic one, really long, lots of dead bodies. I saw it as a kid . . . Burton was Tito and Taylor played his wife, you know the one that's fat in real life, what was her real name?

Man Alright, we'll buy something . . .

Woman Who is their heir?

Man What?

Woman Who is Burton and Taylor's heir? Did they have kids? I don't think so, actually.

Man I haven't got the faintest idea.

Woman They're not alive anymore . . . It could be that it's owned by the state then. But what state is that now? Bosnia, or Croatia?

Man It doesn't matter . . . You can't buy a whole island with this anyway . . .

Woman I would like it, though . . . Haven't you seen it?

Man We didn't have a TV.

Woman It was in the movies.

Man I haven't seen it. Well, I could ask actually.

Woman Ask what?

Man How much an island costs over there.

Woman Who can you ask?

Man Someone has to know. We'll go there and ask. Ask some kind of a lawyer . . .

Woman That costs money!

Man Like the island.

Beat.

Woman How much did you say it was?

Man Six hundred million! It's more than two Nobel prizes. One prize for you, one for me! (*Laughs.*) For having survived it! And it was survival! (*Short pause.*) That's what I was thinking on the toilet. If anyone deserves it, it's us . . . I've always had this feeling . . . When I started to play the lottery, I already suspected it . . . It was such an intuition . . . That it'll work out . . . That there is justice after all . . . This was predestined! It had to be like that! All that shit we had to put up with was meant to make us happier now!

Beat.

Woman That palace over there is worth eighty million . . .

Man We'll be able to buy seven of those with this. We can buy seven palaces!

Beat.

Woman But you'll also have to pay for the bodyguards, security cameras, for the help, everything . . .

Man We'll pay for it. We may just have to go down to six palaces instead of seven.

Woman Why do we need six palaces?

Man We don't, I'm just saying . . . real estate . . . is the safest investment, even if money turns into shit . . . It does happen. Or invest in gold? I don't know. We'll see.

Beat.

Woman If we put it into the bank, how much interest will it get?

Man I don't know . . . If you don't touch it for a year you get more . . . I used to have a savings account, that's how it was then. I'm sure it's the same now if you don't touch it for a year.

Woman Yes, but how much is the interest?

Man How much could it be now? Even if it's one per cent – and it has to be more than that – then it's six million a year!

Woman Six million per year.

Beat.

But how much more could it be?

Man How would I know? Just more.

Woman Could it be two per cent?

Man It could be.

Woman That would be twelve million forints per year?!

Man Yes, that would be . . .

Beat,

Woman Jesus Christ.

She is wiping her face and forehead.

Man No wonder I shat myself.

Beat.

Woman We have to ask!

Man I will ask.

Woman We could then buy a flat with just the interest. The one we looked at when we hoped to sell the house . . .

Man Okay, but it'd be too small now . . .

Woman It's not small, three rooms . . . two and a half. Balcony, telephone line, Sky TV . . .

Man It's not in a good location . . .

Woman Until now it was your dream place. It's close to the school, to the doctor's. You said it yourself that it was a good location.

Man But it's not good anymore . . . Was good enough for us then, but not anymore! No way. It's noisy! Close to the station. Actually it must have sold straightaway.

Woman No, it hasn't been sold. When I went to the cemetery to renew the rent on the grave, I saw in the window that it's still up for sale . . .

Beat.

Man It can't be that good if they haven't managed to sell it since then! (*Beat.*) On the train I decided I'm going to buy meself a helicopter. I'll fly it. You need a different kind of licence for that. And I'm buying the exact same Saab the boss had in Germany. I saw it once, it was silver . . .

Woman Let's put it somewhere else, up there is too obvious.

Man Put what?

Woman The coffee box.

Man You don't dare say 'lottery ticket,' do you?

Woman They could hear it . . .

Man Who? Evil ghosts?!

Beat

Where shall I put it, in the toilet?

Woman I don't know . . . under the bed . . .

Man That's where they look first.

Woman Oh my God . . .

Beat.

Man You won't have to do cleaning jobs.

Woman Why not? Don't knock it. It's good money.

Man You've got A Levels. I won't have you cleaning up after those cretinous Austrians.

Woman I earned more in two months than you did in a year.

Man Yeah, while I was cooking, cleaning, washing up, doing laundry, doing homework –

Woman Alright . . . anyway the Austrian job is unreliable. And I get taxed.

Man We'll go to restaurants.

Woman What for?

Man The rich eat out.

Woman You don't like my cooking?

Man Yes. But we can still go out. Are you going to cook if we go on holiday?

Woman We won't go on holidays.

Man Won't we?

Woman Why, if we have our own villa? We'll have one, won't we? If not an island, at least a villa on the Yugoslavian coast. We'll stay there the whole year. It'll be on the mains, and have plumbing. Look what happened here. We paid good money to be hooked up. They dug down five metres and disappeared. Twenty times we complained to the village council. And still nothing.

Man We'll buy one in Florida too. We have enough.

Woman That's miles away.

Man We'll rent it out when we are not there. Do you remember Ferko? You know the one who inherited from the States . . . that stocky guy, tool-maker . . . He was dealing with them investors, getting rounds for everybody, and six months later, had nothing left apart from his undies. (*He laughs.*) Well, we're not going to be losers like that!

Beat.

We'd need the holiday house to be somewhere else really, or not even a holiday house but a regular house, but not in Yugoslavia . . . The kids would need to learn a useful language . . . They need to learn English or German. That means moving somewhere for two years. They'll learn the language in a year and then we can send them to some posh school . . . Then off to university.

Woman Abroad?

Man Of course.

Beat.

Woman They'll forget Hungarian.

Man Of course not!

Woman And where are we going to be?

Man Well, there . . .

Woman We don't speak any foreign languages.

Man But money speaks!

Woman But if we needed something . . . We'd have to mime and gesticulate all over the place. How will I shop at the market?

Beat.

Man We've been meaning to sell the house and move to town, but it didn't sell – even though I repainted it. It's all because of this rotten mine. People get scared off as soon as they turn onto the road, they don't bother ringing the bell. I don't get the chance to explain that it's not a functioning one . . .

Woman There's no need to sell it now. We'll buy that flat in town. The doctor and chemist will be nearby . . . And if we wanted to, we could come out here too. We'll turn this into our holiday home. We'll renovate it . . . We've never done anything to it.

Beat.

Man When would we have had the time?!

Woman Dad didn't have time either; he still managed to add this conservatory. Granddad didn't have time either, but built it anyway . . . And we did nothing . . . Just ruined it . . .

Beat.

Man I wanted to when we thought we had the money! The council guy said you can't just wing it like that . . . That you'd need plans and permits and whatnot, because of it being a protected nature reserve or something! Here – next to a mine! (*Laughs.*) He wanted money or a job for his mate . . . You didn't want to go ahead with it!

Woman Because you hate it.

Man I don't hate it. It's just that I've never felt that it was ever my own.

Woman This is where I grew up. As shabby as it is, to me it's –

Man I married into wealth! (*Laughs.*) I've inherited an armchair.

Beat.

Woman We'll take it. Take the armchair with us. Poor dad was sitting on it when his . . . foot was already bandaged.

Man Yes, we'll take it. We'll take his nameplate too . . .

The **Woman** *bursts into tears, beat.*

Woman Dad sat here and just kept repeating the same thing: 'I'll slowly get used to being alive, so it will be strange.' He kept saying it . . .

Beat.

Man Alright, we won't sell the house, wouldn't get anything for it anyway. We'll have our own wing built . . . We'll have our own train, a private train driver. A private train driver . . . (*Laughs.*) I'll buy a hand-motored trolley.

Woman What?

Man A car that goes on rails . . . They used to have them in the olden days; you had to pull them by hand, with two stiff arms. It's only six kilometres.

Beat.

We'll have a two-person one. It works like a tandem. I can design it. There'll be two seats in the back . . . and a boot . . .

Woman Wouldn't we need a car instead?

Man (*joylessly*) Of course we would.

Beat.

Woman You'll take your test abroad . . . And get an international licence . . . It's valid here, right?

Beat.

Man I'll have a two-lane motorway built. Only six kilometres! They wrote somewhere that one kilometre's worth of motorway cost millions. The six hundred million will cover it, and no more worries. What else could we waste it on? (*Laughs.*)

Woman And what about the kids?

Beat.

Man Shall we tell them?

Woman Let's. It's theirs too, isn't it?

Man It's especially theirs . . . They'll have time to enjoy it . . . We'll sign them up for swimming, tennis, horse riding and golf . . .

Woman We're not nobility!

Man Of course we are. Prah or whatever it says with its three towers will be our crest . . .

Woman They're the towers of Zagreb, it says on it.

Man We'll be the Turkish-slaying victorious heroes, then. We can buy ourselves posh names. (*Laughs.*) Sir Whatever, and you, Dame Whatever.

Beat.

Woman They've already been spoiled rotten and now this . . . Their only interest is money, now it will get worse . . . Can I get this gear or that . . . high heels, fake nails . . . branded t-shirts, trainers ... Remember when we didn't get something for them, they threw a tantrum . . . It will be non-stop from now on . . . They are not interested in studying . . . They'll sit with a book if I yell at them long enough, but all they do is just stare outside . . . hang out, laze about, they're good for nothing.

Man They won't make it anyway. Even if they went to university or something. They know it too. They're redundant – we are too – the whole country is redundant . . .

Woman We'll live abroad and they'll get their luxury cars, and they'll crash one every week, we'll end up mending them . . . They'll be screwing around, going to prostitutes . . .

Man Don't say that, they're good kids!

Woman Because they don't have any money. But now they'll have some. They'll waste it on gambling . . . on drinking, drugs . . .

Man Why are you saying these things?

Beat.

You're destroying my will to live. Good timing!

Beat.

Should we keep it a secret? There's no way people won't notice that we have new curtains, new beds . . . That we bought a villa by the sea . . .

Beat.

Well, the truth actually is that I've already bought something . . . I borrowed from Joco. . . . It's ridiculously cheap now, it was on sale . . .

He gets up, goes to the breaded straw chair, and takes a box out of his plastic bag. He puts it on the table, sits down proudly.

Woman   A mobile? What do you need a mobile for?

Man   Just want to have one.

Woman   A mobile!

Man   Here's the phone number on the side. It'll need writing down; the box could be misplaced . . . The whole thing was ten thousand, but I bartered off three thousand so only cost seven thousand! I don't get why the kids are allowed it and not me? They'll be able to call me now!

Woman   They won't call you.

Man   Why not?

Woman   They've never called you.

Man   That's because we didn't have a phone!

Woman   They won't call us. No . . . They live in a different world . . .

Man   It's got a camera.

Woman   Have you lost your marbles! Borrow money for this?

Man   The batteries need charging . . . You've got to admit, it would've been handy to call the doctors with it.

Woman   You're overspending and I haven't bought as much as a skirt for myself! I bought one eleven years ago, eleven and a half years ago! I regretted it too!

Man   Why, have I ever bought something for myself?

Woman   The wallet for example. A leather one!

Man   Comes in handy now, doesn't it?

Woman   A wallet! Like you couldn't live without it. A wallet! You could have bought some shoes! I needed that skirt!

Man   You can buy yourself a thousand skirts! Ten thousand! We're rich, get it?

Beat.

Woman   What happens if someone else got it right? What if they've ticked the same numbers? Others could get it right. More than one person, actually . . . What happens if they have to share it out? How much would we get then?

Beat.

Man   That's almost impossible . . . We've got to check how many jackpot winners they have.

Runs out stage left.

*The **Woman** is looking at the coffee box; she goes to it, takes it down, looks around and puts it behind the gas cylinder in the corner, sits back down.*

Man's Voice   There's only one jackpot winner, only one. Come and see there's only one.

Runs into the kitchen.

Can you hear?

Woman   You sure you didn't win more?

Man   What?

Woman   You could have gone in and convinced them to say it was a smaller amount. So that I wouldn't have found out how much you've taken from it . . .

Man   You've gone barmy!

Woman   You kept quiet about your bonus too, we only found out by accident!

Man   Yes, because I wanted to buy you all a present! And it's not a bonus really, but an extra month's pay, because they were state owned!

Woman   Doesn't matter, you lied! And you didn't buy the present either!

Man   The bastards only paid ten out of the thirty days' that I was owed.

Woman   And what happened to that?!

Man   Who cares where a few hundred went when I just got six hundred million?!

Looks up at the shelf, frightened.

Where is it?

Woman   Somewhere else.

Man   What was wrong with over there?

Woman   It's already been there . . .

Man   Have you hidden it from me?! From me?!

Woman   I put it behind the cylinder . . .

*The **Man** hurries to it, crouches down, looks at it.*

Man   But when we swap cylinders . . . it won't be hidden anymore!

*The **Woman** goes to it, picks up the coffee box, exits left. The **Man** follows her, stands in the doorway.*

Where are you taking it?

Woman's Voice   I'll put it behind the telly . . . It's so crap that no one would steal it, they'd look at it and be repulsed by it.

Comes in, sits down.

Man   Lucky you didn't put it in the bed, which we'll get rid of . . .

The **Man** *exits the kitchen left. The* **Man** *looks after him.*

Woman   What are you doing exactly?

Man's Voice   Getting rid of the telly.

Woman   Why?

Man's Voice   Because it's a piece of crap. We'll get a big one, one of those flat ones, the ones you could hang on the wall!

Woman   The football won't look any better.

Man   I'll get cable TV set up. While we're still here I'll be able to watch foreign matches!

Woman   And won't the kids notice the new telly?

Pause, the **Man** *comes in empty handed, sits down at the table.*

Man   I'll get them a video player. DVD. Let them watch it.

Beat.

Woman   They'll be here in a minute and I'm not done! I haven't finished peeling the spuds!

Man (*looks at the clock*)   They won't be here yet, they'll have missed the bus. (*Laughs.*) Or they're already here and waiting.

Woman   What?

Man   They get a free ride on the freight train too. They might even be here already but laying low somewhere until the next bus gets in . . . (*Laughs.*)

Woman   Jesus Christ.

Man   Why, they're saving on the fare . . . They're not stupid. They think I don't know about it. I don't think they've ever bought a bus pass . . . (*Laughs.*) Leave it, I'll peel them!

Woman   No need, this'll do.

Gets up, pours the spuds into the pan, lights the gas stove.

They'll start fussing over my food. They'll end up scoffing all sorts of crap in town. They'll buy chocolate by the kilo . . .

Man   We don't have to give them a bigger allowance.

Woman   You're telling me? You're constantly slipping them extra money. Two hundred for this and a five hundred for that! They can't even drink water anymore, just some concoction that corrodes their teeth and guts!

Man Everybody else drinks that stuff; you can't always deny them everything . . .

Woman They've got mobiles! We can't even afford a landline and they've got mobiles!

Man We can't say no to everything!

Woman You tried to hide the fact that she was thieving. Did you actually think I wouldn't find out?! You and that teacher you paid off have swept it under the carpet . . . She was barely out of my womb that she was already stealing. My daughter! My father has never stolen a thing in his life, even though he wasn't allowed to get an education for being a kulak's son. They took his two poor acres of vineyard off him.

Man She hasn't stolen since! She got scared shitless and didn't go out partying for two months! She'll never do anything like this again! And there's no need to.

Woman We have a piece of paper. So what? And you too! You got yourself into debt right away! You didn't ask me!

*The **Man** sighs, starts to peel the spuds.*

*The **Woman** snatches the knife out of his hands.*

Woman That's not how you do it! You don't know how to do it thinly!

*The **Man** jumps up, moves away, and angrily walks up and down. Beat.*

Woman I've been brought up to be frugal! If it wasn't for me, we would've died of hunger!

Beat.

It's boiling already!

Beat.

Man Why, because I'll be squandering it all away! Oh, yes, I've always squandered everything away! I spent it on the races, women, and booze!

Woman You're not capable of saving! It's a fact. You can't!

Man Dear God!

Woman They'll turn into human rags. All they ever think of is money anyway, but now it won't stop . . . I didn't mean to hurt you . . .

Bursts into tears, pause.

Man It's from joy . . . Joy is like that . . .

Beat.

Woman They won't study anymore; they'll do less than now . . . If you threatened to beat them up they still wouldn't be bothered . . . They'll become trashy and rich . . . and won't give a shit about anything. They'll abandon us when we're old . . .

Beat.

They'll speak some posh language, and we won't be able to understand a bloody word . . . They'll be friends with all kinds of foreigners . . . whores and pimps . . . They'll be tricked and robbed behind their backs. They won't be able to see that they're only being loved for their money . . . they're just a pair of wretched, provincial little pricks who will all of a sudden get a taste of the world . . . Oh God, it'll be a disaster!

Beat.

They'll be involved with the Mafia, taken to casinos . . . They'll get robbed . . .

Man   They won't have money, because we won't give it to them! They'll get the same amount of pocket money as they do at home!

Woman   They'll hire assassins.

Man   Who?

Women   The kids.

Man   What for?

Woman   To get the rest of the money!

Man   They'll have us assassinated?

Woman   Who else?

Beat.

They'll wish us to hell. Why haven't they got it all?! Why are we so useless that they have to be missing out?! Why don't we own a ludicrously posh house in the town centre with a pool and tennis courts? Why aren't you a barrister and why am I not a dentist? Why aren't we rich?

Man   But we are rich!

Woman   We were given a lollipop every other week and we were happy! I was okay with one every other month! I went to the movies twice a year! It was a massive treat for us! Nothing is enough for them! A new Barbie doll, new earrings or trainers, this T-shirt, that T-shirt, a mobile! And they don't enjoy them after the first day.

Man   Hire killers?! I wouldn't have thought . . .

Woman   You'll see. Trust me, it will cross their minds.

Man   I wouldn't have thought that you had so much filth in your heart.

Beat.

Woman   You'll go to whores.

Man   Me?!

Woman   Aging, loaded bloke, with a nagging old wife . . . You're constantly checking women out. You do it in front of the newsagent's while I'm looking for change for the classifieds. You just stare at those pictures of women . . . You think I don't notice? You look at them sneakily from the side, cowardly, so I don't notice . . .

Do you think I can't guess what you go on about with your stupid mates when you're out at the pub?

Man They have four pints and I only have a half. I've always stopped at half pint, ask anyone! I'm not my mother! You didn't know her, but I did and I've seen her drunk far too often! If anyone is vaccinated against alcohol, it's me. I'm too scared to booze, that's why!

Woman You'll be in trouble when they find out you've got money. You'll want to be cool with your mates . . . Soften them up with money and drinks . . . The whores will zone in on you . . . You won't be able to resist!

Beat.

Man If I wanted to screw around, I could have done it . . . When you were in Austria . . .

Woman I wouldn't know what you were up to?! I wasn't at home!

Man I had my tongue hanging out, I was so desperate! I couldn't wait for you to get home!

Woman So that I'd cook.

Man Whores can cook too.

Woman Difference is you didn't have money then. If you had, they would have been cooking. One could have cooked a meatball soup, the other one a stuffed duck, the third one a pork roast. The second you think you've got money, you get in debt! You start buying mobiles!

Man How many, my sweetheart, how many?

Woman While I was away you bought yourself a dressing gown! That's the price of three dinners for the four of us, and you still had your old one!

Man Buying a dressing gown and going to a whorehouse is not the same thing!

Woman It is! You lose your sense of limits as soon as there isn't anyone looking after you! You too, all you ever think about is this rotten money again, just like your kids.

Man That's not fair, I haven't been to a game for ages!

Woman You said it's because they don't know how to play football.

Man It's not about the football. It's a social thing! I still don't go!

Woman You go out drinking with them!

Man I get job leads through them. Don't I? They always let me know if there is any work. Where would we be without them, eh? What do you have against them?

Woman You played the lottery, not me! It's you who wanted to win money, not me! It never mattered to me! I manage with nothing! I've never even played the lottery.

Man Does it bother you that we've won? We've won . . . six hundred million. Why is this a problem for you?

Woman Because it's dishonest! It's theft from the others who didn't win! Are you better than them? They're a miserable bunch too . . . You haven't worked for it!

Man As if you could earn with work alone!

Woman Why did you win it? It's not fair. My father would have deserved it too, he really would have done.

Her voice gets muffled.

Beat.

Man Your father didn't even play the lottery! How could he have won if he didn't even try?!

Beat.

I was the one giving him lifts when he had to be taken in! We never fought! Even when I was dead knackered I played cards with him, I played chess while I couldn't keep my eyes open . . . I changed his bag . . . You did more, but when I was home, I fed him as well at the end . . . Didn't I?

Woman Everybody abandoned him when he got sick, his friends, everyone . . . No one came to see him . . .

Man I didn't abandon him!

Woman You lived here. That helped.

Beat.

I bought you that dressing gown seventeen years ago! And you just go and buy a new one! Why? No one could see the worn out elbow! It was perfectly good for home! Didn't we have everything we needed? What else would you have wanted? I don't need anything! Why did you play the lottery, if it's not money you always think about?!

Beat. The **Man** *walks up and down, then sits down at the table.*

Man Because we have debts. That's why.

Woman I didn't make them.

Man Don't start again. Four more months only, four more to go!

Woman I've never gone into debt. I haven't even borrowed an egg, and flour only once. No, actually, twice.

Man I couldn't watch us struggle anymore, struggle with the kids! I told you a hundred times how it happened!

Woman You shouldn't have done it. An honest man doesn't do things like that.

Man They shut the factory down, didn't they? I had a good trade, a radio parts engineer used to bring in a reliable income, used to be fantastic trade to have! You couldn't predict what's happened. I applied to loads of places. I've been selling myself like a whore . . . Put on clean shirts, polished my shoes . . . I wasn't offered retraining either . . . 'You're too old for that,' they said. That's what they said fifteen years ago! I tried my own business, didn't I? We became partners in the clothes shop – the Chinese arrived. I slaved for that small dark Yugoslavian bloke – got himself shot over there. I became a school janitor – the school closed down. I was managing the sporting equipment – the club closed down. I dealt with bamboo roofs – the chalets took over. The moulding business worked best actually . . . I hated it but it paid well, you can't say it didn't pay well until the multinationals got their hands on it . . . Remember that scumbag, that twenty-year-old new manager, he wanted me to come up with five million forint to make sure I got orders . . . Right. Maybe I should have begged for it somehow, but I was still proud then . . . You, too – you said no way!

Woman Yes. No way.

Man Did I want to live on benefits?! I tried to learn computers, I got laughed at, and that I was too old . . . I went bag stuffing, with my back! I turned into a gypsy! The only thing I haven't done is dig a mortar. You weren't in demand either. You got fired too! God, I've had some shit jobs. And yes, the boss convinced me to accept my salary as a bonus. You get to keep a bigger net sum that way. He kept reassuring me it was completely legit . . . the accountant said so too . . . I know you've heard it a hundred times, but it's me who's speaking now!

Beat.

It wasn't just me who went for it! After paying the boss his fifty per cent, I still got twenty per cent more! Didn't I get more? I brought it all home! Others went for it too, even the smart-arses. How is it my fault that the boss fell out with the director? He obviously didn't give him as much as they agreed and the director got found out. That's why they looked into the books! If they hadn't fallen out, it would have never been found out! I've said it a hundred times that you couldn't have known in advance! So it's me who wasn't careful, me?! I wired the money to the boss via postal check. I didn't just put it into his pocket. I paid a lot extra for it to be delivered, but that scumbag judge didn't accept it because he was paid off by the company! I had to pay it back, no way round it, I did get it unlawfully. The judge said the check isn't proof because I could've won it on the lottery – that's where the idea came from! Until then I never thought of it, not even as a kid. I've never been hooked on the lottery like others . . . I didn't buy lollipops either, bought nothing! I'm glad I didn't sue, some did and they had to pay the suing fees too . . .

Woman An honest man doesn't do things like that.

Man If I hadn't received my salary like that, I would've lost my job!

Woman You lost it anyway!

Man But a year later! Everybody has to work the system! Your dad, too, worked the system and your granddad must have – if he got this house out of nothing! My parents worked the system too by the very fact that I was born! Everybody who is alive today – they all had to work the system in some way. The ones that didn't ended up not having kids, because they starved from hunger before they could.

Woman You were unemployed before and we survived it. Then you wouldn't have got into debt! But this way you worked for them for free! Benefits would have brought in more!

Man An honest man?! The honest man is born rich and has a good job . . .

Woman Did I ever bring it up against you? Have I ever blamed you? Didn't my relatives bail you out when you had to pay it back?

Man Alright, yeah, they did. Because I am so bloody broke, I don't even have relatives. I didn't even have a mother – she drank and then walked out on me before I was ten years old . . . I saved you from a mother-in-law! Oh, yes, you've got relatives, you have indeed. Your precious relatives who let us borrow with twenty per cent interest. (*Laughs.*)

Beat.

Woman What are you saying?

Man The truth.

Woman It's not true; they gave it interest free!

Man That's what they told you!

Woman You did too!

Man Because you would've had a wobbly and I wouldn't have been able to scrape it together from anywhere else!

Woman Who asked for twenty per cent? Who could've been such a shit?!

Man Who? Sanyi and Joli, of course. Who else?

Woman That's not true!

Man They would've been stupid not to lend without interest. Actually, they did reduce it, to be fair. You know how much Joli wanted, the little darling? Thirty per cent! (*He laughs.*) She dropped ten and Sanyi five . . .

Woman I'm going to kill them!

Man Won't make them give the interest back.

Woman What shits!

Beat.

Woman Did Uncle Laci want interest?

Man Nah . . . But he only gave a hundred thousand forints.

Woman   Sanyi and Joli. And after that they had the balls to come and stuff themselves on my food . . . If only you'd known about this . . If only . . .

Man   I paid back two-third of it after six months! Didn't I?

Woman   It wasn't that urgent.

Man   Really? If I hadn't worked the system, we would've had to sweat out eighty thousand a month for three years That's my whole net salary instead of thirty! But I'm knee-deep in shit, I know what to do.

Woman   I wish you hadn't done it.

Man   Hadn't done what? I got us the state's financial aid! That was completely legal! Financial help that you never have to pay back! They never check what you do with it! We've lived off it for two years! Anyway, they wouldn't bother checking whether we built a pigpen or a callous-removing cream factory with it, because we are in a period of overproduction. There is no fucking way that anyone is going to admit to that ever, so they don't bother checking . . . Anyway we've written evidence that we don't have to give it back. I've got the paperwork! The smart-arses won millions – compared to that we got pennies . . .

Woman   It shouldn't have happened. Those awful guys showing up . . .

Man   I warned you well in advance that they'll be back to get half of it. I have warned you. That was part of the deal! They could've awarded it to someone else. It was a blessing that they gave it to me. I made such a stink about it! And the other half was left for us. We've lived off it for two years!

Woman   I refuse to be put through this again, seeing them arrive with that big car. That bald bloke was the worst, the one who was joking and trying to be nice. He was patting the kids' heads and scratching that stupid cat's chin as she was whoring herself around and lying down on her back. I've hated her ever since. While the other two counted the money . . . That bloke was enjoying it! The two retarded morons were harmless, but the one trying to be nice . . . !

Man   I did warn you well in time that they would be back to collect it! I didn't go behind your back! I remember you saying, there isn't much we could do about it!

Woman   They were sitting here scoffing at my làngos! I took some out to the chauffeur, he couldn't believe his luck, didn't want to accept them – thought I'd poisoned the bloody things. Those two bold fuckers were sitting here at this table, counting the money . . . and I tell you this table has repulsed me ever since, even though dad played cards on it . . . Jesus, I never want to be that scared, ever again! I dream about them and their big black car and how he eventually bit into my làngos!

Man   I've told you: Dream something else!

Beat.

I've provided you with a good life, haven't I? Were we starving? We always had something around. We always had potato soup, and the kids always had sausage in theirs or something. Remember how they kept asking about the sausage bush and how long they were at the start? When I married you, remember I told you we're not going to have – we won't have a war between us. Was there a war? No, there was not! Did the kids starve? No, they did not! I also told you I had a good trade . . . And it was a good trade too! For years! Who could've guessed people don't need repairs done, because they just chuck everything out?

Beat.

Those men just did their job. They didn't take more than what was agreed. They could have shot me if they wanted to – These were honest Mafiosi because they worked for the Party and you have to be careful in those circles! Not like my boss and accountant and the judge, who were paid off by the multinationals! The corporations!

Woman I'll never forget the way you were sitting there while they were counting the money . . . Your mouth was twitching when they were counting what you'd already counted five times because you wanted to be sure it was spot on . . . Your face was all red . . . You were sweating . . . The back of your neck was soaking wet. Disgusting it was . . .

Beat.

Man Are you telling me that you've never been upset?

Woman It was my honour at stake!

Man I've stood by you, haven't I? I recommended getting a graphologist, didn't I? You didn't have a clue what that was!

Woman Well, anyone could have got confused! They were pointing at me, 'Look at the informer walking over there!' I'd no idea what was going on, and by the time I got there, they'd stopped . . . I thought they were jealous of my studying opportunity. When they called me in to that what's-its-name place, that office –

Man The People's Control Central Committee. PCCC.

Woman What does it matter?!

Beat.

They called me in, helped me with my coat . . . I thought it was regarding the Polytechnic . . . They sat me down and said that I should tell them in my own words what I'd written to them. I said I didn't write anything . . . Then, they put it in front of me . . . And there it was, my faked signature under an informer's report!

Beat.

Man You shouldn't have given up that education opportunity.

Woman How long did we have to wait to hear that it was not my writing? By that time, everybody thought I was an informer! How could I have gone to school?

Man You shouldn't have left school! By then we had the writing expert's opinion that it wasn't you who had signed it!

Woman   It was too late then.

Beat.

If I bump into someone, I still get stared at. I barely dare go into town! It's bloody shameful.

Beat.

Man   I've stood by you all the way through.

Woman   Every shopping trip was pure torture! It still is! Seventeen years ago it was and I still dread meeting people, in case they still think I'm an informer! How can I look them in the eye?

Beat.

Man   Why aren't you happy? It's so weird that you can't be happy! I'm sprinting home, jumping onto moving freight trains! Why go on about the past? Be happy, for God's sake!

Beat.

Tell you what . . . We'll pay off the drainage guys and they'll spray the whole courthouse with shit for us! They'll scaffold it so the roof can have some too! An overnight scaffolding job, and by morning shit will be pouring onto their heads!

Woman   What for?

Man   Why not?

Beat.

The drainers will get what they deserve too . . . Weren't you raving about how you have to tip them to get them to empty the drains when it's actually their cushy public sector job? I'll get the whole road covered in glue, with a ton of it when they're due to get here. Not here, further up . . . Let them crawl out of it (*Laughs.*), the fire brigade will have to pull them out!

Woman   I hope it's just your big mouth.

Man   We'll buy the mine!

Beat.

I wrote down the lorries' number plates and reported to the police about their dumping rubbish here . . .

Woman   You're not starting up on this one again are you?

Man   They've been emptying their bins in front of our eyes, completely illegally ever since! The cops said that was no proof, but I took photos with Sanyi's camera, didn't I? Shoved it under their noses. They said that it wasn't proof, that nowadays you can manipulate images . . . They said that it's the guard's job to report them. The guards never see anything; a lorry to them is like a tiny mouse . . . I went to the council after that. 'Move somewhere else.' That's all that arsehole could find to say,

'Move somewhere else.' He got paid off, too, or he's just being lazy . . . Lazy, actually – I went to the parliament's representative, I've asked for an appointment five times, he said of course he'll look into it, absolutely he will. He's been looking into ever since in fucking Brussels or wherever . . . Who knows what's killing us here . . . What kind of poison we've been breathing in for years . . . But if we buy it! We can afford to! Do you get it? We can afford to buy it with guards, garbage, and everything! I'll plant figs. I'll bring in earth and heaters, solar panels, wind energy . . . I'll have them dig a private quarry lake! Who needs the sea? A Hungarian sea, a privately owned Hungarian sea we'll have here! I'll have a sign made with big letters saying Dire Mere – do you get it? Diar-rhoea I'll charge an entry fee . . . We can have a nudist beach and everything! We'll be in the tourist guidebooks! We can buy the whole neighbourhood! We'll get everything cleaned up, all the way up to the stream.

Woman They'll dump it somewhere else.

Man Won't bother me.

Woman You'll leave me for a younger woman.

Beat.

Man We'll go halves. Three hundred million isn't that much . . . Not enough for a stunner . . .

Beat.

For fuck's sake, laugh!

The **Woman** *gets up and exits stage left.*

Man What's the matter with you?

The **Woman** *comes back, fussing with the coffee box.*

Man What's wrong with behind the telly?

Woman It's already been there, that's what's wrong . . .

Man What are you doing?

Woman (*puts it up onto the top shelf*) I want to see it.

The **Woman** *sits back, looks at the box, gets up, takes it down, and puts it on the lower shelf.*

Let's put it back to where it was. It's less suspicious there . . .

Beat.

We should do it quickly.

Man Do what?

Woman Get it cashed in.

Gets up, turns off the gas on the hob, sits back down.

Man What's going on now?

Woman The gas cylinder could blow up.

Man It's never blown up.

Woman I'm scared of cooking while it's here.

Man We'll eat raw spuds then. They ate raw potato skins in the war, my father told me. I'll get us horse meat – they ate that too, and we'll eat that raw as well. The kids will be happy with a bit of change.

Beat.

Woman Won't buy a villa actually. We can't do it.

Man Why? Why not?

Woman We won't buy anything. I read you're not supposed to go on a spending spree – can't do anything that stands out . . . I read that you've got to keep it in smaller amounts, in different accounts. And you've got to keep it moving – move the money between accounts. That's what they recommended – I read it . . . They'll break in, destroy everything . . . I daydreamed about winning, too . . . I spend so much time on my own at home . . . My mind is constantly wondering . . . It's awful . . . That's why I read lots, to stop this bloody daydreaming, but I can't help it!

Man What are you on about?

Beat.

Woman What did you say the interest will be on this?

Man We'll look into it . . .

Woman Just a year's interest is a fortune!

Man Of course.

Woman No . . . wait . . . Inflation is higher than the interest rate, right? We'll lose on it if we put it into the bank! We mustn't keep it in the bank!

Man Okay, we won't then!

Woman Where will we keep it?

Man We'll buy shares . . .

Woman No, we won't! We won't become capitalists!

Man If we have money, we will.

Woman We won't buy shares. I won't have you play the stock market . . .

Man It's not like the arcades – not that I go to the arcades, of course!

Woman It's still a no!

Man Alright, so I went there once. I just fired onto a screen, and it's not true that I lost two thousand, because it wasn't even five hundred – Ask anyone!

Beat.

Woman When do they give us the money?

Man When we want it.

Woman How do you get it?

Man We'll show up with a few lorries . . .

Woman It's that much money?

Man It's many floors high if they pile it up . . . We can hire some storage place . . . Or if you want we can buy a bunch of good mattresses, a few hundred to bury the money into them . . .

Woman Stop joking.

Man Do I ever joke?

Beat.

Woman So we'll have to deposit it . . .

Man Don't have to bother picking it up, they'd wire it straightaway. I'm sure they do that. We'll open an account.

Woman More than one then.

Man Yes. Lots. Six little accounts, with a few hundred thousand in each. (*Laughs. A beat.*)

Woman Where do we get it?

Man I don't know . . .

Woman We've got to let them know we're coming to get it.

Man There's a number at the newsagent's that you have to call if you win over twenty million forints. I used to stare at it sometimes, but didn't memorize it . . . Used to daydream we'd win twenty gazillion forints and I'd be ringing that number . . .

Woman Why didn't you get it today straightaway?!

Man Because I came running home with the news! I thought you'd be pleased.

Beat.

Woman Sometimes they can get it wrong . . . They print the numbers wrong. Man I've never heard of that.

Woman Yes, it does happen. You said it yourself that the Germans got something called, 'one winner.'

Man They don't make mistakes like that, either. They screen this live, they pull the numbers out in front of notaries . . . They would've corrected anything in two days!

Beat.

Woman   Did . . . did you play the lottery when you were there?!

Man   No.

Woman   Sure you did! One winner! How else would you know what it meant?! How much did you spend on gambling there?!

Man   Nothing at all.

Woman   You're lying.

Man   Ask anybody! Why don't you hire a detective, an expensive German one while you're at it. Go and look for the Pakistanis, Turks, and Arabs I lived with, they'll know for sure . . . You can buy yourself a translator . . . There was a Greek kid there who spoke Hungarian – they emigrated from here . . . I've got his address, but you can't make out the letters . . .

Beat.

Woman   How much time do you have until you have to claim it?

Man   A few months I think . . . But a few weeks for sure.

Woman   We'd better hurry then, because I can't stand staring at the coffee box . . . Listen . . . We'll ring them . . . You go and check that number, write it down, we'll ring . . . Then we'll throw away the mobile . . .

Man   What do you mean throw it away?!

Woman   Actually, a mobile is no good; we need to call from a phone box! I'm sure they'll see the number displayed or they'll track it and know right away that we're the winners – and they'll flood us with the media, and that'll be the end of us!

Man   What?

Woman   I bet you they'll pounce on us right away, we'd have barely put the phone down and the TV crews will be bugging us . . . They wait for the winners to call in and then they come out straightaway. They'll be able to locate you for sure! But the street phone's number is not good either. They can identify that too, street phones have numbers; they'll send their fingerprinting people out to take our fingerprints . . .

Man   So what? How will they know that it's mine?!

Woman   Can't call from the post office, either . . . They'll hear us . . . Someone is always eavesdropping – they got nothing better to do. Can't call from the town either, it's too close . . . Better to call from somewhere else . . . I got it; you'll go on a trip somewhere far away and call them from there . . .

Man   You watch too many cop shows.

Woman   Me? Are you sure? You're the one always watching shit cop shows. I am bloody fed up with them!

Beat.

The ticket's got a serial number. They can find out it's been sold here . . .

Man   That doesn't matter. Someone travelling could have bought it . . .

Woman   They'll ask the lady who she sold it to. She'll remember.

Man   It was a man.

Woman   If you've always bought it from him, he'll remember.

Man   Fine, I'll go in and wring his neck. They don't usually find murderers.

Woman   You haven't told anyone at work, have you?

Man   No, I haven't.

Woman   No one must find out! Nobody!

Man   I haven't told anybody. I was just relieved to have dragged myself home! I'll have to have the boys over sometime.

Woman   No, you won't!

Man   Relax, I can afford to, just on my wages alone.

Woman   But you have never done it before, and they'll start getting suspicious!

Man   Give over, will you!

Woman   It's no coincidence they tell you to keep it secret! They actually advise you to move house too! For a good reason! Because of all the past bad experiences! People who suddenly come into money, they often get murdered, right? The Mafia kill each other off too. They'll get rid of us too if they find out!

Man   Banks have such things as confidentiality rules. Bank confidentiality!

Woman   But one bloke will know, the one sitting at the other end of the phone line, the one picking up . . . At least one bloke will know! And that one is too many! He's there picking up so he can report it!

Man   Who says you've got to introduce yourself? You only need to discuss when you're coming and if you're opening a bank account with them.

Woman   They'll record and identify your voice.

Man   Where on earth is my voice on record?!

Woman   It will be from then on!

Man   I'll whisper then.

Woman   But when we show it to them . . . They'll need to ask for proof of identity. But even if they don't . . . Anyway, we'll be standing there in front of them and be bloody stared at –

Man   They won't ask for anything, just the ticket!

Woman   They'll copy our fingerprints from it!

Man For God's sakes!

Woman But our faces will be filmed by the security cameras! They're packed with surveillance cameras! They'll look at them, get our pictures from the Ministry of Interior Affairs, and they'll know straight away who won it!

Man Read my lips: 'Bank confidentiality!'

Woman They'll still have to inform the Inland Revenue, they report all larger bank accounts . . . That's how it's done, because of the Mafia. I read it.

Man But it's already the net amount!

Woman You still have to report it and we'll be showing up on their computers in no time! It's there for anybody to see!

Beat.

Man Why does it matter if a few bank employees know about it? They aren't allowed to give out personal data!

Woman If one or two blokes know about it, they'll sell the information for good money. Of course they'll rat us out, rat us out straight away, they will! They aren't allowed to give out personal data? What planet do you live on? And even if they're honest, by chance, still then . . . They can break the secret code and descend on us . . . blackmailing and threatening us . . .

Man Who? Who are they?!

Woman They'll kidnap the kids. Ask for a ransom, hundreds of thousands. They'll call every ten minutes to threaten us.

Man We don't even have a phone! They can't get hold of the mobile number . . . And they won't be able to beat it out of me because I haven't memorized it yet!

Woman In a letter then! Or they'll just show up at the gate with big black cars. Those shameless bastards. They'll kidnap the kids, cut their ears off first, then their pinkies, their noses, you'll have to remove them from the post box . . . No point telling the cops. They'd be in on it . . . They'll be tied together at the bottom of a hole, won't be fed, heads covered by some sack for weeks and months . . . Why did you have to play the lottery at all? You're really winding me up now . . . You always talk shit, such and such a mate or some dodgy business, and we always lose out at the end!

Beat.

Man People have been winning and they have always got their hands on it in secret! If you don't take it public, your name doesn't get published!

Woman How do you know? It could well be that none of them are alive! (*Short beat*)

Man That's crazy!

Woman Maybe no one has ever won, maybe they lied to the population, so that the winnings don't increase . . . Get it? . . . They've saved millions for the state . . . They probably got some bonus for it, it would make it worth their while . . . Have you ever seen anyone on TV, somebody who raked in a lot? Have you? Because I haven't. Because they never existed!

Man They didn't want to be bragging in public, it makes sense!

Woman The whole thing is a con. No one has ever won anything!

Man But we did win! Haven't you seen that they picked out our numbers?! *Beat.*

Woman They'll deny it. We don't have the money in our hands yet. We'll go there and they'll tell us we've forged it.

Man How could we have forged it? With what?

Woman With a copier they'll say.

Man Where do you see a copier here?

Woman They'll make one appear, lie and say your fingerprints were on it . . . If I can make these things up, why couldn't they?! They won't want to pay it, or they could say that it was last week's or last year's ticket! It's not last year's, is it?

Man No!

Woman They'll come up with something else then. Whatever. They'll deny it. They always deny everything. They'll say that somebody has already claimed it, and they paid the cash to them . . . Good luck in suing them. No point. They could also ask to check your winning ticket, disappear behind a door, and never reappear again. Meanwhile they'll politely ask us why we're standing there, are we by any chance about to rob the bank? . . . You'll have no time to realise you are already handcuffed. They'll find a hundred witnesses who'll testify to seeing you whipping out a gun . . . They'll manage to find the weapon. They'll do a house search and find the heroin that they'll have planted there themselves . . .

Beat.

Man You never used to be like this, so . . . evil! You never used to be like this!

Woman No, because until now I was poor . . . But now I'm rich! And you've got to think like that!

Beat.

Man Why only remember all the bad stuff? Why now? When everything will change. Our whole life will . . . How come you only remember the bad stuff?!

Woman That's what they're like though, aren't they? Like when your mate lied and said you were driving his car!

Man He was never a mate!

Woman Whatever, your colleague then. It was a massive speeding fine! You didn't even have a driver's licence! They weren't shits in your opinion? You went and told them that you don't even have a licence, they had actually taken it away and you never got it back because you didn't attend the course . . . You were a coward, got scared of not passing . . .

Man   There was no point; we'd just sold the car because we couldn't afford to run it!

Woman   Then they had the nerve to say that driving without a licence would be an extra hundred thousand forint fine . . . If I hadn't spent the whole night screaming under his window, they'd have made you pay one hundred and fifty thousand!

Man   Yes, and I had to do the begging to get you released from jail!

Woman   Doesn't matter, he shat himself and paid the fine! So, I remember only the bad stuff, do I? What else could I remember?!

Man   But I thought that we'd forgotten all this stuff ages ago! Really ages ago! Why choose to remember it now?

Beat.

We'll ask someone . . . give them a bit of dosh and they'll open the account . . .

Woman   Have you lost your mind? They'll walk off with the ticket! And actually we don't know how much we'll have to deposit in the bank . . . Almost the whole lot! They'd be idiots to give us all that money!

Beat.

Woman   Anyway, we need to get out of here . . . even if they give it to us.

Man   It's not exactly –

Woman   Not out of the house – get out of the country!

Man   Why would we have to do that?

Woman   Because everybody will be on our case! Everybody! Your mates, acquaintances, the whole country! How much did you say it was? Six hundred million?

Man   Six hundred and five million. (*Laughs.*) We could actually leave the five there, let them wipe their arses with it . . .

Woman   Won't leave anything. It's two years' good living money.

Man   Okay, we won't then.

Beat.

Woman   We'll be hunted down by everybody! We need to get out of here right away! Even if we don't want to!

Beat.

Man They won't find out. We'll live modestly. I'll keep working . . . Better to actually, I won't get bored . . .

Woman They'll still find out. They'll know the second I start throwing out the beds. We need to leave straight away! Remember how everybody started hating you when you got that bonus? You came crying to me that they didn't ask you to the pub!

Man I wasn't crying. It felt crap, that's all!

Woman How much did you get? Was it enough for a few rounds? And look, they got on your case!

Man Not great to leave just before their A Levels?

Woman They'll get them abroad. Like you said, in a useful language – (*Beat.*) I won't get anything for this shit house, anyway!

Man What do you mean, shit house? Your granddad built it!

Woman I despise it! My dad was unhappy here!

Man We lived here alright!

Woman We only went to the cinema once, just once in nineteen years!

Man When I was working abroad I had to sleep in sheds and hostels with some dodgy people around. They were times when I was the only white one! And that's worse than being a gypsy here. I was too scared to fall asleep. You were living in a hotel at least, only sharing with four! And what about when I cut my hand and it got infected and they wanted to amputate it from the wrist down? I didn't let the fuckers do it, did I? And what about when the ladder broke under me and I couldn't go to the doctor's because I was working illegally on the black market – and I was in pain for months every time I took a breath. Of course, I couldn't see a doctor, I didn't have health insurance.

Beat.

Woman You've no idea what it was like weeks and months on my own with the kids! I had to learn bloody maths so that I could check their homework! And I had to learn physics and chemistry! I almost failed my maths in grade 7 because by then I was already helping mum!

Man Don't you think I did exactly the same stuff when you were abroad!? *Beat.*

Woman Let me tell you, Sanyi will be the first one to send his bouncers on us. He'll claim that as family he'll be entitled to such and such an amount. Oh yes, the family! Joli will be crying her eyes out all day long, whinging about how many thousands and thousands she needs for building materials. She'll bring up all that business about her mum giving money to Dad for his crutches . . . She'll make us a scene, Joli. She asked for the crutches back! She wanted them back because she paid for them. She didn't even need them! My dad's crutches, for God's sakes! (*Cries*)

Man I thought he'd misplaced them . . .

Woman (*crying*) I had to give them back . . .

Man I am so lucky to have missed out on relatives!

Woman Why didn't my dad win it? He could've had his operation abroad . . . (*Cries.*)

Beat.

The school will ask for donations for the gym, the Attila statue and God-knows-what.

Man We can give a little. There'll be enough to go around.

Woman You'd waste the whole lot, wouldn't you?

Beat.

Man On the train coming home I was thinking, why me? There're plenty worse off than me . . . I see them in Budapest on the street, sleeping rough. We should give the whole lot to the homeless. (*Laughs.*) I was thinking that . . . Crazy stuff . . . I must be insane too . . . The whole lot! (*Laughs.*)

Woman You've lost the plot!

Man Alright, we won't give it to the homeless. Just a thought.

Woman How much would each one of them get, did you work that out?

Man No . . .

Woman How many homeless are there? Sixty thousand I think.

Man I don't know.

Woman Whatever, let's count with a hundred thousand. How much for each then?

Man (*counts for a while*) Six hundred forints.

Woman You see? Is it worth it?

Beat.

Man But I don't want to give it to them!

Woman It'd be enough for one meal. They make more with one day's begging. Actually, they wouldn't even get hold of that six hundred. You can't just go up to each and put it into their hands. You'd have to give it to some organisation for distribution. How much do you think will be left? They'll steal half of it or . . . three quarters of it. No, they'll steal almost the whole lot. Best-case-scenario is that each homeless person ends up with a hundred forint. Is that what you want?

Beat.

Man What about . . . kids with cancer?

Woman Oh, God no! They're a bunch of thieves, it was on telly. When they were collecting for their picnic trip, how much do you think was left, eh? Not even a tenth of it. They were fed bread with dripping and onions for two weeks and only twice a day. And they had three thousand for each day!

Beat.

Take it away. Hold it and take it away. I won't get any rest until it's here.

Beat.

I can't sleep with this crap being around.

Man   With what crap?

Woman   The coffee box.

Man   Put it under your pillow.

Woman   It would burn my neck.

Man   I'll put it under my pillow then.

Woman   It'd still burn my neck.

Beat.

We're now arseholes just like that bold tosser with earrings in his open-top car who wanted to run me over on the pedestrian crossing. He even returned to kick me in the back when I was trying to get up! Everyone just stared and laughed while I was trying to pick up the surviving eggs. They just stood there laughing. Jesus Christ, no one moved a finger to help!

Beat.

You'll have to get the same car and the same sunshades and shirt. You'll have to shave your hair off . . . You'll have to run over pedestrians at the crossings . . . Because if you don't, they'll figure out that you are not one of them. Course, they'll suss it out, you're a bastard like them. They'll always be able to push you around.

Man   That's not true!

Woman   You're a fathead, you are! A dawdling sloth. A big cowardly blabbermouth. A phoney. All you can think of is your spree. You could never grow up.

Man   That's why you fell in love with me.

Woman   They'll love you for your money from now on. I was the only one who didn't love you for your money. Your kids only loved you for the money they could milk you for.

Beat.

You should have won less. Like three hundred or six hundred thousand, an amount that they wouldn't want to take off you . . .

Man   Well, I'm so sorry it's too much. But even three hundred or six hundred thousand is too much. They broke into Jani's for only two thousand, beat up and crippled his mum . . .

Beat.

Woman   Let's give it back.

Man   What?

Woman   Take it back.

Man   To who?

Beat.

Woman   This came too late for us and too soon for the kids.

Man   Why would it have been any better twenty years ago when we got married? Or in twenty years' time when we won't be around? When is better?

Woman   Take it. I know that you want to steal the whole lot. Of course you do!

She takes the coffee box down, puts it on the table.

Here you are. The coffee box is yours. Prah.

Beat.

Man   Let's give it all to the kids, they can decide what to spend it on.

Woman   That's the perfect way to completely destroy them.

Man   Why, is being poor good for them? I can't look them in the eye, I'm so ashamed. They come home and what's for tea? Cabbage or potato soup . . . What did I, their dad, provide for them? I'm so embarrassed at parties, other kids smiling, running around, and ours just standing there broken . . .

Woman   It's been fine like that. They can learn how to fight in life. If they don't want to, then it's their business. If they want to steal, let them – that takes some effort too. But if they're rolling in it, they'll never fight for anything.

Beat.

Man   You're afraid that they'll grow up and leave you. But they're going to grow up and they'll leave the nest, they will. That's your problem, that's what's scaring you!

Woman   The whole thing is artificial . . . With you it's been like that for ages and same with them. The whole thing is a lie . . .

Man   What are you on about?

Beat.

What's hurting you is that I managed to do this! Yeah, that I got this for us on my own! I was the one who stuck with it. Yes, I stuck to it, me! I wasn't a loser after all, that's what's bothering you! My success gets to you!

Beat.

Woman   What do you get for it?

Man For what?

Woman For the money. You can't exchange the past. A big pile of misery is what it was. You can't take it back now. What's the point?

Beat.

Man We're not that old . . . We've got twenty good years left in us. A hundred thousand for each year! They won't let you die properly nowadays anyway. In top hospitals, they plug you into some tubes, you don't even have to bother chewing, and you get fed from underneath. (*Laughs.*) It won't be us waiting this time. It'll be a bunch of doctors waiting for us to hire them. And it'll be us telling them stuff. (*Laughs.*)

Woman (*shouting*) What do you want to say to them?

Man Whatever I feel like.

Woman What do you want to say? Tell me what! (*Cries.*) I hate it! I hate my whole life. You included! It was bearable until now . . . but now that you've become rich, (*Sobs.*) I can't bear it.

Beat.

Man But why? We were doing fine, you and I. Weren't we? We were okay. Don't ever say stuff like this . . . Why now? What's happening? What have I done?

Beat.

Woman (*calms down, wipes her tears*) Who will you hang out with when you're abroad? In what language? Who will you go to the pub with? You'll be lurking around ports, hunting for Hungarian mates. You're not the type to be alone and they'll fleece you, just as your mates do.

Man They don't and I won't hang out there then!

Woman You'll be clinging to me all day long. You'll stare at the telly and go crazy.

Beat.

My father died here . . . Where else can I feel at home after that? We'll have to watch all this from somewhere . . . You want me staring at them while they're washing up, cleaning up after me? They're slaves just like I was. (*Shivers.*)

Man I am sure you'll get used to it.

Woman I can just imagine you bossing them about, shouting.

Man (*shouting*) When have I ever shouted?

Beat.

It's you who wanted the Adriatic island!

Woman Of course I didn't! I'm not that daft. Take this crap away from me. I don't want it! You won it, so get out of here with it!

Man   Is this paper cursed? For God's sake! Is this some punishment, or what? How can you reject such luck? It's a sin.

Beat.

What about the kids?

Woman   I'll raise them myself.

Man   With what?

Woman   With cleaning jobs and child benefit . . . We'll manage. Take it then! It's yours! I don't want it!!

Beat.

Man (*stands up decisively, a short beat*)   Okay. I'll take it with me. I'll start a new life without you all. On the train I'd already imagined myself flying the helicopter, and you weren't on it. I was flying alone! You were nowhere to be seen! I saw myself landing with staff fussing over me and it was me bossing them about . . . That's what I've been seeing in my mind then and now. And I also saw that if only I hadn't let my father go out that day, he wouldn't have got knifed. I could've hidden his uniform, and he would still be alive today!

Woman   Go, now –

Man   Wonder what it would be like if my parents were together. They couldn't possibly drink more than what they drank . . . Just better booze, maybe.

Woman   How many times have you promised to fix the roof? But you were too scared to fall off it! Wouldn't let me call a specialist because you would always do it. You're a cowardly loser!

Man   I painted it on my own!

Woman   But it was me on the ladder. You get vertigo!

Man   I had knee troubles at the time!

Woman   Be brave just for once in your life. You've got money for it . . . Go, go!

Man   I AM GOING!

Goes to the wicker chair and picks up a bag.

What can I take with me?

Woman   Anything

He is a bit aimless.

Did you buy any yeast?

Man   What?

Woman   Yeast. I asked you this morning.

Man   I forgot.

Beat.

Woman And bring the telly back in. It's too heavy for me.

Man In here?

Woman In the room, of course!

Man I never took it out!

Woman Yes, you did. You threw it out.

Man Only talked about doing it!

Beat.

He goes to the table, picks up the coffee box. Stands there.

If I wire you some money from it, you will use it, right?

Beat.

Look, you do with it what you want, I won't get involved. You can spend it on what you want . . . just let me stay . . . If you could put up with me all this time, why not now? You said, when you went nuts that time and took off, that you came back because you'd got used to me . . . You didn't mention the kids' smell, but mine! So how come you're used to it now?! It doesn't work like that!

Woman Take it to hell!

Beat.

Man I'll leave the box here. Prah . . .

Woman Okay.

Beat.

I'll take the bathrobe, the old one . . .

Beat.

Let's wait for the kids, see what they say . . .

Woman Will you go now?

Beat.

The **Man** *opens the box, unwraps the ticket, puts it on the table, and sits down. They look at the ticket.*

Man Where will I sleep tonight?

Woman Go get the money and get a room . . .

Man They don't give it to you so quickly!

Woman I have seven thousand in my purse. Take it.

Beat.

Man Why do you want to get rid of me? What have I done?! I was allowed to live here until now. Why am I not allowed to anymore?!

Beat.

Woman You can't pity a rich man.

Beat.

Man Let's burn it. Let's burn this crap. If we burn it, can I stay?

Beat.

*The **Man** gets up, gets the matches from the cooker, goes back to the table, sits down.*

I'm lighting it. Shall I light it?

Beat.

Woman Could we just keep a little bit of it? Not much, just enough to get a tombstone for Dad . . .

Man It's not possible.

Beat.

You seem to like your dad a bit more now.

Beat.

Woman You'll take the mobile phone back.

Man I won't take it back.

Woman You won't have enough money to use it anyway.

Man I'll put it on my bedside table and admire its beauty!

Beat.

Man I'll light it. Shall I light it?

Woman Not at the table! By the sink!

*They get up. The **Woman** is holding the ticket, the **Man** the match, they're walking to the sink.*

Beat.

Man We'll regret this. It'll drive us mad right after we do it.

Woman Doesn't matter.

Beat.

Man Oh God, make them catch AIDS, cancer, bird flu. Have bailiffs descend on them – have their electricity cut off – make them eat fat dripping morning day and night. Don't let them enjoy a good footie game ever again – contaminate their water – let their balls rot off – make them go blind – take away their paid holidays – bury them alive – make their guts, ball sacks, and feet blow up – let terrorists kill them –

bury them in a hole up to their necks – make them get diarrhoea and give them constipation at the same time – take their driving licences away – let their mother tongue die out – don't let them sleep . . . If I had money, I'd buy a machine gun and shoot, shoot, shoot!

Beat.

I am going to light it.

Woman Light it.

The **Man** *lights the match. The* **Woman** *holds the ticket, which catches fire. Darkness, with only the burning ticket. The flames slowly die out. Darkness.*

The End

Prime Location
A Comedy by György Spiró (2011)

Translated from the Hungarian by Szilvi Naray

Characters

Mr Sneak
Miss Judith
Husband
Wife
Woman
Mother
Daughter
Old Man
Three Men (Beaters and Turks)
Three Women (Turks, Old ladies)

Hungarian Premiere, 12 October, 2012, Pesti Theatre, Budapest

Scene One

Trees, bushes, bulrushes are being blown by the wind. Three men enter from stage left dressed in hunting clothes. They stand.

[Translator's note: **Beater 2** *speaks German;* **Beater 3** *speaks Russian. The Russian words are phonetically spelled.]*

Beater 1 (*reads from a notebook*)   High aim?

Beater 2   Die Kanzel.

Beater 1   And what else?

Beater 2   Der Hochstand.

Beater 1   High aim?

Beater 3   La Bazz. Vurshka.

Beater 1   Hunting ground?

Beater 2   Der Jadgbezirk.

Beater 3   Ur gordyer. Paulyer ahortu.

Beater 1   Woodland of Peace?

Beater 2   Die remise.

Beater 1   Woodland of Peace?

Beater 3   I don't know. Not on my notes.

Beater 1   Doesn't matter. Prey?

Beater 2   Die Beute.

Beater 3   Der bee-oocha.

Beater 1   Hunting horn?

Beater 2   Das Horn

Beater 3   Valtorna.

Beater 1   What?

Beater 3   I've got Valtorna.

Beater 1   Really? Strange. Sure it isn't Faltorna?

Beater 3   It's Valtorna. What is Faltorna? It is Valtorna. The accent is on the long o.
Beater 1   Don't mind me. Beaters' Drive?

Beater 2   Die Laufjagd. Die Kreisjagd. Die Triebjagd. Die Streifagjd. Die Streifhetze.

Beater 1   Beaters' Drive.

68   Prime Location

Beater 3   Ahorta Zagorn.

Beater 1   Beater?

Beater 2   Der Treiber. Der Hetzer. Der Kaiser.

Beater 1   Beater?

Beater 3   I don't have anything like that written down.

Beater 1   If you don't have it, you don't have it.

They exit stage right. The trees, bushes, bulrushes disappear.

Scene Two

OFFICE. Desk with a computer screen on it, keyboard, and files. A leather swivelling chair behind it. **Husband**, **Wife**, *and* **Mr Sneak** *enter.*

Sneak   Please wait here. Miss Judith will arrive shortly.

Wife   Isn't she called Mary?

Sneak   That was the one before, ma'am. Miss Judith has been the new boss for six months now.

Husband   We would have come before but no one ever mentioned anything.

Sneak   Well, then there was nothing wrong. Don't you worry nothing about it. Please wait here.

Usually people wait in the dining hall, but they're getting ready for tonight's party, cleaning, setting up tables, and all that stuff. When Miss Judith gets here she'll give you the entry permits.

Husband   To where?

Sneak   To them, little oldies.

Husband   You never needed a permit before.

Sneak   Well, you need one now. With so many overnight guests staying, they could wander in. Or the little oldies could walk out, which would not look good.

Husband   They're not locked up, are they?

Sneak   We are sensitive to their resting needs. And that is why you can't just visit as you please. You've got to book yourself in first, and Miss Judith will sort you out with an appointment.

Wife   We had no idea about any of this!

Sneak   It's no problem, we're flexible. I'm just telling you for next time. You can still go in now. Miss Judith is very understanding like that. No worries about going in this time, as you didn't know. She'll allow me to open the ward as I've got them keys. But next time, book by email and Miss Judith will write back with a slot.

Wife They're not allowed in the garden.

Sneak Of course they are, when it's scheduled in they can. The ones that can't walk get pushed out . . . we roll them out. 'Mr Sneak, will you roll me out, please?' And then I go and roll them out. I've got time, me, so I roll them out into the garden. Mr Sneak, that's me, that's what I go by. I used to be Snape but became Sneak . . . It was before I got this job here. I am the opposite actually. Always speak my mind, me, say it as it is. They just won't believe me. (*Laughs.*)

Husband You used be able to park right by the gate. Can't believe that they had the nerve to put a security-gated, paying parking lot in the middle of nowhere!

Sneak It's the new development.

Husband And what are all these Russian and German four-by-fours doing here? Who are these people?

Sneak They're the hunting holiday adventure guests.

Husband What do you mean by hunting holiday?

Sneak The one over here. In the west wing of the castle.

Husband The bit that's been renovated?

Sneak Yes, building new business is the only way. The council had run out of money, they got them overdrafts fees, can't be too much, but still . . . it meant they couldn't have got them zero tax returns, which they would need for the grant application . . . Then the finance manager showed up and made it clear what you can spend the money on. It wasn't the mayor or the committee, you see . . . So that's when Mary left, the boss before, and we came on the scene, because they wanted to recruit Miss Judith.

Husband Excuse me? Can you clarify this for me? Are you saying that they took the main castle section away from the residential home and then piled the old people on top of each other in the ancient bit that was left in ruins?

Sneak Even like this, there's plenty of space for our little oldies. We get a lot of interest; we've a good reputation, you see. It's not in such a bad state inside. Next year, we'll be replacing the ventilation system . . .

Wife How many share a room?

Sneak It depends, ma'am. You'll see for yourself, when you visit your lovely old man. It is your old man, if I'm not mistaken. You did say it before, am I right?

Wife My father.

Sneak Lovely old man then.

Doorbell rings.

Sneak Excuse me, I've got to go. Please wait here . . . Don't sit in this chair. Miss Judith don't like it. I'll bring you some chairs.

He leaves.

Scene Three

SILENCE.

Wife Jesus Christ, I told you we should have come before!

Husband Relax, there is nothing wrong with him. They didn't contact us. And he didn't call, either.

Wife He can't 'do' mobiles.

Husband He could use it. We've taught him. But he never picked up when you called!

Wife No reception, or it got stolen.

Husband We'll buy him a new one.

Wife It'll get stolen too.

Husband We'll chain it to his wrist.

Wife We should have visited. We never come!

Husband We're here now, aren't we? He was perfectly well last time.

Wife They built an entire hotel since then.

Husband They renovated a wing. What's the big deal? It was done in three weeks. No shortage of manpower . . . the building sites are deserted.

Pause.

Wife They've moved him to another room, to a shared ward. We should arrange for him to be . . .

Husband We will.

SILENCE. **Husband** *walks to the back of the stage.*

Husband The garden is still beautiful. A bit on the wild side now, but still beautiful.

Wife *also walks to the back.*

Wife I can't see anyone around.

Husband Quiet time.

Wife In the morning? They won't let them out during the day.

Husband Of course they do. He said so earlier. They roll them out.

Wife We'll have to pay him off, this Mr Sneak guy.

Husband Okay, we will.

Wife And what if they moved him to the top floor? He can't walk down by himself. I'm not sure they've got a lift here . . .

Husband Then they'll bring him down. It's their job. No big deal – we'll just slip the nurses a backhander. Everybody will get slipped one, whether they want it or not.

SILENCE. **Husband** *sits down on* **Miss Judith***'s chair.*

Wife Don't sit there, we've been told not to.

Husband You must be joking?

Stays sitting, turning, swivelling on the chair.

Wife They'll take revenge on Daddy!

Husband Of course not! (*Swivels.*) They'll have been paid off. It's not my fault that there are no chairs here. I'm not going to be standing around for hours.

Scene Four

A **Woman** *and* **Mr Sneak** *enter. The latter is carrying three folding chairs used for hunting under his arm.*

Woman Good morning.

Wife Good morning.

Sneak I've brought three chairs. One has one leg . . . You get used to it.

SILENCE. **Husband** *gets up in silence.* **Mr Sneak** *puts down two chairs and pulls open a three legged camping chair.*

Sneak They're willing to sit on this for hours. I couldn't do it.

Sneak *opens another three-legged one, puts it down. He plants the one-legged one down, sits on it, loses his balance, laughs.*

Sneak Out there they quickly disappear into the ground, 'cause it's too powdery. So you have to move it somewhere else from time to time . . . and where the ground is hard, it feels like you've swallowed a pole.

Gets up. To the women

Sneak Miss Judith is on her way. She must be at the tailor's because of them costumes. They love the folkloric stuff and Gypsy music. This is a Gypsy-free area, so you need to bring them in from elsewhere.

Husband Gypsy music?

Sneak For the feast. They love it.

Husband What feast?

Sneak For the hunters. You've got to include everything in the package, otherwise they won't come. The in-laws will snatch them off us otherwise. Are you with me? The Austrians.

Husband Aren't the Gypsies too loud?

Sneak They're loud, alright, sir.

Husband   Can you hear them in the old people's home?

Sneak   The ones who aren't deaf. They love it too.

Wife   All his life my father hated Gyspy music.

Sneak   We only book them good bands.

Wife   It makes him want to slash his wrists. He hates it.

Sneak   I'm sure he got to like it. They're lovely, our little oldies.

Husband   Whose idea was it to take out half the castle?

Sneak   I don't know nothing, me. I was in tourism before . . . Me and Miss Judith was asked to come here, because of the new hotel and the castle. Miss Judith worked in Germany for years. They did tourist office stuff and all that. And me, I was at the Spa Hotel . . . Miss Judith saw I was a jack-of-all-trades, so that was it . . .

Husband   Hasn't she got a related professional qualification?

Sneak   She sure got them qualifications. Not a softie, Miss Judith, oh no.

Husband   What about the other boss lady? Did her contract end? Did they sack her?

Sneak   I'm the doorman, me, the garden is my responsibility, and other things, but I don't know what goes on up there. I was brought here by Miss Judith, me, but I know Mary is the only one who left. The psychiatric nurse and the physio nurse stayed and all the others too . . . It's hard to find employment around here . . . the whole region is unemployed. Everybody is happy to have the old people's home. And they were pleased that the hotel came along. The hotel is completely separate, apart from Miss Judith, who manages both. Two separate divisions, only the boss is shared, as manager. And the kitchen is shared too! They get unique gourmet food here, our little oldies, and don't cost more, you know what I'm saying. Guess how much it costs? It's shameful to say, really . . . With that you have to cover their breakfast, lunch, dinner, vegetables, fruit too . . . the diabetics need two extra snacks, they end up licking their fingers, because of the hotel's catering. The committee gets their lunch from here too, I mean the council, which is now the government's office.

Pause.

Wife   Are the diabetics also allowed some sweet stuff? Suppose a small amount won't do any harm!

Husband   Wait a second. Someone bought half the castle?

Sneak (*laughs*)   Or the whole thing, maybe. Wasn't expensive. The deal being that they'll be keeping some of its functions, like the old people's home. It was left out of the capital when the assets here were stripped. The trust took it out.

Husband   You mean the finance manager?

Sneak   Yes.

Husband   And he sold it? But who valued it?

Sneak I wasn't there. But must be a real estate guy . . .

Husband They made a deal . . . The finance manager gets a cut.

Sneak At least ten thousand forints after each deal.

Husband So, it was a good deal to sell it cheaply then.

Sneak They're asking for one to ten per cent of its official value. And they don't have to sell it at an auction either. They often don't even bother advertising. The one per cent isn't that much. You get ten thousand for the value of a million. But what can you do? It's legal. (*Laughs.*)

Husband And you could have gotten a loan on that one per cent, couldn't you? If we had known about it, we could have bought it without any cash.

Sneak But you didn't know nothing about it. (*Laughs.*)

Woman I would have come before but couldn't manage it. I kept putting it off for the following week. You don't realize how time flies.

Pause.

I've been here and stayed the night, but today I've got to get back.

Sneak We haven't got them guest rooms no more, because of the merging . . . Can't stay overnight now. You can at the hotel of course, but you've got to book it and it's expensive . . . It's luxury stuff. Hungarians can't afford that. We've got new house rules, please look on the boards in the corridors. It's on both, on the women's too.

Husband New rules?

Woman My train leaves late afternoon, actually, not in the evening, but I can just about make it . . .

SILENCE.

Husband How much is the daily food bill?

Sneak The Germans ask me that too. I tell them a euro and a half. But they don't believe me. Not possible to cover the costs, they say. Ausgeschlosschen . . . But that is how much it is, and if we didn't have the hotel . . .

Wife Euro and a half for a day.

Sneak You can ask Miss Judith, she'll tell you exactly how much. She is coming soon. Please take a seat, these chairs are fine.

Wife A euro and a half isn't much really.

Husband Hang on. You can only sell something if it's on the inventory. In the nineties not everybody did one, when they passed on the state's capital, so in fact, we don't really know what the country's assets consist of. Is it possible that you lot didn't actually buy the castle, but MISS just occupied it?

Sneak Well, I bought nothing, me, you can find out from Miss Judith, you can. She'll tell me off for blabbering on too much, she says I shouldn't hang out dirty laundry. (*Laughs.*) But nothing ever came of it. I like to chat and get to know people. But I do my job on time, me. I'm a social man, with a friendly character . . . Miss Judith will soon be here.

Leaves.

Scene Five

Woman   Mum or Dad?

Wife   Dad.

Husband   It's Dad for me too. He's seventy-one, and that's not that old nowadays.

Wife   If he's not ill.

Woman   Well, yes. He left me and my mother when I was little. I couldn't even remember him. I grew up searching for him. I put ads out, but he didn't see them. Someone who knew him told him one day. I hadn't seen him for twenty years. He was so happy to see me. My mother was upset; she didn't want me to see him. Then she died. My father became ill. He would have needed a carer, but who can afford that? Apparently you can employ these Transylvanian women.

Wife   We had two of those.

Woman   But if you need them for twenty-four-hour shifts, and pay someone who can attach the intravenous stuff, that's five months' salary for me!

Pause.

Woman   I checked out so many old people's homes, until this . . . just this one's name: 'Sweet Home.' It's a lovely name, isn't it? And I was sold on the garden!

Wife   Yes, the garden . . .

Woman   The castle itself is not a big deal. But the garden is great.

Wife   When the Russians were here it was a stable. Then a storage place, when they took it from the aristocrat who owned it; and after that it became the farmers' agricultural co-operative's office. They were growing cabbage in the park, and the pool became a lake for geese . . . The kids destroyed it, when it became a school. Mary told me the whole story because she was from around here. Amazing how much of it is still in one piece, actually – with some of the original plastering, even. You can see bullet holes in some places . . .

Woman   Dad had a small one-bedroom courtyard apartment; he lived alone, 'cause his partner died. I didn't know her. You know, third-floor courtyard, no lift. I thought that at least now, at the end of his life, he could enjoy a big garden! Someone recommended this place. The director was such a nice lady, too; she didn't ask for any backhanders.

Husband   The state ones can't ask for it. Only the charities and the religious ones. Well, the religious ones can't ask for it officially, but of course, you can 'donate' to

Scene Five 75

the church. (*Laughs.*) Or if it's a charitable trust. And if it's a church, then of course you can donate to the priest, or the reverend. They're people too, after all . . . and who knows – they might put you ahead on the waiting list and give you a single room. (*Laughs.*) The rate is between three and five million, but for this you'll need to sell your flat.

Woman That's not why we sold Dad's place though; he simply wasn't using it anymore, and I already had my mum's apartment where I was registered, so why let it go to the dogs? And why would I want two flats? Double the utilities. It would've been hard to rent it out – a run-down, centrally located courtyard apartment in a Gypsy area . . . I put all the money in a bank account and haven't touched it ever since . . . It's his. But he's never asked about it. I put it in a bond, it's not much though . . . Mary said he'd be well looked after here. Dad doesn't even know he's got money, first time in his life . . . It reassured me that I brought him to a good place. I was finally able to relax. He was put into a shared room, with another old man, who never, ever said a word . . .

Husband They have dementia. More than half of them. Alzheimer's and stuff like that.

Woman So your dad ended up in a good place.

Wife I've wheeled him out in the garden every time we've come. He used to be strong enough to push himself. Mentally speaking he is one hundred per cent. The nurses take them out every day, in the winter too. They wrap them up really well. If you slip them a backhander, they'll take them out. It's just this mobile he can't cope with. He can't even answer it.

Woman Can't he? That's it then! I bought him a mobile too, but can't reach him for the love of God . . . though you see some oldies, on the tram they are like kids, texting all over the place. I don't know why he can't . . . He might have dropped it . . . Got to get a new one.

Husband They can be exasperating.

Woman And he doesn't write either.

Wife Dad doesn't. It's gone out of fashion.

Woman Last time I visited, I shared a room with a twenty-year-old girl. It was in room number three downstairs on the right. There's a big walnut tree in front, dark during the day, but we were there just for the night . . . Her mum is only forty-five, and already here. Awful story . . . She only visited her twice a year, there was something wrong with her mum . . . she cried to me all night, for having been a shit, and not visiting her mother – she kept me up all night.

Pause.

Husband There are more women than men, sixty-five per cent – in some places, sixty per cent – but they are all demented. The state spends a fortune on them – well, you and I actually . . . the insurance company spends the most in their last years of life, when it's too late anyway. The whole thing just doesn't make sense. You should support the healthy ones, those who are still useful to society. Those who work. Why throw money out the window for nothing? It wasn't an issue in the past, people died at forty, fifty. There are still places in the world today when at sixty, they tell them, 'Goodbye, old fellow, you've lived enough, let the young live now', and the old men take themselves into the rainforest, walk up the mountains into the clouds, and the situation is resolved.

Wife   Where do we have mountains that big and rainforests around here?

Husband   We used to have them, they got taken off us.

SILENCE

Woman   I didn't see him for twenty years. And then for ten years only saw him every couple of weeks for lunch. Always sharing the bill down the middle. But then I had to bring him here. And for the past eight years I've hardly seen him. I don't get much time off, no car, and on the train it takes all day. That's the problem with this place, it's too far out.

Wife   It's only an hour and a half by car . . . So pretty and quiet. It's still unspoilt here, and it's safe. The air is good. I even suggested to my husband the idea of relocating here. In America they don't mind about having to drive two hours to work and two hours back. It's only for us here that it seems so difficult. We could buy a house on the hillside. This is still untouched territory, prime location; no heavy industry here – there never was, really. People are kind. It's the countryside, nature!

Pause.

Woman   You can't get home in the evening from here. Even from the bigger towns you don't have trains going to Budapest after six o'clock, so you can guess what it's like from here. The country stops functioning at six o'clock in the evening. I looked into the buses, but that's even worse. You've got to change, wait for three quarters of an hour in a vandalised waiting room, with the wind whistling in. I'm not sold on the country . . .

Pause.

Wife   The village is full of houses for sale, nice big ones. There are some real new ones, can't cost too much . . . They say that now it's the right time to invest in property . . .

Husband   They bought them on credit. And now they need to get rid of them. So – they'll give them away for nothing. But the prices will drop further.

Stabs down the one-legged chair, sits on it, balances on it, laughs.

I couldn't be a hunter, that's for sure, not for any money in the world.

Sits, tries to balance.

You really can't fall asleep on this.

Gets up and pulls out the chair from the carpet.

Can you imagine a seventeen-stone guy on this?

SILENCE

Woman I really could do with going in now . . . I've got to catch a train this afternoon . . .

Wife Kids will be done with their A Levels soon, then off to university. You and I would be alright here – good air, peace and quiet.

Scene Six

Mr Sneak *comes in with* **Mother** *and* **Daughter**. **Husband** *and* **Woman** *stand up.*

Sneak Please come over here. They call me Mr Sneak here. I used to be Mr Snape, but Sneak stuck with me from me primary school days. I'm not sneaky in the least, though, but they don't believe me . . . These people here are also waiting for Miss Judith, as you can see. The canteen is being cleared. There'll be a party tonight. I'll go and find some chairs. Especially for the lady.

Mother No need, I'm fine standing. I'll survive.

Sneak Please do take this.

He pulls the chair from behind the table.

This is Miss Judith's chair. She doesn't like it if someone else uses it, but she will forgive us this time.

Mother I won't sit though.

Daughter We're just here for a quick look and then we're off.

Sneak Just until she gets here then, please.

Daughter We'll take a quick look at the rooms and the garden and we'll be off.

Sneak If Miss Judith gets here, and if she'll allow it, I'll open the garden gate. You can't just go out there. Miss Judith runs a tight ship. I've got them keys, but she'll eat me alive if I decide to open it, just like that.

Daughter You can't go out in the garden.

Sneak You can, but not at any time you like.

Daughter Why can't you?

Sneak Because we have house rules. They are hanging on the corridor walls. When Miss Judith gets here you'll be able to look at them.

Daughter Are they locked in?

Sneak The door is locked, but it's for their own good. We don't want the hotel guests and relatives bothering them.

Daughter Relatives?

Sneak They're the worst, ma'am. But I don't want to offend nobody. But the little oldies get real upset after them family visits. And it's hard to deal with them afterwards . . . The peaceful ones too get angry . . . And we've got some phoney relatives, who are only collecting, thieving, or converting them to Jesus, or making them sign wills, wanting to get their hands on everything. You can visit, but you've got to email first. You've got to let us know how you are related. Plus give us your identity number.

Daughter (*to her* **Mother**) Are you hearing this?

Mother It's a beautiful castle. In a beautiful place. The garden is also beautiful.

Daughter You're not even allowed to go into the garden!

Sneak You are. But not always.

Daughter (*to* **Mother**) Are you listening?

Mother You can look at it from your room. You can look at the garden, can't you?

Sneak Sure you can. I'm responsible for it. I sometimes get some help because it's big. To mow the grass, trim the hedges, watering, I've got tons of other stuff too. But people like it that it's gone a bit wild. The little oldies, they like it, that it's not like an English garden.

Mother It's really beautiful.

Sneak I prefer the weed myself, me. The colour is not as washed out as the grass is, don't you think? Ragweed has got a lovely colour. I feel bad getting rid of them. I've got to pull them out, otherwise Miss Judith will eat me alive. But I don't like to, me. It should be able to live anywhere, it should. It's so bright and green; it's got lots of chlorophyll in it. It's not its fault that it gives allergies, is it? It's happy just being.

Mother Nowadays they can cure allergies, can't they? Homoeopaths with ragweed.

Sneak I had a feeling, me! The bushes too should be left alone to grow. They were not made to be round, but bushy and tall . . . I'll bring more chairs in.

Leaves.

Scene Seven

Mother It's a beautiful castle.

Wife It is.

Mother I'm going to move in right now.

Daughter Let's not get carried away. She's perfectly okay at home – she's just got this thing into her head.

Mother You can't expect your kids to sacrifice themselves for you.

Daughter Right. Can't expect it.

Mother Young people should enjoy living their own lives.

Daughter She's got it into her head that she is stopping me, that she's the obstacle . . . that it's because of her that I'm not dating. It's not my fault that there aren't any men in this country.

Mother I'll be alright here.

Daughter We haven't seen it inside yet!

Mother I don't need much, just a bed, a cupboard. I'm lucky not to be fussy. That's how I survived everything . . . And we've got the luxury garden here!

Wife It's a good place.

Woman It is good – I wouldn't have brought him here otherwise.

Wife My dad was in another place in Budapest. He would have put up with it, he's like that – a trouper, doesn't complain, just puts up with it. But it was me – I couldn't bear to see it. We moved him back home with us after a few weeks . . . but, we both work full time, and you can't expect the kids to care for him. They're busy with school – private lessons, sports. Dad required full-time care. We couldn't have made it work at home.

Husband In that place, they were constantly arguing whether to leave the windows open or not. They managed to argue about that all day long. We were told that in another residential care home, that's how the nurses tried to get rid of them, by opening the windows and leaving, and then hoping they'd catch a deadly cold. (*Laughs.*)

Pause.

Wife As soon as you stepped inside, the worst smell of urine hit you. It was like a primary school – even worse.

Husband Encia, mencia, demencia, incontinence . . . cia.

Wife The incontinence pads were thrown around, left by the wall for days . . . the bedsheets never got changed. They had marble flooring everywhere, the rooms, the corridors . . . The heating was on, but it made no difference, because the cold was coming up from underneath.

Husband It didn't have a basement. Used to be a factory outlet. Then a hostel for workers. And now an old people's home . . .

Wife We wanted to bring him in an electric heater but they wouldn't let us, as the electricity bill was so high already. We offered to pay the difference; but apparently they couldn't work out what we would've owed. Others weren't so fussy, apparently, and we were told that dad should just put on thick socks. They suggested that he put on two pairs.

Husband They had eighty people on the waiting list. There's more than two thousand waiting in Budapest alone!

Wife We brought him home after a few weeks, though it wasn't easy to get him in there. You had to slip them a backhander to jump to the top of the list. We never saw that again, but didn't ask for it either. We were just so pleased that we'd freed him. Dad would have put up with it. Didn't complain. But I couldn't bear it!

Woman   We were lucky to come straight here.

Husband (*laughs*)   Every room had its own TV with the three free public access channels. My God, they could fight over it. All three of them wanted to watch different channels. If they had four channels, each of them would want to watch four different channels. They had lights out at ten p.m., but they kept watching it on mute. (*Laughs.*) The nurse couldn't care less, as long as they had the volume down. They were deaf anyway. They would stare at the moving mouths, well into the night. I suppose they got used to reading lips.

Wife   The common room had a TV, but it served as a smoking room too, and dad doesn't smoke . . . So he didn't watch any TV. But this one here, I'm pleased with this one now. We've looked everywhere in the country. I don't exactly know now where they've moved him to, but I hope that . . .

Pause.

Mother   I don't mind if we have to share a room – much more entertaining.

Daughter   You've never had to live in a dormitory. I had to. They don't let you sleep, people turn on the lights, chat, bang the doors, snore, grunt, throw up.

Mother   People entertain me.

Daughter   And what if they have bunk beds? How will you climb up?

Wife   They don't have bunk beds . . . At least, not that I know of.

Daughter   You've got the master bedroom at home, why would you leave it empty?

Mother   The box room would do for me too.

Daughter   I don't want your room! We've got space, she can go on walks, go shopping. When she is off to the chemist, she stops to have a chat at every corner. Why does she need this, then? There is no reason for you to go into a hospice!

Woman   This is not a hospice! It's a residential home for the elderly.

Daughter   Of course it's different. These guys only get a quarter of the care that a hospice would offer and with less medical staff. I've done my research!

Mother   I'm sure they have a doctor, too.

Wife   He comes twice a week, right?

Husband   Yes, the GP comes twice a week.

Wife   That's when he writes the prescriptions. It's the nurses who give out the majority of the drugs though. They have registered nurses here.

Mother   You see, this place is okay.

Daughter   Let's get out of here! We weren't even allowed to take a look!

Mother I'll wait 'til we can. I've got plenty of time. You go if you want to.

Daughter And how will you get home?

Mother I'm not. I'm staying here for good.

Daughter You can't just stay here! You've got to fill in the paperwork. Takes weeks. We haven't brought your stuff!

Mother I'm staying, and if I need anything, I'll catch the train home.

Daughter Jesus Christ.

SILENCE.

Husband (*laughs*) At election time, they would make them vote by passing the ballot box around the room. They brought it to those with dementia and showed them where to put the X. Surprisingly, everyone had to put an X for the same representative and party. They got shit scared and X'd everything. Encia, mencia, demencia, incontincen . . . cia. I reckon they should not allow the over-seventies to vote. Take back their voting rights, I say; they don't even know what time it is. Only the young should vote, the ones who support them, right. The dried out tree should turn to dust. Actually, take it away from them at sixty, they're nuts enough by then. The Indian way is to charge them when they move in and then make them work. They have to work on carpets, do embroidery, stuff like that. In the evening, it's collection time so they go out to beg. They've got to work to get fed. They're not bored to death, at least. If the state is broke, why should we have to pay?

Pause.

Mother I'm sure I'll be able to get a lift from these lovely people. They probably drove here.

Woman I came by train too . . .

Mother Then we can go together. This lovely couple will take me to the station.

Wife Of course.

Husband How can people who don't work but stare at the TV all the time understand what the world is about? The TV's on day and night. They don't even talk to each other. They just stare. Don't even know what at.

Wife Don't we all do the same? We sit and stare. Except we drink, too.

Husband It's not against the rules for them, either. They are allowed to bring drinks in. Well, you could six months ago. They'll sneak it in anyway, so it makes no sense to ban it. Mary was alright in that respect. She only took it away from the drunks.

Wife Dad doesn't drink. Hates it. When his health declined, we brought him a wheelchair, so he could get around.

Husband A good chair cost a hundred thousand forints plus VAT, not even a motorized but just manual one. You have to buy everything separately – headrest, the ramp. That in itself is six hundred thousand.

Wife But you've still got to help him get onto the toilet. He's got a really heavy body because he's disabled. He needs to go more often. When the lift was out of order, we couldn't take him down. You can't live like this. He kept asking to be booked in somewhere . . . kept saying that he didn't need his flat. It wouldn't have been big enough for both kids and their future families . . . they're constantly fighting anyway. We have decided to sell Dad's flat. We'll help the kids later on, so they can buy one each. His place is not small, eighty-six metres square. But it was just a bit lived-in. We're updating it now. Some people say that you'll never get your money back. But others say that you can't sell it if it's in bad condition. There are so many on the market.

Husband That flat's not worth much now. It's not in a bad area, not exactly Buda's leafy suburbs, but it's not bad at all.

Wife We've got new plumbing in, and a new boiler instead of the coal-fired burner. When dad was living there, no one minded about the peeling wallpaper, or the damp walls, or the crackling of the floor with bumps in it . . . but now that dad isn't there, the place will be as good as new . . . So we've got the new kitchen, we got rid of the old table, and the pantry cupboard. We've got a marble-style counter, easy to clean, if you get water on it. Dad was really keen on having that done. Well, now it's going to happen. The bathtub has got new taps on now; we got rid of the heater. Dad had always wanted to keep it. But you can always change it back to multi-energy if you run out of gas. Which according to him we will soon do. We'll still be able to have heating.

Husband (*laughs*) My father-in-law has catastrophic thinking. Didn't trust the Russians. (*Laughs.*) Hated the Germans. (*Laughs.*)

Wife I've never plucked up the courage to tell him that his bunker from the cellar got stolen. When we were allowed to buy it off the state, a good twenty years ago now, they forgot to add it to the inventory. We were so happy to finally own something that we didn't notice that someone had walled it off and put a lock on it. When we brought it up, it turned out that you couldn't prove anything, couldn't prove it belonged to us.

Husband They got paid off on time. We overslept on this.

Wife If need be, there's nowhere to store the coal or the wood. Dad wanted us to take care of it. He was only interested in his work, and we messed up. They stole the bunker. (*Wipes her tears.*)

Pause.

The flat will be gorgeous. Like never before. We'll have another toilet added to the bathroom, a suction one, so you can advertise it with two toilets . . . Dad will never get to see it . . . We should take him to see it, shouldn't we?

Husband Of course not! He wouldn't realize that he used to live there.

Wife There's nothing wrong with him mentally! He remembers everything!

Husband You mustn't bother him with this. Or anything else. He's fine here.

Wife It's not right we're selling the flat when he's still . . . Maybe we should wait a little . . . there's no hurry for the kids. Real estate prices are at their lowest, so why rush it like this?

Silence.

I do know that he wouldn't even have dared to dream of a garden like this. The garden was a priority! Dad always lived in downtown Pest, he used to say he wouldn't like it in leafy Buda, even if it was free; thought people were different there. Still, for a garden, it would be worth it. For him, this garden will make up for it.

Woman The garden is really something! That's what I was thinking too at the time.

Wife Still, it's – when they lived in their flat, they never did anything to it . . . they couldn't afford it during those forty years with my mum, or when he was alone. And now when it gets redone, he's not . . .

Husband He wouldn't have put up with the mess anyway And actually we planned this when he was still walking. It was after your mother died. But we thought he would be better off without all that business. He wouldn't have wanted it anyway. Don't worry about it. We're here now, and it isn't true that we don't visit him!

Wife He should have moved in with us when my mum died. He would have had a completely different life with us.

Husband Where, sweetheart, where? We had the kids by then!

Wife We talked about doing an exchange swap, swapping his and our flats for a bigger one, which would have been big enough to have him live in it as well.

Husband You can't be serious, my sweetheart! Sharing with your dad, the know-it-all?

Wife To this day he knows everything. He's smart – was born that way. He predicted stuff that ended up happening. He just let himself go because he was so into his work, nothing else interested him. He could have become a millionaire if he had left in fifty-six, before I was born . . . But oh no, he was dedicated to his work and the country. This is the only thing that he didn't . . . Why do you have to hate smart people? It's not their fault that they were born that way. They're harmless, and still everybody bugs them. It's pure jealousy!

Silence.

It's a pity that the kids didn't inherit it . . . Neither of them . . . I didn't inherit it either, so no chance that they could have got it from me. This gene business is not fair.

Pause.

Husband They must have put a new heating system in the castle. I reckon they have had to do it from scratch, with all the wiring, unless they closed off the old part, which would not surprise me.

Silence.

Woman I don't know, my father was a drunk. All his mates drank. All of my mother's colleagues drank too. It's a miracle that I don't . . .

Daughter It's not like that with us. (*Pause.*) We had plenty of room, the kitchen is big too. And the box room is eight metres square. We've got plenty of space for all my stuff. Why would she need to leave? Why would she voluntarily choose to go to a prison?

Wife It's not a prison! That's an exaggeration!

Woman Not a prison at all, it's a fantastic place!

Daughter Okay, not a prison, but a prisoner's camp, for a life sentence. Why do it if you don't have to? Mum's got some twisted pedagogical thinking. This is her way of blackmailing me into standing on my own two feet. So that way, at least I'll make some friends, because apparently if I pour my heart out to her, then I'll stay immature. Fifty-one per cent of women in America live on their own. I mean completely alone, with no pet dogs, cats, no friends, no husband, no boyfriend, and without a woman friend either. Over there the lesbians are lonely too. And they don't have mothers either . . . Over there they have a name for them. They push themselves so hard, from morning till night. By nighttime they can barely drag themselves to bed. No time for a relationship that's for sure.

Husband America's America. They're rich. You can put up with it, if you've got money.

Mother I don't want to be anybody's burden. If I pay for it with eighty per cent of my pension, that's fine, and fair. At least it's a clean deal.

Daughter A burden. Do I grind my teeth and poison your food? Do I?

Mother It would be more honest.

Daughter She's obsessed with this! I can't talk to her!

Silence.

Husband (*to* **Mother**) The elderly have tons of savings. They're actually rolling in it. But they don't want to spend it, because they're worried about not having enough for later on. Mind you, it's true they do get taken for a ride in their last years, with the cost of prescription drugs and all. They'll buy into some so-called new procedures, the newest drug, the miracle ones, the alternative-whatever cure – natural healers, charlatans, magicians, confessors, Reiki healing. They promise you a separate room, with an ensuite bathroom, when in fact the whole floor has only got one toilet. And apparently you're not allowed to build extra bathrooms. It's the young who are skint. They really could do with that money now. Economists say we should earn more when we are young. We should start with a high salary and reduce it gradually! Where can an old guy go? They push him out to the garden, leave him out in the sun, let him burn to cinders, meanwhile the money is rotting, in the bank or the pillowcase. So, let me warn you, dear lady, that you will be squeezed and fleeced in this place.

Daughter You see? If you don't believe me –

Mother If I always saw the glass half empty, I could have hung myself sixty years ago.

Wife Dad has not been fleeced!

Husband   He hasn't! We have!

Wife   His own pension covers his bills.

Husband   It only pays for half of it, so in fact they're getting the other half from us.

Wife   They might get exploited somewhere else, but not here! We wouldn't have brought him here otherwise!

Husband   There's no escape from it.

Wife   We looked around, didn't we? You always assume the worst of everybody, the very worst – everybody is a thief, a cheater, a robber. That is all you think about! Next you'll be accusing them of mass murder!

Husband   But aren't they like this? In politics too . . .

Wife   But not here!

Husband   Okay, of course not here – this is an exception, I was talking generally.

Scene Eight

Mr Sneak *comes in, bringing in two stools, and a folder.*

Sneak   Sorry about this, but had to get it from the kitchen . . . Why don't you sit down? Please sit, and if Miss Judith doesn't like it, I'll explain.

Puts down the stools.

This is the application form . . . Please go and sit down by the table, it's more comfortable to fill it out there . . . It's just a few pages. (*Laughs.*) We are very thorough . . . (**Sneak** *puts the folder on the table, pushes the chair back under the table.*)

Mother   Alright. But just until . . . (*Sits down, takes her glasses out, puts them on, takes the documents out of the folder, takes her purse out of her bag and puts it in front of herself.*)

Does anybody have a pen?

Sneak   There're some in them drawers.

Mother   I don't rummage in other people's drawers.

Husband (*takes out a pen from his inner pocket*)   Here you are.

Mother   Thank you. (*Disappears in the paperwork.*)

Sneak   We've got enough chairs around . . . No one else should arrive now. People don't arrive after late morning. It gets busier sometimes. You can book a visitor's dinner too . . . Not cheap though . . . We have higher-than-average prices . . . Miss Judith's brought in a chef she's worked with before . . . Miss Judith would make a good chef too – she's qualified.

Husband As a chef?

Sneak She's got a hospitality and catering background. They took cooking exams. So yes, she can cook.

Mother You have to fill in your religion?

Daughter What? Religion?

Sneak Well, of course if someone needs last rites . . . Wouldn't want to give it to someone who isn't entitled . . . (*Laughs.*)

Mother Fine. I don't mind filling it in.

Daughter It's none of their business. Don't write it down. Don't fill in anything.

Sneak Miss Judith will help you fill it in . . .

Mother 'When did you last go to confession?' You've got to write that down?

Sneak If you don't remember when, she'll type in any date.

Daughter On the website it said that this is a state-run home, not a religious one.

Sneak Of course it's state run.

Daughter (*to her mother, looking over her shoulder*) Chronic illnesses, it's none of their business! That is sensitive personal information!

Sneak It's for the doctor! What is the matter with her?

Husband (*to* **Daughter**) Excuse me, but this is an obvious one . . . How can they possibly treat her if they don't know what's wrong?

Woman Obviously they'll need to know.

Daughter 'When did you last confess'?

Husband If you don't remember, just put down anything. Why get hung up on that? And if you are a Protestant, they will have it on file, and you won't have to confess.

Wife This is a good place. We wouldn't have brought Dad here otherwise. Why would we have brought him to a bad place?

Woman It's a good place and the care is good. My dad was all skin and bones, and they fattened him up. They are very humane here. The nurses too. It's clean too, and it's quiet. This was the most important for him. All his life he was shouted at.

Wife When he needed round-the-clock full-time care we started to look around. We wanted the best place. One day we had gone and looked at three places in different towns.

Daughter 'Your savings'? None of their business. If you pay the monthly fee, it's no business of theirs to know what your financial situation is.

Mother We don't have anything to put down anyway. Why are you making a fuss?

Daughter Because it's none of their business.

Husband Of course it's their business. They need money to live on too. They'll live off your dear mother's pension, for example, and off our money, and they'll get some state contribution, too.

Sneak Six hundred and thirty-two thousand. Been the same for years. Hasn't followed inflation. The faith-based ones cost much more. Some charge one million. That's state money, too, from our taxes . . .

Husband He could have gone to a faith one – I don't mind . . .

Wife Dad is not religious.

Husband He was fighting against it, had a tantrum. 'I'd rather you killed me. Kill me!'

Sneak The ones with dementia pay an extra hundred thousand forints more. You've got to pay the hairdresser and pedicurist separate. I'm sure you'll want them services, as you seem to look after yourself. The cafe waitress comes over and brings you whatever you want – coffee, hot chocolate, chocolate bars. The diabetics can get diabetic biscuits. Some homes are run like pawn shops. For four weeks they sell you food on credit, then charge you a huge interest rate when the pension check arrives. In a few months, they got nothing left.

Husband Pawning?

Sneak Sure thing. Well, we don't have that here! Miss Judith wouldn't put up with it. Oh, before I forget, you'll have to pay for your medication if you don't get them on the national health. And that's a lot of money. Anyway, Miss Judith won't ask you stuff that isn't important.

Daughter Did Miss Judith write the form? Isn't it a standard form?

Sneak Of course she did. It's different in all homes. The house rules are different too. Please go and take a look at them when you go in. Ours are different.

Silence.

Daughter 'Permanent place of residence . . . ' You mean the home isn't going to be the official registered address?

Sneak Of course it will.

Mother Give it back now! It's my form!

Sneak Excuse me, ma'am, but what some people ask about is death and funerals. This is not awkward for us at all. We talk about it more openly, and don't tell no lies. Death is a simple matter here with us, ma'am. And quite frequent. There are days when we have three or four . . . then a few weeks off, and more again . . . The doctor shows up – he comes twice a week anyway . . . or the ambulance. If someone kicks the bucket in the ambulance, then it's those guys who do the paper work . . . But mostly it's the doctor. He was here this morning and signed all the necessary paperwork. The death certificates are in the folder here on the table. We deal with all that business right here. The relatives don't have to do nothing . . . They get given the filled-out death certificate, which of course requires a signature, so as to avoid further complaints. We take care of the funeral too. I do it. The relatives don't have to do a thing. They like to have the funeral here . . . often they don't come. You don't have to, the priest gives a speech, or an official from next door. Miss Judith will send an email, saying it was lovely and how much it cost. It's not expensive, believe me. We can account for every penny . . . And the ones without relatives, well, I take care of those . . . basically you couldn't wish for anything better.

Pause.

Husband   I heard that in some places they don't tell you that someone died, so they can keep claiming their pension from their account.

Sneak   It's not like this here with Miss Judith. We let them know straightaway. We wouldn't be caught cheating over something like this. If you require a gravestone, you can just give the inscription to our wood sculptor, he's real good with his hands. He can also do figurines, very popular, that. He'll sculpt you dates, tulips, stags, patriotic stuff, anything. But you can have gravestone, if you wish. It won't be done here locally, but you can order it from us, too. Anything from imitation stone to marble . . . Plenty of space in the cemetery, worth taking a look, if you can go home that way – it's just after the turn. We're in the country here, and everything is cheaper, and we really do take care of everything, we do. Makes it simple.

Pause.

Daughter   Do you also do euthanasia?

Mother   It's completely fair that they talk openly about everything. Why shouldn't we talk about death? Especially in a place like this! I really like what you said. Finally, a straight talking person!

Sneak   I could see right away that we'd get along, ma'am. But if the lady weren't so intelligent, we'd get along too. Miss Judith doesn't tolerate just anybody around her – she's got high expectations. You get guaranteed quality with her, that's why I came to work for her.

Wife   This home is perfectly in order. You'll be in good hands. Your mother will be in a good place. From a care-treatment point of view.

Woman   We were lucky about being having been recommended this one first . . . And 'Sweet Home' – the name itself was catching . . .

Sneak   Miss Judith will be here soon – Oh, and the wood sculpture is separate. We can contract them for you, and we don't charge a broker's fee. Miss Judith has learned her work ethic from Germany, you see; she's worked over there for years. She's got contacts over there. She's fluent in German and speaks English to the Russians . . . Not easy to manage a hotel . . . there's a lot of competition . . . Especially Austrian competition. You've got to offer lots of extra-special deals or they won't come here. Miss Judith even brought in big cats.

Husband   Big cats in Hungary? You must be joking.

Sneak It's true though, I always speak the truth, me. No exaggeration or lie has ever been uttered by these lips. Miss Judith brought in big cats!

Husband Jaguars, cougars, leopards?

Woman And panthers, snow tigers, tigers . . .

Daughter Hyenas, pumas, wild cats . . .

Wife And marble-printed cats. That's a separate species.

Woman Cheetah?

Daughter Yes, cheetah.

Husband Which ones do they hunt then?

Woman We left out the lion!

They laugh.

Husband Where did they get them from? This must have been crazy money! Unless they were domestic cats gone feral.

Sneak They cost a lot, so Miss Judith stopped it. It wasn't financially viable. But you have to offer something different to these guys. They want sensational stuff. They will hunt absolutely everything in the world. Birds, four-legged creatures, two-legged creatures, as long as it's exotic. (*Laughs.*)

Wife How come they hunt two-legged ones?

Sneak That's why she got the sack from Germany, because those know-it-all German lawyers didn't like it that a non-German made a successful business over there . . .

Wife What kind of two-legged ones, monkeys?

Sneak Human-sized ones. (*Laughs.*) Believe you me, ma'am, I am known for always speaking the truth and never exaggerating. Often they don't believe me, but when they find out I was right, yes! (*Laughs.*) I'm a straightforward man, friendly, open-minded, welcoming. And if I say that it's worth staying for dinner tonight, then you must believe me. I don't know what the menu is, but please stay. It will be worth it.

Scene Nine

Same place. Same people.

Sneak They start cooking it in the morning. The sweet little oldies get the same, if the dietician nurse allows it. So every other week they, too, really look forward to the hunters' visits. One nurse, her daughter, actually, takes care of the pickled salad. The meat is from the farmers' market, and the wine comes direct from the vineyard. It's got to be quality. The Russians have been well spoilt recently. We get wholesale beer for the Germans. Kolsch or Pils.

Husband The oldies are allowed alcohol?

Sneak Sure, if they pay for it.

Woman How much is a beer?

Sneak It depends on the exchange rate of the euro.

Woman I'll sign up Dad. How much are they allowed per person? I'll pay for a month, two months, six months – how much does it cost?

Sneak I can't tell you all the prices, you've got to ask Miss Judith.

Husband What about Schnapps?

Sneak We got it.

Husband Is it homemade?

Sneak Sure it's homemade. The Russians drink it at sixty degrees. Germans can't take that, so they get it at forty degrees.

Husband This is paradise.

Sneak Yep. When the school had a power cut, and had no heating, we had everything working fine here. The hotel takes care of the whole castle.

Husband What kind of heating does it have?

Sneak It's got a mixed combustible wood-fire. We can bring the wood in from the forest.

Husband Who does the forest belong to?

Sneak No idea, me.

Husband Thought you knew it all?

Sneak Yes, I do. (*Laughs.*) The point is, even in the winter it's warm here.

Husband Who gathers your wood?

Sneak It gets brought in. The locals like the castle; we maintain a good relationship with them. It's important to us.

Husband You must need a lot of wood for such a big castle. Yes, especially since you've got to keep heating it when you don't have gas, so the walls don't go cold.

Wife And because of the residents, too.

Sneak Of course, ma'am.

Daughter What happens if you run out of wood then?

Sneak It doesn't run out.

Daughter And hot water?

Sneak Boiler.

Daughter How many bathrooms on each floor?

Sneak One. At the end of the corridor. That's where we've got all the plumbing. I mean in the old wing. Because the hotel has got ensuite bathrooms.

Mother I don't mind walking out to it.

Daughter And how many people in a room?

Sneak You'll see for yourself, love, when Miss Judith gets here.

Mother The more the merrier.

Daughter Oh my God!

Sneak I can see that you're a smart lady. We'll get along just fine.

Daughter What size are the boilers?

Sneak I've got no idea.

Daughter You don't know? Aren't you supposed to know everything?

Mother Leave him alone, I'm the one moving in, not you. He'll get upset with me.

Sneak We don't get upset with nobody, ma'am. We understand that old age is difficult. But to be honest with you, there are times when we run out of hot water and you've got to wait. They run the hot water and then forget about it. They forget to turn off the taps. In that case the boiler gets cold and you've got to wait. But it's not a big deal because some don't wash for a week.

Daughter You don't wash them?

Sneak Of course we do – just that sometimes they forget. Their nurses are on it though. You've got to shave them too. Many if not all women have hanging beards. (*Laughs.*) But there is a hairdresser, who needs to be booked and paid in advance. You walk into the TV room, and you see them with beards blowing about.

Daughter Can they go out into the garden?

Sneak I'm in charge of opening the door; you've got to be careful that no one wanders in. We don't have thefts here. Miss Judith makes sure. They leave everything out and about, these happy-go-lucky oldies. On chairs, tables, we don't have no safes here.

Husband A few years ago they fitted them in all hospitals. It cost a fortune, and then they banned them. They took them down and someone walked off with them. That's how things work in this country.

Sneak Yes, that's how. I used to be in charge of ordering stock. You won't believe the things I saw. I used to work in hotels too. That's where Miss Judith poached me from. She noticed I'm good with people. After high school, I worked in leisure, at the union's package holiday company. Oh, those were the days! Date nights, trips, singing, dancing games. A new group of people every week . . . They used to love my matchbox trick. They were supposed to put it on their noses without using their hands (*laughs*). Then we would visit the wine-cellars . . . then ping-pong tournaments. I was able to involve the awkward ones as well, 'cause I'm a people person, me . . . That's when I realized that you don't have to get married, what with getting a new group every two weeks, and another get-to-know-each-other evening! (*Laughs.*) Czechoslovakian knee-high padded trainers with airing holes in them, tights, nylon turtlenecks, tight jogging outfits . . . I wasn't Mr Sneak in them days. I was Sandor, dear Sanyika, and so-forth. (*Laughs.*)

Pause.

Husband   When is Miss Judith getting here? We're busy this afternoon . . .

Sneak   Very soon now. She likes to do everything in person. She trusts me, of course, but has her doubts. She got used to precise work – but none of it over here. She was sought after in Germany too. She used to organize fantastic trips to Africa. They hunted absolutely everything there – four-legged, two-legged, a hundred-legged creatures . . .

Wife   Hunted monkeys?

Sneak   Not monkeys. The local Blacks. (*Laughs.*) You had to book a year in advance. That's how popular it was. Of course the legal guys came in, made a fuss, they reported it. The business was too successful . . . Not easy over there in Germany either. They've got different types of people there too. I used to go there when I was a tourist guide. I learnt a bit of German from home – we could watch Austrian TV. Everybody watched it. I don't speak as well as Miss Judith, of course. She's phenomenal! She just picked it up from over there . . . I get to welcome them here. Bitter schon, Ya vol, I'm doing okay. (*Pause.*)

Mother   I'm signing it.

Daughter   You haven't seen what it's like inside! For God's sake, don't do this! Let's look at it first at least.

Mother   Will I be done by signing it?

Sneak   Almost, ma'am. It will be passed on to the directorate, and they'll make a decision.

Mother   Who are the directorate members?

Sneak   Miss Judith.

Mother   It only depends on her?

Sneak   Of course it does, but she'll be here soon.

Husband   Couldn't you give her a call?

Sneak   She won't pick up and I don't know her German mobile's number. She didn't give it to me, but she has got one. She has a Russian one too. A manager type if there ever was one.

Husband   You can't call her? What kind of a caretaker are you?

Sneak   A jack-of-all-trade kind. My contract says doorman, but if Miss Judith wants something, she'll call me. But we prefer talking face-to-face. (*Laughs.*) Phones could be tapped. Wouldn't surprise me.

Pause.

Daughter Don't sign it until we have seen it!

Wife It would be better, you know, if you did take a look! Would set your daughter's mind to rest . . . help her accept the separation. It's very difficult, even if it's a relief. But you really seem to be in a very good shape . . .

Mother There is nothing wrong with me! That's why I've got to do it now, while I've got my wits about me.

Woman Don't worry about signing it. This is a good place. My father is completely satisfied with it. Miss Judith is a very good director. She's strong, strict but humane. A lot depends on the director . . .

Sneak There are some places where they leave everything they've got to the care home. Big money, too – just like that, a new will appears . . . They must beat it out of them.

Husband I read somewhere that in some care homes, they kept the corpses in the fridge to avoid paying for the funeral.

Wife Stop talking utter nonsense!

Husband I promise, somewhere in Romania . . . They did business with secondhand clothes, the ones they left behind. To get a place, they had to forfeit their house. After they died the house became the care home's property. They made them sign official charitable donation forms.

Sneak I've told you. They beat it out of them . . . out of these poor little oldies . . .

Wife It's awful!

Sneak In some places they sedate them, stuff them with sedatives so they don't fight back . . . Well, we have nothing like that here.

Daughter Do you hear that? They'll give it to you, even if you don't want it!

Wife The point is, they don't do that here.

Mother You don't even hear what they are saying, you.

Woman It's alright here, you'll see. I wouldn't have brought him to a bad place. He's ignored me for twenty years, and I searched for him all the same. Didn't even have a new family, or a new kid. Found out that he didn't have one. Still he never . . . I never made him feel like . . . he was shit though. I get it with my mother. But with me, his kid, what had I ever done to him? Others had fathers, I didn't . . . I kept making deals with myself, that if I ever found him, that I would take revenge and burn down his flat. I learnt how to do it from the movies. You pour petrol down and throw a lit match on it . . . I used to practise in the park, how to throw away a burning match, but the wind always blew it out before it fell down. It would've worked in an enclosed space. I didn't think of it then. Shame mum let slip he was alive – I wouldn't have looked for him otherwise. It's easier to live with the idea that someone died, especially if you don't know them. I haven't seen a photo of him either, so I was shocked when I . . .

Pause.

Mother I'm going to sign it now. (*Silence. She signs it. Puts the pen down.*) Until the director gets here, I'm going down to the garden.

Sneak You can't go there unless she allows it.

Mother But you've got the keys to the garden, haven't you?

Sneak I do, I've got keys to everywhere, me. But it's not a good idea for them to socialise. I mean the patients and the hotel guests. There could be misunderstandings, you see, and the hotel guests have not come here to make friends . . . They might be turned off by the whole thing! (*Laughs.*) They couldn't speak to each other anyway; the patients don't speak Russian or German.

Wife My father does.

Sneak They speak with such strong dialects, that it's impossible to understand them. I don't understand them either. I just nod. But when there are no guests they can go outside. Accompanied, because they could wander off. Not everybody knows where they are.

Daughter What do you mean by no guests? So if the guests happen to stay for days, it's house arrest?

Sneak They are here every other week for two or three days. The other days the hotel is empty.

Husband Is that good business?

Sneak Sure it is. Please don't ask me the details, but I tell you, they pay a lot for all the extra activities, and we offer tons of extras here – four-legged, hundred-legged, two- legged. We've got a good reputation. Big companies organise their bonus trips with us. We created the 'Woodland of Peace'. We took trees and bushes from the garden here, pulled them out by their roots and replanted them . . . Gardening costs would've been massive.

Wife What is the Woodland of Peace?

Sneak It's a small wood with bushes and trees in the clearing where the beasts go to hide.

Wife You brought the trees from the home?

Sneak We bring the people, the trees . . .

Wife With their roots?

Sneak Used to work in gardening, after the event-organiser job. So I know what I'm doing. Carried the bushes in a wheelbarrow and the trees in a trailer, we stood them up, we pegged the tall ones down, we watered them, and they all survived.

Husband You've moved them from the home's garden?

Sneak But we've planted new ones. There's plenty left still. It's either trees or dinner, we get to choose, we've no other option. They had no heating or food at the school, so they had to shut it down. The kids had to go to another local school. They promised a bus route, but it never happened . . . Here with us at least, you've got heating as well as food. The little oldies have got it good. They've got plenty of padding on them. You'd want to eat them. Look at me for example; I eat what they eat. Am I skinny? You've got to become entrepreneurial, Miss Judith says – we shouldn't give in just like that.

Husband No, we shouldn't.

Sneak Whinging about difficult circumstances – that is all you hear. We need action, not moaning.

Husband You are absolutely right. Moaning is a Hungarian damnation. As well as passivity and showing off. We really need to break out of it.

Sneak Miss Judith has learnt to fight for everything. I've learnt that, too. But she really has. I've met hard girls before. But she's hard as nails.

Mother If I give you my application form today, when can I move in?

Sneak We too got a waiting list here. But you don't have to wait as long as in other places. As Miss Judith says, we've got a quick turnaround, every two weeks. Every other week there are three or four new places, sometimes five or six. It depends on the weather, more frequent in season too.

Husband These guys are sensitive to heat waves. Apparently more people give birth then, and when there's a full moon.

Sneak They don't hunt at night, these sow hunters. They can't even manage to finish eating their dinner. They get totally trashed and pass out. Russians on vodka, Germans on beer. It's us who got to drag them back to the hotel. You can imagine how we struggle. They're overweight, and heavier when they're unconscious. They fall over in the woods too, not used to walking. I follow them with a hunting chair, but they can't even sit down on it. They rented it, so I'm bringing the damn thing. I am also dressed as a beater. Miss Judith bought us hunting outfits, and checked that they fit okay. She thinks of everything. She knows what she wants and how to get things done. She's got contacts abroad and at home too. A rare woman! Born to be a leader – from a small village. Isn't that amazing? I am from a small town, me. But I'm not as hard as she is.

Mother I'm going out into the garden.

Sneak Just a little patience, ma'am. It's no good if the hotel guests and the little oldies meet before it's time . . . You see, you've now become a sweet little old lady. The rule is that they can only meet in the Woodland of Peace.

Wife What is the Woodland of Peace?

Sneak It's the part of the field where the beasts hide.

Wife You take them out? Into nature? (*To* **Husband**.) You see, they get fresh air. What about those who can't walk? My dad, for example . . . ?

Sneak They get wheeled out. We wheel them out, to be more precise. I do it too . . . On the boggy bits, we put some planks down so the wheels don't lock in the mud, and for the ones with crutches, so they don't slip. The ones who are still running around – and I mean it metaphorically, because they are wobbling – they walk around in the garden here, when it's possible. We don't really take them out to the hunting ground. It does happen, but not typical.

Pause.

Mother I'm going down.

Daughter Don't go! – She's impossible . . .

Mother *leaves stage left.*

Scene Ten

Daughter Go after her!

Sneak She'll come back alright . . . They like to wander about until they're able . . . They don't usually get lost . . .

Daughter She's got a bee in her bonnet. Her auntie from New Zealand wrote to her. She left in 1956 when she was fifteen. My mother was ten at the time, worshipped her whilst she was away. She imitated her, put her on a pedestal . . . They didn't write to each other, but all the way through it was Buffy this and Buffy that. Buffy can barely speak Hungarian. Writes appallingly. She's called Lizzie now, not Buffy. Buffy's gone to a residential care home now. It's fabulous, dream-like, and so my mother got it into . . . I tried to explain that it's not the same in New Zealand . . . but she's never really listened to anything in her whole life. (*Pause.*) Bring her back, she'll break the door down.

Sneak You mustn't force it. Let them be. In the end, they'll do what they are told.

Daughter She's completely bonkers. We used to bring over bedsheets from Poland, across the Czech border on the train. We stored them in the cellar, but couldn't sell them because they all rotted . . . She forced me to study engineering at uni because women have the same rights now. I got a place. Tried the entry exam four times. Got ill from it. The constant drawings killed me off. They kept sending them back. Destroyed my guts. She wanted a small plot in the outskirts nearby. Wanted to grow vine spinach, because it's high in vitamin C. Not surprised my father left her . . . then we got stuck with unripe bitter melons, all kinds of tropical crap. She grew the stuff in the bathroom, until the Japanese mushroom pushed it out. It's good against cancer, diabetes, blood pressure, we grow it in the bathtub in Japanese soil. It's as expensive as gold and I can't take a bath! She always seems to want something.

Wife The Woodland of Peace must be beautiful.

Sneak It's beautiful, peaceful, and quiet. When they shoot, the ducks and pheasants escape together in a flock, the sky goes dark with them.

Woman They shoot?

Sneak Yes, ma'am, they do where they hunt of course. In some places they provide bows and arrows. It's becoming popular because it's quiet, but they are so crap they can't hit anything. So we don't use the bows.

Pause.

Wife Could we go and see the Woodland of Peace?

Sneak Sure thing, but there is nothing there. No one is interested in it in the village. They don't go that way, they've got no business there. Others who wander in here don't know of it.

Husband But the hunters do.

Sneak We take them there – though we've got to be careful so they don't fall into the lime pit. Because there is a big lime pit out there. That's why us, the beaters, we're there to stop accidents happening. I'll soon need to get changed . . . I would've never thought I'd become a beater on a hunt. It's amazing how many jobs you can end up doing! You just have to live long enough, don't you? (*Laughs.*) They could tell you a lot about what they went through, these sweet little oldies. Of course, they babble nonsense, makeup stuff, have visions, get reality and dreams mixed up . . . many of them are like that . . .

Woman My father does that too. It's from the booze. We were sitting in a pub, and he was telling me about his daughter, describing her – all the time I'm sitting there facing him. He didn't know he was talking to me, about me.

Pause.

Sneak What's bad is that you do get to like them. Then you have to mourn them. So many I've met aren't here anymore.

Wife It's awful!

Husband Sweetheart, this is the natural way of things.

Woman That's why I don't have pets. A few years with them and then you have to start grieving them. I'd rather not have one.

Sneak During the seven months, we had five hunts. It took two months to get the first batch . . . Everything sorted itself out after that . . . That is about twenty-five oldies in six months. I haven't counted exactly . . . Oh, what can you do?

Daughter How many are on the waiting list now?

Sneak Miss Judith will tell you, but I reckon about thirty. It'll be six months till we can admit the last on the list.

Scene Eleven

From stage left, three women and three men dressed in Turkish costumes enter. The men are not wearing shirts but sleeveless waistcoats, baggy puffy trousers, and each has a different coloured turban on their head. The women are wearing turquoise, red and blue bra-like tops, with tasselled bits hanging off them. On their waists they are wearing tasselled scarves. In front of their faces, white veils. Their eyes and foreheads are showing. Baggy shiny trousers and red leather boots with spurs on.

Man 1 Where's Miss Judith?

Sneak Isn't she in the costume room?

Man 1 She isn't.

Sneak Oh dear. We've got new outfits from the costume's rental. They had to be fitted on them. They're going to be Turks today. They got nuts for the folkloric outfits. That's how they wait on them. Usually they're dressed in traditional Hungarian clothes. The boys in shirts and breeches, but the girls, oh the girls . . . headdress, skirt, apron, sometimes it's Indians or pirates – depends – or Romans in togas or Egyptians in God knows what. We advertise it on the web like this: themed costumed waiters. Miss Judith has bought the hunting clothes, and it's not just for us – the guests can rent them so they don't need to bring them. We get to charge them a rental fee that way. We've bought capes for example. Officially they're hussar collars. They're waterproof, and in the sales they go for fifteen hundred thousand plus VAT. But we also bought trousers that you can warm up. They cost thirteen hundred thousand each. Not cheap. And we also got waistcoats that you can warm up, fifty thousand a pair, and ambush trousers for thirty-four thousand, and kidney protectors, for nine thousand. It pays off in the long run, you only need to invest once. But when it works out cheaper, we hire it too. We get a ten-member group discount, and you've only got to leave a deposit. Of course the rental shop makes a continuous profit. But it's still worth it for us . . . We've regular customers who like to see the girls dressed differently every time. As if that made it new to them! (*Laughs.*) Whoever was an Egyptian goddess last time will become a country maiden, and so on. It's the boots that are a problem, because we don't have enough. They've got these soft boots in sizes thirty-four to forty. They cost two thousand three hundred plus VAT for three days, which is all we need them for, but you have to reserve them three days before. And the deposit is twenty thousand. To buy them would cost thirty-five thousand. We don't buy them; then again, here are the boots that go with the pirate, sheriff, or military girl outfits. They simply don't make them anymore. There is no demand. So they have to wear red boots when they are Egyptian slaves, nuns with cleavage and bonnets; so as you can see, the boots are an issue. You've seen it for yourselves.

Man 1 Shall we wait for her?

Sneak She'll be here soon. As you can see, we are entrepreneurial. That's how we make sure the little oldies get heating . . . And that they have more to eat than spuds and cabbage, which is what the daily food bill would cover. You've got to be resourceful, that's what Miss Judith keeps saying. These Turkish things are quite cheap. So we hire them. With everything, it's five thousand, plus VAT. On the day of the hunt, everybody has to have a bath, wash hair, shave, put on deodorant, and all. Shoe shining too. We've got lacquered, long-pointed shoes from the rental place. They've got high heels, can barely walk in them, but that's all they had in the lacquered style. We actually ended up buying them shoes, and coats too, as well as hunting hats with the badges. The Russians love those hats; they think it's part of the Hungarian folkloric costume. (*Laughs.*) The boys and girls also have to bathe before dinner, isn't that right, kids? At the beginning Miss Judith would go round and sniff everybody. But sometimes she will just appear and sniff you (*Laughs.*) The bike repair kits also belong to us. The wheelchairs break down quite a lot, they get a flat, or the spokes get bent. There are tricycles made out of old bikes too, out of the old Csepel R26. That's why we've got to park so far, because that's where they are, the rickshaws . . . Weren't they around there today? The rickshaw drivers are out looking for our hunting guests' business. They'll become beaters, too, if they get in there first.

Husband This mouth cover makes it look like there's an epidemic going on. (*Laughs.*)

Wife Don't be crude.

Husband Alright. But it's weird that they're not wearing real veils.

Sneak Because it's more expensive. They do have them, black ones, though with matching hats, and mourning veils. If they ask for it, for a funeral. Everybody walks out in a line, in any costume you wish, it's simply a matter of paying for it . . . And I go in, in my doorman's coat, me. When they come down for dinner I greet them in my knee-length doorman's coat. They got it especially for me. It's light blue baize with gold laces. The hat is eighteenth-century Hungarian style. And I salute them, like that – freshly shaven, Miss Judith insists on that. You wouldn't recognise me. I salute them throughout the evening and the night. One time they booked a funeral with twenty-five mourners – they, the family, never showed up. But they sent a spy – just to check that there were enough mourners. They wouldn't pay for them otherwise. (*Laughs.*) We're not going to be caught out with something like that. Would you like us to sing to you? Shall we sing? Something happy. I've taught it to them. I picked up this skill from my cultural organiser days. Okay, boys and girls! (**Mr Sneak** *lifts up his arms like a conductor.*)

Sneak Rasvetalie! (*Gestures silence.*) What's going on, have you got frogs in your throats? Rasvetalie, and one, and one and two . . .

Choir sings a Russian song.

Sneak You see! They know all five verses. The last one is the same as the first one though. Right, listen to this one now. (*Gestures.*)

Choir sings a German song.

Sneak And who sings all this? The Turks! (*Laughs.*) It's good, right? – It's good fun, right?!

Scene Twelve

Mother *enters stage left.*

Mother How lovely, how lovely!

Sneak You won't believe it but three of them have degrees. Hands up, ones with degrees!

Two women and one man tentatively put up their hands.

Sneak I don't have a degree, me, but they still have to do what I tell them, because I'm Miss Judith's right-hand man. Did you enjoy your walk, sweetheart? Did you not change your mind?

Daughter You are at the bottom of the list. It will take six months; you've got time to change your mind.

Mother I haven't changed my mind. The dining room is huge with brand new fixtures!

Sneak They were made to order!

Mother I just can't believe that you're not able to jump ahead on the list.

Sneak Of course you can. But you can't say you heard it from me, sweetheart. I haven't said a word. I just chat. But you can ask anybody, I have never lied to anybody. 'Mr Sneak is not a lying rascal,' they will say. No, in fact no one has ever accused me of exaggerating, either. You see, I never exaggerate – why would I? It would make no sense, would it? Let's look reality straight in the face.

Husband That's right. They try and make you believe all kinds. You mustn't believe a word of what they say. When they're not speaking, they're still lying. They twist it inside out; they're very good at it. Good at screwing you over, that's what this country is good at!

Sneak Well, I was never one of those, who wraps it up in lovely packaging, someone who speaks nonsense. I'll always tell you how it is, me. I'll tell it to you factually. (*Laughs.*) Usually they don't believe me, when I'm being completely straight to their faces. I enjoy it.

Husband Hungarian people are straight talking, they're known for it.

Sneak Absolutely right. My mother used to say that I've been doing this my whole life.

Pause.

Mother We're grateful to you. What's your name again?

Sneak Mr Sneak.

Mother We're grateful to you, Mr Sneak.

Wife And if you could take Dad out regularly . . .

Woman And if he wants a few spritzers, here and there, it will be okay.

Husband Salaries are so very low, in places like these; even if one is a jack-of-all-trades, the more stuff you get to do, the less money you get for it, right?

Sneak I can't really complain. Miss Judith appreciates her staff. But of course if it looks half decent before them taxes, the net number is not so . . .

Husband   Don't you worry, Mr Sneak.

Sneak   You too mustn't worry. You guys – Look away.

After considering it, the **Husband** *takes out an envelope, which he gives to* **Sneak***, who whips it into his pocket. The* **Woman** *takes out an envelope, gives it to* **Sneak***, who whips it away into his pocket.*

Woman   You'll take my father out for a walk too, won't you?

Sneak   Of course I will.

Woman   Take him into those small woods.

Sneak   Into the Woodland of Peace.

Woman   There, yes!

Sneak   It's Miss Judith who decides whose turn it is to go to the Woodland of Peace, when there's a hunt. We take them out, but it's her decision, who goes out that day.

Mother   Can you please pass my bag?

Daughter *takes the bag to her.* **Mother** *takes out her wallet.*

Mother   What's the going rate?

Sneak   Twenty thousand, let's say thirty.

Mother*, searching in her wallet, gets the money, counting it out.*

Daughter   Eight thousand four hundred.

Sneak   It will do.

Daughter *takes the money over and gives it to him.*

Mother   Here you are.

Sneak *steps towards them, spits on the money, and whips it into his pocket.*

Husband   We won't say anything to Miss Judith.

Sneak   Miss Judith hasn't got heart problems, so you can tell her, don't worry about it. She suspects it. There's always someone who likes to enlighten her. (*Laughs.*) It's not really our main subject of conversation. She'd rather tell you what to do than chat. She was born to give out orders. From a small village, she is.

Mother   Miss Judith is a wonderful creature. She's determined, strong, a good manager. You have to keep order in a home like this. How many of us are here?

Sneak   Seventy-three without you, ma'am.

Mother   And you've got the staff on top, and the whole hotel! This is not an easy job. But Miss Judith can tackle it, she can.

Daughter   You haven't met her, haven't even talked to her on the phone!

Wife   Everybody knows Miss Judith.

Woman   Miss Judith is humane. She wrote to me, asking me to visit my father, 'cause he missed me. But some stuff came up and I couldn't come. When did she call, maybe eight months ago . . .

Husband   Eight months ago.

Woman   It could be nine.

Husband   Mary was the boss then, right?

Woman   Could have been, but it doesn't matter. I knew that he was in a good place here with Miss Judith.

Mother   The name itself. 'Sweet Home'. Others don't have names, or if they do, it's something cheesy, like 'Fairy Garden', 'Pearl Wreath', or 'Autumn Blue', 'Oasis', 'The House of Beautiful Age'. Why can't they simply say home for old people? Why give it diminutives, or nicknames? 'House of Joy'. I am sure it's full of song and laughter. 'Silver Bridge'.

Daughter   'Sweet Home' is as revolting as those other ones. 'Autumn Rose'. 'Diamond Gate'. 'Sun Ray'. 'Beautiful Dawn'.

Woman   It isn't. It's got some warmth to it, something spiritual.

Wife   Heart-warming. It spoke to us too. Miss Judith's done a good job with that.

Daughter   Okay, fine, we've sorted it. You're top of the list now. Let's go before you give out our petrol money too.

Sneak   I'll give you money if it's for the petrol. There's a station two kilometres from the cemetery. Their petrol comes from the Ukraine. Our guests use that one, much cheaper.

Daughter   Thank you. Let's go now.

Sneak *takes money out of his pocket.*

Sneak   How much do you need?

Daughter   We'll be alright.

Sneak *puts money back in his pocket.*

Mother   I'm going to stay and wait for Miss Judith. You can go of course.

Daughter   I'm not going.

Mother   You can climb in through the windows.

Daughter   Don't start now.

Mother   She uses her window to go in and out. Her box room opens onto the courtyard. She does it to avoid me. She had it fixed so you can open the window with keys, from the outside. All this so she won't run into me in the hall. We're the laughingstock of the whole building. She's climbing in through the window when she could have added a door! She can't stand my smell, but she pretends to. And now that I want to leave so that she can finally have the flat to herself, she's stopping me. She's ashamed of her hatred of me. She shouldn't feel ashamed. Her face is scarlet right now.

Daughter *crying, having a tantrum.*

Daughter She's crazy! She's crazy!

Mother Isn't she? Look at her, she's about to explode. Shame on you, doing this in front of strangers. They're laughing at us, everyone's laughing at us, and it's revolting.

Daughter *cries loudly, has a tantrum, and slowly stops. Silence.*

Wife Let your mum do whatever she wants. She can always go back home if she isn't happy.

Mother I'm not leaving. Never!

Wife We brought Dad back home once.

Mother Because the fortuneteller didn't tell you anything, but she told me.

Daughter Oh, of course not, it's not possible.

Husband Be glad to get rid of her.

Wife It's none of your business.

Pause.

Sneak She really should be here any minute now. I'm off now – I'm getting changed into my beater costume. If you aren't going to sit down, then I'll take the seats back. It's lucky that they're so light, they easily fit in the weapons bag . . .

Scene Thirteen

Miss Judith *enters stage left.*

Miss Judith Good morning.

She goes behind the desk. **Mother** *gets up and stands farther away.* **Miss Judith** *sits.*

You haven't made appointments.

Sneak I've told them.

Miss Judith Can you please register your visit next time? Our email address is on the Internet. We give out visiting-time slots. If you come at a different time, we won't be able to let you in. I'll make an exception now. Mr Sneak, please be careful, because the earth is flooded near the pit. The fresh lime arrived. I was out there and they poured it straight into the pit. Tell the others that it's slippery.

Sneak Of course.

Miss Judith Let me see your heels.

The girls, like horses, hold their legs up. **Miss Judith** *checks their heels.*

Miss Judith Okay, you can put them down.

The girls put down their legs.

Miss Judith (*to the others*) They usually wear the boots all day long, that's how it's always been. But from now on, the spurs will have to be worn as well. Please use them carefully.

Sneak You think of absolutely everything, Miss Judith dear, don't you?

Miss Judith You can leave now.

Man 1 Goodbye, ma'am.

The Turkish-dressed people leave annoyed.

Scene Fourteen

Miss Judith Mr Sneak, open the corridor, there's half an hour for the visit.

Sneak I'm on it. (*Takes out a bunch of keys.*) Should I open the garden door too?

Miss Judith Not that one, because they've arrived. We don't let them mingle before it's time. Our guests can only use the garden when the hunters have left.

Sneak I've told them that too.

Miss Judith Any questions, any wishes?

Pause.

Mother Miss Judith, dear, I'm moving in here.

Miss Judith Fill out the admission form, please.

Mother I've filled it out, got it from this gentleman.

Miss Judith Has he also told you about the entry fee?

Mother There was no mention of that . . .

Miss Judith One million. Due on the day of moving in. In case you don't have this amount, we have a payment plan to offer you. Our bank gives us a ten-year loan. The interest rate is below the norm and well under the legal limit. The monthly payment is thirteen thousand, eight hundred and sixty-seven forints. We don't ask for a processing fee, nor for a first payment. When you sign the contract we will also need proof of ownership of your flat. The documents must be less than two weeks old. In the eventuality of multiple owners, all owners need to be present.

Husband What is this, house swap?

Miss Judith If you compare the lending rates on a comparison website, you'll get the banks' most recent offers.

Husband *takes out phone and starts to tap it.*

Miss Judith You'll see that we're not more expensive than any other bank.

Husband Are you legally allowed to offer bank deals?

Miss Judith Our co-operative is run according to the rules and regulations of the business and credit bureau.

Husband And they agreed?

Miss Judith You've got to have a good relationship with them.

The **Husband** *laughs out loud and keeps tapping his phone.*

Husband So you're right! You're not more expensive! So where's the business in that? Is it a scratch-card game?

Miss Judith There's no lottery, no, we're not a commercial group, and we don't promise you high interest, so no . . .

Husband But the people who get the loan don't actually get the cash in hand.

Miss Judith That's true, but they get a receipt.

Mother I don't quite understand. Do you?

Daughter *shakes her head.*

Husband In return for your mortgage, you'll get a million-forint loan. If you accept it, you can move in.

Wife Jesus Christ. Do we have to do that loan?

Husband Why would we have to? He's already in there.

Miss Judith This deal only concerns new admissions.

Daughter Excuse me, but who will own the flat? Will we lose it?

Miss Judith It'll remain yours. The flat can only become the co-op's property if the monthly payments stop. The first reminder is sent out after three missed payments. And it's only after three more months that you get a note on your property documents, but only if you haven't paid up to date by then. This is all in the loan contract.

Husband And where do you send the warning?

Miss Judith To the registered permanent address.

Husband But if they're registered here with you . . .

Miss Judith It would still be sent out by post. It'll be sent by recorded delivery and signed by the addressee. Everything is legal.

Silence.

Husband And let me ask you . . . If the person in question passes away, without next of kin, then you'll own their flat, is that right?

Miss Judith That's right.

Husband But if there is a next of kin?

Miss Judith   They have to continue paying the monthly payments.

Husband   And what happens if they don't know that their relatives died?

Miss Judith   We send out the death certificate, by registered and insured mail.

Sneak   I've said that too.

Husband   But still people can miss payments, right?

Miss Judith   We then send an attorney's warning, and yes, it can happen that despite that, there is no payment received.

Husband   What's the percentage? One in ten?

Miss Judith   We started six months ago, there's no history yet.

Husband (*laughs*)   Don't tell me that you haven't calculated it! If they're forgetful or slack, the flat is yours!

Sneak   So what? The contract is legal!

Husband   How many new oldies do you get a month?

Sneak   Ten or twelve, depending on how many die. We're quite small.

Husband   A flat a month. If we calculate with cheap flats, let's say ten million forints each, that's already a hundred and twenty million in property.

Miss Judith   You can't guess the current market prices, especially not nowadays.

Husband   It's clever, but I wouldn't have the balls –

Miss Judith   Mr Sneak will give you information about these conditions. Do we have enough copies?

Sneak   Yes, we do. I copied some. I'll give it to them at the reception.

Miss Judith   Have you taken down their names and ID numbers?

Sneak   Right away.

Miss Judith   You're not allowed to visit unless we've got these. We can't be responsible for unauthorised visitors . . . We accept full responsibility for the welfare and property of our guests.

They search in their pockets or bags.

Daughter   I don't get this. What happens if I pay one million in cash up front?

Husband   You don't have to pay anything up front, if I understand it right. They get your mortgage and then you pay a smallish amount each month as repayment.

Daughter   But what if we don't ask for the loan and want to pay it in one go?

Husband   I don't know, then. What would happen?

Miss Judith   We're not in the business of ripping off elderly people. So that's why we don't accept anybody without a loan. If you have one million in cash, spend it on something else. It would cover the nursing care in your own home for a while.

Daughter   You've got to take out a loan. Are you saying that this is the condition to get a place here? Why?

Miss Judith   Because the company's owner decided it for humanitarian reasons.

Daughter   Miss Judith, are you also one of the owners?

Miss Judith   The ownership information is not public. I'm mainly a managing director.

Daughter   Can you see what they are like?

Mother   They're very nice . . .

Daughter   You've always warned me against living in debt, never accept credit, why now then?

Mother   This is different. We're not spending beyond our means. We're not overstretching . . .

Daughter   But you're buying the right to live here!

Mother   But you don't pay for it, isn't that what they said?

Daughter   Oh my God.

Husband   That's what the state will end up doing. (*Laughs*.) First they will bring in property tax – that most won't be able to pay. Secondly, they will add the tax to their mortgages; thirdly they will start evicting the ones who can't keep up with the payments for their own house or they'll be forced to take in some lodger. Anyway, that's what I would do if I were the state, easy peasy.

Miss Judith   Most deals are dead easy.

Pause.

Mother   Where shall I put the form?

Miss Judith   Here on the table.

Mother   When will I get an answer?

Miss Judith   Soon.

Daughter   This whole thing stinks! This loan is very suspicious!

Mother   Will I be the first on the waiting list if I get the loan and pay cash on top?

Miss Judith   No, you won't. We don't make exceptions. It's first come, first served with us.

Daughter   You need to look around first, for God's sake – let's see what it's like. It could be awful. You could pass out from the stench of urine when we walk in.

Miss Judith   Please don't rush it, take a look around. We're a bit tight since the hotel is in business, but it's not too bad, go and see for yourselves.

Mother   I've seen enough. It'll suit me fine.

Daughter   But you haven't seen anything. Don't do this. because I am getting fed up with all of this. Don't do this; we'll lose our flat!

Mother This is none of your business, so why don't you stick to climbing in and out of the window?

Daughter I own it too.

Mother I've signed it. Done deal!

Miss Judith (*to* **Daughter**) Now that we have the visitor's details, we're in a position to give out a carer's agreement stating that the next of kin will be looking after their parents. We don't charge for this certificate, but only charge the mailing cost. In the future, certain benefits will depend on this document. I agree with the state's endeavour that the family is what society is founded upon. And if you're going to ask me if I'm married, no, I'm not; I haven't found Mr Right.

Pause.

Sneak The doctor has signed the death certificates this morning.

Miss Judith Take them to the authorities tomorrow.

Silence. **Sneak** *gathers the certificates and starts copying numbers into a notebook.*

Pause.

Miss Judith Please use capitals to write the guests' names and your relationship to them next to your own names and ID numbers. I won't ask you to verify your relationships with documents this time, but next time, bring them with you.

Husband Documents to prove I'm visiting my father-in-law? How can we prove that? Isn't her maiden name enough?

Miss Judith Both guests and visitors need to present their birth certificates.

Husband I don't know where they are . . . it's a pain to get a new one.

Miss Judith You'll need it anyway for the death certificate. We need to protect their safety and peace of mind. In old age your mental resistance is diminished. The mobile phones aren't good for them either. Their blood pressure jumps up. We don't recommend their use.

Sneak *hands back the identity cards. They put them away.* **Wife**, **Husband**, *and* **Woman** *write in the book.*

Woman You've written to me a little while ago telling me I should come to visit, but I couldn't until now . . . I was thinking no news is good news . . .

Miss Judith My predecessor must have written more than six months ago. It's not our style to scare relatives. We either send them a death certificate or we don't.

Woman Well, I haven't received one of those, I don't remember getting one. Mind you, the postman just tosses in the recorded delivery mail. We'd agreed that he can sign it himself so I don't have to queue at the post office . . . It could have got mixed up in the junk mail, which I get rid of straightaway. I can't stand junk mail, the smell, colour . . . (*Shakes.*) Disgusting, they are, especially the one-page ones, the colour is revolting, the feel of it . . .

Silence. **Sneak** *walks stage right.*

Wife (*to* **Husband**)   Will you go in, please? If he sees me he'll get upset. If you think he's going to cope, then bring him out. That's okay, isn't it?

Miss Judith   The dining room is the visiting area, but since they're busy in there for tonight's event, it's fine for now.

Wife   Thank you very much.

Woman   Very kind of you, Miss Judith.

Daughter   Let's go in finally – Let's see what it's like!

Mother   I'm low maintenance; it'll suit me fine.

Pause.

Daughter   Fine, I'm going without you.

Mother   Go.

Daughter   I know you won't believe what I'll say.

Mother   Of course I won't.

Daughter   When have I lied to you? Why can't you believe me?! Can you never believe anything?

Miss Judith   Mr Sneak.

Sneak   Are you coming in?

Sneak *and* **Husband** *exit stage right.*

Scene Fifteen

Miss Judith (*turning on the computer*)   If you don't mind . . .

Wife   Of course, go ahead . . .

Woman   We don't want to bother you. We could leave, actually.

Miss Judith   I'm organising a new group, coming in two weeks' time. During the hunting season we have more competition, we've got to book at least twenty people.

Wife   What do they hunt?

Miss Judith   We've got that already.

Wife   What, are they wild boar, wild geese, deer, stuff like that? I'm a city girl – don't know what's protected and when . . .

Miss Judith   I didn't know either.

Pause.

Woman Hunting must be exciting, but tiring too.

Wife It's a kind of passion, some people fish. I'd lose my wits, waiting through the night, but there are some who put up with it.

Woman They drink while they do it, that's why they do it.

Pause.

Daughter Miss Judith, do you really have to get the one million forint loan?

Miss Judith No, of course not, but you don't have to move into the residential care home either.

Pause.

The loan has nothing to do with 'Sweet Home', just like the hotel doesn't either. But without the hotel our guests would starve, just like they do elsewhere. It's thanks to the loan that the business is working. It's non-profit.

Pause.

Mother But you don't have to pay anything when you move in, right?

Miss Judith You don't have to.

Mother That's what matters, you hear this? That's what matters.

Scene Sixteen

Husband *wheels the* **Old Man** *in.* **Mr Sneak** *is behind them.*

Miss Judith Mr Sneak, get changed and bring out the others too!

Sneak Yes, ma'am. I'm not saying goodbye yet.

He leaves.

Scene Seventeen

Wife Dad. Do you recognise me, Dad? It's me, Dad. Does he recognise me?

Husband Of course he does. You haven't changed that much in six months.

Wife What's it like inside?

Husband Not too bad, a bit tight really, but . . .

Wife He's looked after all right, is he?

Husband Yes, he is.

Wife Dad, you're alright here, aren't you?

Pause.

He doesn't understand us. He did last time.

Husband I think he understands. He didn't object to me pushing him out.

Wife Does he recognise us?

Pause.

Old Man I miss them – that's the horrible thing. I miss them.

Wife I miss you too! A lot! All the time!

Old Man The ones who didn't come back. They took them out and they never came back.

Pause.

Husband Sometimes these guys mix up reality with dreams. They have visions.

Old Man They were taken out to get some fresh air . . . they never came back . . .

Wife He's talking about the war. He was a kid but remembers it well.

Old Man They shot them.

Wife I told you – the war . . .

Old Man You can hear it.

Pause.

Wife He's in good shape, isn't he? Looks well.

Woman The food is good because of the hotel.

Wife He doesn't look unkempt, does he? His nails have been cut.

Old Man Don't let them do it.

Wife What?

Old Man Take me away from here! They'll shoot me!

Husband I've told you. He's starting again.

Wife Oh God! Dad – no one is going to hurt you. You're in good hands!

Old Man They've not brought them back. They won't bring me back either.

Wife Miss Judith. What is he talking about?

Husband It's not unusual for them to say stuff like that.

Woman My father has hallucinations. The stuff he used to say. Because of the side-effects. Or maybe it's because of the withdrawal symptoms. It was awful. I didn't like seeing it, that's why – I kept delaying it too. It's no good. And it makes you feel so helpless. At the end he was completely dependent on me, like on alcohol, he was depending on me, cried when I left – for twenty years he had ignored me, so then I kept a distance between us. He was already here by then, he didn't want me to leave, even though we had agreed about it beforehand – and in fact it was Mary who suggested I come less often – she said that I shouldn't give my life over to him.

Mother That's right, that's what I keep saying too. This isn't real sacrifice, but fake devotion.

Pause.

Wife This blanket is nice and warm. Is it a 'Sweet Home' blanket?

Miss Judith Yes, pure wool.

Wife It's got a tasteful design.

Miss Judith We try our best.

Pause.

Wife He's freshly shaven.

Miss Judith We shave them before we take them out.

Wife That's very good.

Pause.

Wife Where in the garden do you take them out?

Miss Judith Different parts. But when we have the hunt, they get taken to the Woodland of Peace.

Wife Don't they catch colds?

Miss Judith No. If need be, they get hats and scarves. They're a hundred per cent wool too.

Wife Wonderful.

Woman Miss Judith thinks of everything. Of absolutely everything. Everybody knows these things, but still – she's so good that she makes a point of it . . .

Mother I can still walk, but when I won't be able to, and not even able to wheel myself because my arms will be too weak, will you still take me out to get fresh air?

Miss Judith Not a problem. We'll wheel you out.

Old Man Don't let them. They don't bring you back.

Pause.

Husband Right, what can I say? This is what he's like now.

Wife We should take him home with us, shouldn't we?

Husband We couldn't cope at home. We've tried, haven't we? We tried and it didn't work out. It crippled us too. We can't offer specialist care. That's why he was brought here, am I right?

Scene Eighteen

From stage left, **Mr Sneak** *enters wearing a hunting jacket and boots.* **Three Beaters** *in hunting outfits also enter.*

Sneak   You see, this is the hussar collar I was telling you about. They used to call it a pig thief, because a whole pig would fit under it . . . Fifteen thousand plus VAT, it's worth it. The boots are my own. I would prefer walking boots, but Miss Judith won't allow it. That's how she is, tries to save here and there . . . Miss Judith, who are we taking out today?

Miss Judith   Well, if this gentleman is already here, let him go. And what room shall we choose from the women's ward?

Sneak   Number eight will do.

Miss Judith   How many in there?

Sneak   Three.

Miss Judith   Good. Four people will do for today.

The **Three Beaters** *leave stage right.*

Sneak   You see, it's convenient to take out the whole room – much easier to clean up after them. No one gets to be difficult this way. You can finally open the windows and let some fresh air in, without them complaining and squealing.

Husband   Yep, opening the windows or not is their biggest problem.

Sneak   And the TV.

Husband   That's a general issue though. If you're finally home, you must stare at something . . .

Old Man   I don't want to . . .

Wife   What don't you want, Dad? What doesn't he want?

Husband   I don't know, I don't know.

Old Man   I don't want to . . .

Sneak (*laughs*)   He doesn't want to go for a walk! It happens. Not everybody enjoys the fresh air.

Wife   Some fresh air will do you good, Dad. You've got to get out sometimes.

Old Man   They won't bring me back either!

Wife   Dad, please stop. We'll come and visit – everything is fine! I promise we'll come more often, it's just that . . .

Woman   Same here . . . And then comes the guilt . . . But it's true, things always crop up.

Wife   Is your father also like this . . . ?

Woman   Oh yes! Ever since I've known him . . .

Wife It takes a while to realise how your parents have difficult personalities. And that with time they change, but not to their advantage. It's not getting any easier for them.

Old Man Don't let them . . .

Husband We won't let them, Dad. You've got to leave them to it. Everything is fine, Dad! We won't let them. He doesn't get it anyway. We should soon –

Wife Is it time to leave?

Husband It's time.

Wife But we haven't chatted!

Woman How time flies . . . My train is leaving soon . . . But it was always difficult with my dad . . . Doesn't say much . . . just sits there in silence. Makes me freeze up, that does. Maybe if I'd known him from childhood. But that's not my fault . . .

Wife Of course not. Not your fault at all. Not everything is down to us.

Woman Will you give me a ride to the train station?

Husband Of course, we've already promised.

Daughter We could take you all the way to Budapest.

Woman No thanks, the station will do.

Daughter But we've got room in the car!

Woman I like travelling by train. I stare out of the window, daydream, not so easy to leave someone here.

Wife Oh God, it isn't easy. My God, it's hard!

Husband Right, so we should really get going.

From stage right, the **Three Beaters** *wheel in three chairs with an old woman on each. They are wrapped up in blankets.*

Miss Judith Put a hat on them, the red ones.

Sneak Miss Judith, you really think of everything. Well – I'm going to say my goodbyes. It will be a sensitive one, as they say. (*He smiles in a childish way to the* **Woman**.) I'm glad that your dad . . . Do visit. We'll be looking forward to it. (*Shakes* **Woman***'s hand. To* **Husband**.) Lovely chat we had. Rare to meet someone as intelligent as you. (*Shakes hand with* **Husband**. *To* **Wife**.) Goodbye, ma'am. Please don't worry, everything will be according to plan. (*Shakes hands with* **Wife**. *To* **Mother**.) I'll see you anyway. I can't wait. (*Shakes hands, gives her a hug. To* **Daughter**.) I know what you must be feeling. I've found it hard to become independent too – but won't be difficult for such a nice lady . . . You'll come and visit, won't you?

Old Man Don't let them . . .

Sneak (*laughs*)   Don't be scared, it's not going to hurt. Pleasure to have met you, goodbye. Tallyho! Tallyho! Tallyho!

Sneak *and* **Three Beaters** *wheel the three wheelchairs.*

Scene Nineteen

Miss Judith   I'm going to the kitchen.

Husband   We're leaving two woman.

Mother   So you've got my admission form?

Miss Judith   Of course. It's over there on the table.

Mother   And how long will it take?

Miss Judith   Six weeks, two months . . .

Mother   It's not that long. I'll be able to hang on in there.

Daughter   I wasn't able to become a homeowner. You did, but remember you did it when it was doable!

Mother   Have I ever expected it from you?

Daughter   No, you just made sure that I knew.

Mother   Me? When?

Daughter   When you got your flat it was different; it's not like that anymore!

Mother   The six weeks would be better than the two months, Miss Judith.

Daughter   Twenty-four-seven, you're trying to prove I'm unable to do anything. You've done that all my life.

Mother   Best thing would be tomorrow.

Miss Judith   We'll try our best. Three places on the women's ward just got freed up. Please drop off your entry passes at the reception when you leave. I hope you got given one.

Husband   We did, we did, please come with us. We'll take you to the station.

Woman   Thanks.

Miss Judith *exits left, the others also exit left.*

Scene Twenty

Trees, bushes, bulrushes are being swept by the wind. An approaching dog barks, and a rhythmical shooting sound is heard. From stage left, the **Old Man** *and the three* **Old Women**, *looking panic stricken, speedily push themselves on their wheelchairs.*

116   Prime Location

They have red hats on, as they quickly wheel themselves, trying to escape to the right. Dogs are barking. Loud shouts are heard, sounds of rattling. A quick succession of five, six shots are heard. Cries of fleeing birds and the rustling of their wings can be heard.

Silence. From the right, **Three Beaters** *and* **Mr Sneak** *come out, pushing four empty wheelchairs.*

Scene Twenty-One

The office. **The Wife** *and* **Husband** *enter stage left. The latter carries a big package in his hands.*

Wife   He could already be asleep.

Husband   We'll put it by his bed then.

Wife   Let's put it by his bedside table.

Husband   He hasn't got one.

Wife   How come he hasn't? He did have one!

Husband   There was no more space in his old room. We'll put it by the foot of the bed.

Wife   He'll get frightened.

Husband   He won't even notice.

Wife   Should have given it to him.

Husband   Why did you put it in the trunk? I'd have seen it on the back seat.

Wife   Lucky that I even remembered.

Husband   After twenty kilometres!

Wife   Still better than at home!

Husband   We could have eaten it. A sack of sweets for a diabetic! What if the corridors are locked?

Wife   Are they?

Husband *takes off to the right. Stops at centre stage.*

Husband   They are.

Wife   We should call Mr Sneak.

Husband   Leave it, he's probably having his dinner.

Wife   Okay, let's leave it here on his desk. We'll put his name on it. She's a decent woman; she'll probably give it to him.

Husband *takes out a pen from his inner pocket, writes on the package. We suddenly hear Gypsy music.*

Husband Here we go.

Some god-awful singing with unclear lyrics can be heard. Very loud sound of violin. Then quieter.

Husband Wow – they're really going at those strings! What a party!

Wife He'll be woken up by this!

Husband Even the dead will.

The violin is playing a folkloric song: 'My Father Loved to Sing.' It is accompanied by singing. **The Husband** *puts the package on the table. The music becomes softer.*

Wife We'll pop round in two or three weeks.

Husband Of course we will. We can come more regularly. He'll be pleased to see us.

They play very loudly, then quietly.

Wife So lucky that Dad ended up liking Gyspy music.

Husband Your dad is in a good place here.

He's pushing his **Wife** *towards the door.*

Scene Twenty-Two

Mr Sneak *in a doorman outfit enters stage left.*

Sneak Oh, good evening. Are you still here?

Wife We forgot the present . . . came back . . . It's just some chocolates.

Sneak Chocolates for Dad, that's not a good idea, ma'am. Feel free to leave them here for me. I'll eat them.

Laughs.

Husband (*laughs*) That'll be best.

Gypsy music stops, applause can be heard.

Sneak I've come back for the death certificates. I left them here . . . I'll quickly get them signed by the doctor – he's dropped in, he's eating in the kitchen. I'll take them all in tomorrow to avoid having to go twice.

He takes out some forms from the drawers, puts them into the folders on the table, and then snaps them under his armpits. He's listening to the sound of the applause from inside.

Sneak They must be at the Beautiful Legs Competition . . . They love it. Only men can enter, and all they can show are their legs. Their bodies and hands are hidden by a stretched-out sheet – that's how they walk onto the stage. The man whose legs get the most votes wins a trophy of carved wood . . . It's done by the same guy who carves the headstones.

Applause. Cheering.

Wow – that really must be a good leg. We've got a winner, then. A beef stew will do you a lot of good . . .

Wife   No, thanks, we don't –

Husband   With dumplings?

Sneak   Homemade! Come on in, there's plenty.

Wife   We can't . . .

Husband   Why not? They're asking so nicely. At least we won't have come back for nothing. Let's eat.

Sneak   Don't make me beg you, ma'am!

Wife   Alright, but only a bite.

They leave. Applause. Cheers. Gypsy music plays.

The End

Sunday Lunch
A Drawing Room Drama by János Háy (2010)

Translated from the Hungarian by Szilvi Naray

Characters

Girl, *twenty-six years old at the beginning of the play*
Mother, *over fifty*
Father, *close to sixty*
First Man, *the Girl's first husband. An operation engineer in his thirties*
Uncle Laci, *the mother's brother, well into his fifties*
Second Man, *the Girl's second husband, a mathematician in his thirties*
Kid, *by the Girl's first marriage, around eight*
Eldest Kid, *by the Girl's second marriage, around eight*
Youngest Kid, *by the Girl's second marriage, around six*
Kati, *the Girl's colleague, in her thirties*
Aniko, *the Girl's colleague, in her late twenties*
Matchmaker, *a woman in her forties*

In the second act, all of the characters are eight to ten years older.

Premiere, May 2012, Tivoli Theatre, Budapest

Act One

Scene One

*A converted attic flat in which the **Girl** and her **Husband** live. It is the evening, and the husband arrives home.*

First Man   Where's the kid?

Girl   He's already asleep.

First Man   He's always asleep when I get home.

Girl   'Cause you come home when he's asleep. If you didn't come home when he was asleep, he'd be awake.

First Man   Stuck at work.

Girl   They let you do that there?

First Man   Do what?

Girl   Drink.

First Man   I am there for the overtime. So we can have more. You said there wasn't enough.

Girl   It's too late.

First Man   I have tried everything.

Girl   Don't do it for me.

First Man   Could we . . .?

Girl   No. Not anymore. You come with too much baggage.

First Man   I can change things.

Girl   Some things you can't.

First Man   I can change anything!

Girl   In twenty years' time, we would still be living here in this attic. With you, it's as good as it gets.

First Man   My father built this with his own hands.

Girl   Shows on his hands too.

First Man   We can do an extension. He has planned it that way. You could extend the other side of the roof, towards the back garden.

Girl   Your parents would still be living under us. So why not pour concrete over them and move them out into the garden, as sculptures.

First Man They're my parents. And they've done so much for me.

Girl For you.

First Man And for you too.

Girl For me? What?

First Man Always ready to help with the boy. Didn't even have to ask . . .

Girl Don't need to ask them to come, have to beg them to leave.

First Man It's because they love you.

Girl But I don't love them. They are not my parents. They are just two pushy people who always have advice for you. It's a running commentary on how to do things; as soon as I walk in it's like they are reading them out to me. I don't want to live with them, I don't want to hear your mother's voice, I don't want to eat her Sunday lunch.

First Man We'll be at your mother's on Sunday.

Girl That's lucky then.

First Man I've never said, let's not bother and stay home instead.

Girl Why would you have said that?

First Man What I mean is that I made allowances. I managed to go with the flow.

Girl That's what you are supposed to do. Why wouldn't you have managed?

First Man Wasn't easy for me either. It's not so straightforward with your parents. I know full well that I wasn't a good enough catch for them because they had someone else in mind, someone who would have been a better match for their daughter.

Girl And they were proven right.

First Man But you are not the daughter that they had in mind.

Girl I had never wanted to be. That daughter was exactly like them – boring. She spoke in her mother's voice and thought that her father was the ideal man. So, as a matter of fact, no, I am definitely not like that.

First Man Then you can't get the man they wished for.

Girl In the past, maybe not. But now, yes.

First Man Why now? What has changed?

Girl I know I can get him. I used to believe that it could only be you. Now I know that it can be someone else.

First Man But we have a life together.

Girl Had.

First Man I can change whatever you want.

Girl   No chance. You can't erase your mother from here. She will always be here, even if she is not here.

First Man   It's easier for us with them here, plus they give us all they've got.

Girl   I don't want it. I don't want that money; they pay us to be here, and they want to buy us. But I don't want to stay here. I want move to Buda where my parents –

First Man   You don't even like them!

Girl   They are not the reason; I am used to that place.

First Man   But this is Buda too.

Girl   You really don't understand anything, do you? You and I are so different. Even with your big degree, you have become exactly like your parents. You don't know what I want. You only know what your parents want because that's all you have seen. You have no idea how to live for other things or in different ways.

First Man   I haven't had a drink today.

Girl   It doesn't matter.

First Man   It doesn't?

Girl   No.

First Man   Until now, that was your reason.

Girl   No. If you weren't you, I wouldn't mind if you drank. But you are you.

Scene Two

Entry hall. Doorbell rings. Inside: A man looks at his watch, his wife glances toward the wall clock. They open the door. The **Girl** *enters.*

Father   What about the boy?

Girl   Oh – didn't I bring him?

Father   Why not?

Girl   I need to talk about something.

Father   What is it?

Girl   I am getting divorced.

Father (*astounded*)   And you just simply announce it like that?

Girl   How else am I supposed to do it then?

Father   Somehow more gently.

Girl   I am the one divorcing, not you.

Father   And how about your mother? Have you thought of her?

Girl I have always thought of her. Now I can't.

Mother (*approaching*) What's going on?

Father She says she is getting divorced.

Mother What do you mean divorced?

Girl I can't stand to live with him anymore.

Mother We don't get divorced in our family.

Girl No. But I will anyway.

Mother What do you mean you will? Look at me, did I divorce? No, I didn't. I have carried on, because in our family everybody carries on.

Father And me too, I didn't divorce either. Because then your mother would have been a divorcée. Your mother is not a divorced woman. When half the kids in your class had divorced parents, we were still together.

Mother Only this has true value. If you untie the knot of marriage, then nothing makes sense. We become like dogs, happy to lie with anyone.

Father Dogs don't do it lying down.

Mother What are you involved in this for? I just mentioned the dog thing, the emphasis was not on the sleeping or the position – and anyway, I don't have time to watch documentaries on dogs' mating habits. I have a house to run, so don't criticize what I am saying. The point is that you can only break things once, because after they're broken, they will stay broken.

Father Marriage is like football. It's fine when the players are up and running, but rubbish when they're injured on the ground.

Mother Is football the only thing in your mind?

Father It's the World Cup soon.

Girl He drinks.

Mother He drinks? So what? All men drink; drinking is not a reason to divorce. There would be no marriages left in Hungary.

Father How much?

Girl More.

Father That's a problem.

Mother Why would it be a problem? You always drank more. Even on our wedding anniversary. Still no divorce.

Father That is exactly why.

Mother What is exactly why?

Father Because there was still no divorce after so many years.

Mother Drank because you were happy, right?

Father I don't know, I don't remember. I really overdid it, but nowadays I forget everything when I drink. I even forget why I drink.

Girl He is aggressive, too.

Mother Aggressive? I haven't known him like that. I can't believe that someone who is as polite and well mannered as he is could be aggressive.

Girl It's all an act. Everyone thinks that he is not like that, but he is – he is just good at pretending.

Mother I don't think so. It's only actors who have a need to perform in life; they are the ones who get muddled up with their roles, but not Tamàs. He is an engineer.

Girl You shouldn't look down on him so much because he is an engineer.

Mother Me? Of course I don't. But I just don't believe that he can pretend to be different.

Father No, I can't either. I got on well with Tamàs; we understood each other quite well.

Mother Yes. Especially when you have to get wine.

Father Yes, but also about women.

Mother Women? What women?

Father Not about specific women, but women in general. We really understood each other well on the subject of what women are really like. And look, he is the one proven right, since he is the one being dumped just because he likes his drink.

Girl Dad, it's me who is your daughter.

Father Of course you are.

Girl Then you shouldn't defend him.

Father I am not defending anyone; I just want to be fair.

Girl To be honest, I can't go on living with him. I have already made up my mind.

Father Then don't blame the alcohol if that is your decision.

Girl The alcohol is part of my decision.

Father I can't believe that.

Girl But it's true.

Mother And where will you live? You can't stay with your ex-mother-in-law.

Girl No, not there, not for a minute.

Mother Then where? Where can a divorced woman with a six-year-old kid go?

Girl Home.

Mother Home here? That's a no. Your father has high blood pressure – you can't do that to him. And me too, I've got heart problems. And anyway, your father has been sleeping in your bedroom since you moved out.

Girl I was just about to say no, not home, because that is why I got married – so that I could get out of here.

Mother You got married because you got pregnant.

Daughter I got pregnant so that I could leave, because I couldn't carry on with you two. I couldn't breathe around you. You were constantly on my case. When am I getting back home? Who am I going out with? What shall I wear? . . .

Mother Parents have responsibilities.

Daughter I was not a child anymore.

Mother To a parent, the child is always a child. Even when they grow up.

Father On top of that, you were only seventeen, legally a minor.

Mother Why do you always have to be so insensitive? We are talking about our child here, not a legal matter.

Father Fine, I just meant that even if we set aside the emotional aspects of things, she is our child legally, too.

Mother Oh, let's leave it. The point is that we wanted you to be happy, for you to go to university, for example. We only wanted what was best for you.

Daughter You? Wanting the best? You drove me into this marriage. Even Tamàs looked a better option than you. So anyway, I am not coming home; you don't need to worry about that.

Mother Renting then? How will you afford that? Tamàs won't give you much because he doesn't have it himself. He'll be lucky to give you what the court orders.

Girl What about Grandma's flat?

Mother Grandma's flat?

Girl Yes. It's sitting there empty since she died . . .

Mother We've only just buried her.

Girl It's been over half a year.

Father Isn't it convenient that she died now instead of dying next year? Because then you couldn't have mentioned it . . .

Mother Leave my mother alone. At least now she is dead.

Father That's why I don't believe in God, because everyone's resurrected. Even your mother.

Mother How can you hate someone for so long? Especially someone who isn't alive anymore?

Father   But there was a time when she was alive. Her memory still is.

Mother   No, you can't have that flat.

Girl   Why not? It's sitting there empty – no one is using it.

Mother   It's there because it isn't just mine. We both inherited it. And we can't decide what to do with it yet.

Girl   It could be mine, then.

Mother   Don't you understand? Only half is mine . . . of course I'd give it to you right now if I could, but I can't without Uncle Laci's permission.

Girl   I am sure Uncle Laci won't need it. Why would he? He lives by himself. What would he do with it?

Father   Right, and what if he marries a young secretary from work, who will then take it from him?

Mother   Who will take it away?

Father   A woman. These things happen. Women are capable of anything if their eyes are set on a free flat.

Mother   It would still be his.

Father   Well, that is true too, but still – a flat is a valuable asset. It's not every day you inherit a flat from your parents.

Mother   Once.

Father   Twice maybe, if they were divorced. Actually, it's quite likely the kid of divorced parents will be better off than if the parents stay together. I never thought of this until now. And on top of it all, everybody feels sorry for them.

Mother   Who feels sorry for them?

Father   The teacher at school, and the psychologist who sees them because of their problems as a result of the divorce.

Mother   That's why they get seen, because they've got all these problems. They've got them because their parents are divorcing.

Father   The others have got problems too, but they don't dare to take them to the psychologist. Shrinks are afraid to hear that the kid is full of traumas even though they aren't divorced. No one treats those kids. Only the divorced parents' kids get seen. They need a shrink for the custody hearing anyway. If, for example, your parents had divorced, you wouldn't have had to go through all this with Uncle Laci because you would have inherited two flats to begin with.

Mother   But they didn't divorce, so this is the only one we've got and it has to be shared.

Girl   Then that's the solution. You have to ask Uncle Laci.

Mother   You ask him!

Girl Me? Ask . . . him? You can't be serious. (*Looking at her* **Father**.)

Father I am sure your mother . . .

Mother I always have to do everything around here. If it's anything difficult, I have to do it.

Father He is your brother. I can't tell him to give away his inheritance.

Mother You're behaving like this because you haven't inherited anything.

Father I did inherit, but the value of a flat in the middle of nowhere here in Budapest was only worth a Russian car. That is not my fault.

Mother A secondhand Russian car.

Girl I used to love that car.

Father Me too. The Russians knew what they were doing then. Later they manufactured shittier cars and at higher prices.

Mother I will give him a ring tomorrow.

Girl Uncle Laci always liked me.

Mother Uncle Laci likes everyone. He is that type of person.

Father It's easy to love without responsibility.

Mother His work was his responsibility, not family.

Father Families are different. You can't just say you don't feel like it and go on sick leave.

Mother He never took a day off – not like others who can't wait to get the flu and their pension.

Girl I have to go.

Mother So soon?

Girl The kid . . .

Mother That's right. The kid is the most important. Especially now that he'll grow up with divorced parents.

Father Does he know yet?

Girl He knows something.

Scene Three

The Girl *and the* **Kid** *at home.*

Kid Dad?

Girl At work.

Kid What's he doing so late?

Girl What do you think?

Kid I don't know. Working. He said he has to work a lot. He's at work.

Girl At work? No. He is not working.

Kid What's he doing?

Girl He is drinking.

Kid At his office? Where he works?

Girl Or at the pub.

Kid He is that thirsty?

Girl His kidneys are always dry.

Kid How do they get dry?

Girl It's an expression. Dried out kidneys, like the Sahara.

Kid Sahara?

Girl The Sahara is a desert. There is only sand there.

Kid And kidneys?

Girl They are a body part.

Kid Like hands and feet?

Girl Yes. Like that. We have two kidneys too, but they're in our belly.

Kid When will he be back?

Girl Don't know. When you're asleep.

Kid Does Dad love me?

Girl He loves you. But not me.

Kid Not you?

Girl No, he doesn't.

Kid He probably doesn't have time. And you? You love him, don't you?

Girl No, I don't either.

Kid Why? You don't have time either?

Girl No, me neither.

Kid When will you have time for it?

Girl For what?

Kid Time to love each other.

Girl It's possible that we may never again.

Kid Never, ever?

Girl Never. These things happen sometimes. You understand that, don't you? It means that now we have to do things separately, just like your mates at school.

Kid There are three in my class, actually four, because now there is Gabor's family too.

Girl Gabor's too?

Kid Yes, but I am the only one who knows.

Girl There will be more and more. By the time you are in the eighth grade, there will be . . .

Kid But not you, right?

Girl Well . . . to be honest.

Kid Not you, right?

Girl Well . . . actually . . . There is no other way.

Pause

Kid Does it mean that you are moving out of Grandma's? Will you not be around anymore?

Girl I will be around, because I am moving out with you.

Kid With me?

Girl Yes.

Kid That's good. But what about Dad? Will he not be around then?

Girl He will be around too. On weekends. You can be together at the weekends.

Kid That's not the same as always.

Girl But he's never home anyway. Not even on Sundays.

Kid But he comes into my room at night and in the mornings.

Girl From now on, it will always be me coming in. I will always be with you.

Kid Will it be us two?

Girl Yes.

Kid And sometimes Dad too?

Girl (*caressing him*) Yes, sometimes him too.

Scene Four

*Room, The **Mother** is putting the phone down.*

Father   So, what did he say?

Mother   That it's all okay.

Father   That he is giving it to her?

Mother   Yes.

Father   Just giving it away like that?

Mother   He is.

Father   Why?

Mother   Because I asked.

Father   Because you said we needed it, and then he just said okay, have it then? I don't need it?

Mother   Basically, yes. I also said something about our childhood.

Father   What?

Mother   That they loved him more.

Father   Did they?

Mother   I felt they did. Love is a feeling, after all.

Father   But it's not so straightforward.

Mother   It is for me. I also said that when we needed help, when mum was already bed ridden, it was me who went to her. I thought it would never end.

Father   But it did.

Mother   It did, and I was there with her. Even then she wouldn't say that it was good to have me around but asked where Laci was. Even then.

Father   She couldn't ask where you were because you were there.

Mother   I was. Laci never lifted a finger for mum.

Father   He wouldn't for himself either. He has a cleaning lady.

Mother   Fair enough, but our parents were our parents; we had to look after them. He could never make time.

Father   I still wouldn't have given away eighty grand, just like that.

Mother   But he did. Because he felt he had to.

Father   That had to feel like shit.

Mother   Not for him. He's not like that.

Father Everyone is. Everything has a price. This will too.

Mother It won't. He is close to our family, since he's without kids. Ours feels like his own to him.

Father Got divorced before he could have any.

Mother His marriage didn't work out. They were a mismatch.

Father He wasn't up for it. He didn't want the commitment.

Mother He would have with the right person. It just didn't happen.

Father He could have found someone. His engineering career was more important; make it to manager, work affairs, one-night stands.

Mother Do you envy him?

Father No. Actually, I don't know. Yes, a little.

Mother Why, did the family thing not work out for you, then?

Father Yes, it did, but I can also picture things differently.

Mother You couldn't picture things then. You couldn't believe you'd become team leader; you thought only others could get it, not you. And without me you couldn't have done it.

Father There is no way of knowing what I would have become if things hadn't happened the way they did.

Mother Nothing probably. You needed the family, and it's me who was there to help you, who could tell you what to do.

Father I thought that for a long time, but I may have become successful too on my own – maybe more. But different, that's for sure.

Mother Everyone is the way they are. No one can be someone else. You are who you are.

Father I have become like this.

Mother You have become like this because you couldn't have become anything else.

Father Life events also shape a person, not just their character.

Mother But events are shaped by you. You needed someone to motivate you; you needed a family so that you could see why it's worth doing.

Father It was you who wanted it this way. I never had the guts to change things because I was afraid that you'd leave me and I'd lose the kid. But actually nobody would have wanted you. I know that now.

Mother If only you knew how wrong you are. Have you got any idea how many men were after me?

Father They only wanted you because you were my wife. They only wanted bits of you; no one wanted you as a whole.

Mother You just carry on believing that.

Father Not just believing it, I know it, but it's too late. Things can't be changed now.

Mother You couldn't have done it anyway.

Doorbell rings

Father Let's drop it. They're here.

Father *opens the door.*

Father By yourself?

Girl He is with his father.

Father Not coming to Sunday lunch?

Girl Can't, because he is with his father.

Mother I won't stop seeing my grandchild because you are divorcing, will I?

Girl He needs to be with his dad too. A boy can't grow up without a father. He needs a male role model.

Mother An alcoholic shouldn't be a role model. Especially not for my grandchild.

Girl He isn't one. He is just a drinker.

Mother Will be one in five years. Without a wife they all turn into one. It's me who pulled your father back.

Father I am the one who said I've had enough. Me, you get it? Me. And, no one can possibly say something like that in someone else's name. I said it when it wasn't fun anymore, when I felt that physically and mentally I –

Mother You said it too, but only after I did.

Father I said it, but it's enough for me to know that I did.

Girl (*taking her coat off*) What did Uncle Laci say?

Mother Are you curious?

Girl Of course I am.

Mother He didn't say anything special.

Girl But go on, what did he say?

Mother That we are his family.

Girl I know that already. So is he willing to give it away?

Mother He is.

Girl He doesn't want anything for it?

Mother Nothing.

Father That's what I can't quite believe.

Mother Not everyone is like you. Some stinge bag! Hanging on to your old clothes . . . rather than let me donate them to charity. I had to sneak them out of the cupboard.

Girl Really, Dad?

Father No, that's not true. I only wanted my favourite tracksuit bottoms, because I love those.

Mother But look at the state of them! You can't even take out the garbage in them.

Father But I loved them. Don't you get it?

Mother You? You don't love anyone, not even your old tracksuit bottoms, only yourself.

Father Why are you saying this? Why are you always bad-mouthing me?

Girl Yes, mum, you really shouldn't always go on about Dad; it's bad for me too. After all, Dad is Dad to me. Actually, I was a daddy's girl for a long time.

Mother I didn't mean anything really, but the fact remains that your father has a very low opinion of everybody.

Father Not because I don't like them, but I am just a realist with my friends. I don't want to be biassed just because they are my friends.

Mother But if you liked them, you could understand them better.

Father I do like them. If they need me, I am always here to help – just a phone call away.

Girl Okay, let's leave this. I have heard this thousands of times. I don't even know how you can stand it – it's like you've memorized the same bunch of phrases.

Father Because this is our life. This is what was put on our plate.

Mother Not that one again.

Father I have heard 'I have heard it a thousand times' a thousand times –

Mother I am only saying that in thirty years, you have said everything that can be said.

Father I won't say another word then.

Mother That doesn't make you interesting either. I don't think there is anything going on up there. Just nothing, plus all the stuff you've already said.

Girl Could I get some attention, please? Or can you give it only to yourselves?

Mother We've always given you lots of attention. You were what we lived for.

Father And I got left out along the way.

Mother Of what?

Father Let's drop it.

Girl So did it go smoothly without any hiccups?

Mother It did.

Girl When is it possible to move?

Mother Tomorrow, if need be. Next week is better though. A few things need clearing.

Girl Mum, this is . . . good.

Mother Isn't it?

Father Really good, right?

Mother You had nothing to do with it, so don't you get involved.

Father Because he is your brother.

Girl I would never have thought it could go as smoothly as this.

Mother You know how I am when it's about you.

Girl I'll still give Uncle Laci a call though.

Mother Absolutely. This needs a big thanks.

Girl Actually, how big is the flat?

Mother I looked on the papers. Sixty square metres. The smallest room will do for the kid, the bigger for you. You'll be alright for space.

Girl For now, yes.

Mother As long as you wish.

Girl But not if we are three, we wouldn't.

Mother But there are the two of you.

Girl At the moment.

Mother What do you mean at the moment?

Girl It's possible there will be more of us. The family may grow – two can become three.

Mother Did you split up because you are seeing someone?

Girl No, of course not.

Mother If you are, that would explain the breakup.

Girl Don't you understand? There is no one.

Mother What kind of loser would break up a marriage? It's usually secretaries in their thirties, because their only chance is a married man. But why does a man want a woman with a family? They can lay their hands on someone younger – even in their fifties.

Girl I am telling you I am not seeing anyone, but I don't want to stay single.

Father And you don't need to. You mustn't. The boy needs to have a father.

Mother He has a father.

Father Yes, but they need one at home.

Girl That's part of it. And it's bad for me, too, to be alone.

Mother It's better if you prepare yourself for a single life.

Girl Why?

Mother With a kid you don't have much chance.

Girl You really shouldn't encourage me this much.

Mother It's better to face reality.

Girl I am facing it.

Mother If you had been, you wouldn't have divorced.

Girl If I stay, nothing changes in my life.

Mother No change is good because then it can't get any worse.

Girl But can't get any better, either.

Scene Five

Office, name-day celebration drinking. Female colleagues are a little drunk.

Kati So you're single now?

Girl I can't find anyone.

Aniko Have you looked everywhere?

Girl What do you mean, everywhere?

Aniko Under the bed? (*Laughs.*)

Girl Silly cow . . .

Kati It doesn't matter whether you are single or not.

Girl What do you mean?

Kati I am repulsed by him.

Girl By your husband?

Kati Just the sight of him . . .

Aniko Don't look.

Kati I don't. He climbs on me anyway.

Girl Don't you like it when he does? You don't feel like it?

Kati I'd vomit if it wasn't for the sheets.

Aniko Wow. That's brutal.

Girl I miss it.

Aniko But you look great. I can't believe that there is no one out there for you.

Girl The single ones over thirty always have something wrong with them, you know. They are either ugly, stupid, or they drink.

Kati Or they're gay . . .

They laugh as they all look towards someone in the room.

Aniko Oh, like . . .

Girl He isn't. Is he?

Kati Didn't you know?

Girl No.

Aniko You can even tell by his walk . . .

Girl It didn't seem any different to me.

Kati Well, he is.

Girl So that's him out.

Aniko Yes, count him out. That's one less available.

Girl I don't want to be on my own.

Kati Then why did you leave your husband?

Girl Because I ended up hating him. And I realized that he wasn't the one. I did it so I didn't have to breathe the same air as my parents.

Kati Well, what can I say? I am staying because I have got two kids and I am not as brave as you. But then, twice a week I have to put up with his grunting and moaning. I would have never thought that ten minutes can be so fucking long. And it's disgusting when he touches me; however much I try to rationalize it, my skin crawls. I am doing it for the kids, because they need a family. They need to have parents they can love and feel safe with.

Girl But this is exactly what I didn't want. I don't believe that there isn't an alternative. It must work out for some people.

Kati I don't think so. They just don't talk about it.

Girl   Just like my parents. I will make sure I don't bury them in the same grave.

Kati   Two graves are double the price, and you have to water the flowers for both.

Girl   I am still not going to stick them together once they're dead.

Kati   It doesn't matter to the dead.

Aniko   Thanks a lot, guys. I've still got everything ahead of me.

Kati   That's the best time, because everything is still possible.

Aniko   Like what?

Kati   You still can dream about all the good stuff and not just the shitty future.

Scene Six

In **Mother** *and* **Father***'s living room*

Mother   I told you that you shouldn't leave . . . If you ended it, it's part of the deal, this goes with it, you will be alone . . . Who said that they will be queuing up for you? I did tell you that with a kid, no one will want you . . . What will you do if you have to be alone? . . . Is this my problem now? I can't resolve it for you. I helped with the flat . . . You should be grateful you are not renting, at least, and that newest loser of yours has somewhere to stay . . . You say you don't want the leftovers? Only the real one will do now, will it? That the real one will be next . . . Do you think your father was the real one for me? . . . Well, no. But he was the one around when needed, and then you try to choose the lesser evil . . . Others are lonely too. And the ones who don't feel it yet will feel it later. No one has got anyone; they just live together because they think they have to – . . . I have told you that . . . It's definitely not my fault, that you are alone at thirty; I am not to be blamed for that.

Mother *puts the phone down*

Father   What is she saying?

Mother   Same as always, upset that she hasn't got a husband.

Father   She had one, but didn't want it.

Mother   That's what I said too, that she had one.

Father   What does she want then? At least she has got a kid.

Mother   It's not enough for her.

Father   She'll eventually find someone.

Mother   Apparently her generation are all married.

Father   They'll divorce.

Mother   She doesn't want to break up a marriage.

Father Not good to anyway. Actually, it wouldn't have been ethical either.

Mother It's a pity that you have only just realized that.

Father Realized what?

Mother What is ethical.

Father I didn't just realize – I have always known.

Mother Then somehow you must have forgotten.

Father When?

Mother When you were seeing that stupid bimbo from human resources.

Father Why do you always have to bring that up?

Mother I am just saying that you could have remembered your ethics then.

Father I needed someone – you know that. I needed someone because you weren't interested in me.

Mother I did the laundry and kept the house in order. That is a woman's job at home.

Father Other things needed doing, but you were always too tired.

Mother A person can get bored with that. You can't do the same old things in bed over a lifetime – everything always the same. As soon as the kid fell asleep, grabbing me, all frantic to get what you wanted.

Father I'd been waiting for hours.

Mother But we couldn't do anything when the kid was up.

Father Even after that, you were in the kitchen. I was in bed waiting and was thinking you were waiting for me to fall asleep so that you didn't have to.

Mother With women it doesn't work the same way. You have to create something . . .

Father What?

Mother A mood.

Father The mood was I wanted you. For years I did. Ten years went by and I still did. Then twenty and I still wanted . . .

Mother You didn't give me any attention. I barely got under the duvet and you were pulling me under you. You had no idea what a woman is like, what she needs, you thought it was the same as for you. Well, it isn't.

Father Because you didn't love me.

Mother The basic rule of marriage is that we love each other. There is no need to constantly prove it.

Father That girl was different. She understood me. She wanted me, not a husband.

Mother Didn't she want you to marry her then?

Father Only so she could give me more. More love.

Mother And you believed it.

Father It was true. She didn't have the opportunity to love me, just a few hours in secrecy.

Mother If it had been more, she would be the one sitting here – not me. And she'd be exactly like me, just ten years younger. No one is better than anyone.

Father I only stayed because I didn't want to harm the kid, I didn't want her not to have a father.

Mother No. You stayed because you didn't have it in you to start again. This marriage only worked out because of me.

Father I stayed for the kid so that I could love her and she could love me.

Mother You don't need to stay because of her now.

Father She left because of you.

Mother Who looked for her at night?

Father Because you said it would be my fault if something happened to her.

Mother You would have gone anyway.

Father You didn't allow her to make her own decisions in things that she easily could have made. You did with her what you did with your mum and dad. You were always right.

Mother Why didn't you say something, if you didn't like the way I did things?

Father I couldn't say anything because you said that if someone keeps a lover, they better shut up. And I did. Everything is like this because I shut up and let you reorganize everybody's life. But I didn't want what you did.

Mother You didn't want anything.

Scene Seven

Dating agency's office

Girl I am a little embarrassed to be here, actually. I am not here as a last resort, I just would like to look at my options.

Matchmaker Miss, everyone is embarrassed in these situations, but this goes with the territory, and I understand exactly. If I didn't, this wouldn't be my job. But there is no need to worry. Up to now, all our customers have left satisfied.

Girl It's just that . . . this is not how it's supposed to be. You are supposed to fall in love and then –

Matchmaker You need a little help. Nowadays, everyone is so busy. People don't get the chance to meet anyone because they don't have the opportunities.

Girl Yes, but it's hard to accept it emotionally . . . that you can do things this way too.

Matchmaker Not to worry, Miss, I will find the right man for you. I have been in your shoes myself.

Girl Really? The same happened to you?

Matchmaker Worse – I have got two kids. I know it's a bit like losing a coffee maker and opening a café. (*They laugh.*) But life goes on and I was able to hold on to the coffeemaker and the flat, actually – because of the kids, really.

Girl That's lucky.

Matchmaker I know what it's like to be in this situation. Believe me, you've come to the best place. If you had gone to a shrink, you wouldn't have got anywhere, not even after a year. You would just pay and talk for years, analyse everything and come up with the idea that when you were a baby you were in love with your father's penis . . .

Girl What?

Matchmaker They can find out stuff like that . . .

Girl It's that advanced now?

Matchmaker A lot of water has gone under the bridge since Freud.

Girl Well, this is still hard for me, really . . .

Matchmaker We are action people, so there is no need to fear any talking, or guilt tripping, or any other phobias. Simply tell us what type you would like.

Girl You mean, looks wise?

Matchmaker That too, and personality wise – the whole person, really. And then I will try to get a close match . . .

Girl Well, six feet tall . . . Prefer darker hair, and if I can be choosey –

Matchmaker Of course you can. What age?

Girl Over thirty really . . .

Matchmaker With a degree?

Girl Yes, he would have to have one.

Matchmaker Any hobbies, activities?

Girl I don't care as long as it's not something crazy like bodybuilding or gambling.

Matchmaker Of course not, I wouldn't wish that on my worst enemy. Basically, we wouldn't even have anyone weird like that on our list.

Girl Good. It's just that you meet so many different people, and I am a bit cautious. I wouldn't want to get involved in anything weird, but I know that having a kid makes it harder.

Matchmaker Not necessarily.

Girl Really?

Matchmaker (*turning pages*) If it works, the kid won't change anything, he will just fit in with the new ones.

Girl Which new ones?

Matchmaker Well, the ones that the other partner brings.

Girl I wouldn't want one who also has –

Matchmaker Not with kids, then?

Girl No. It's enough that I have one.

Matchmaker So this is a deal breaker for you?

Girl It isn't for others?

Matchmaker We will find someone without a child then, someone who is okay with you having one. You will be different from each other in that regard.

Girl In what?

Matchmaker Regarding the child

Girl I wouldn't want to raise someone else's.

Matchmaker I can understand that. You will have more anyway.

Girl What will I have more of?

Matchmaker Children. Don't you want any more?

Girl I couldn't even think of it while single, but with the right person I probably wouldn't say no.

Matchmaker Well then, your partner, Miss, oh let's not be formal, as we are talking so intimately. You don't mind, do you, as I am older anyway?

Girl I thought we were the same age.

Matchmaker No, I am past forty. But all these successful love stories here have made me look younger . . .

Girl You didn't have any work done?

Matchmaker Nothing, just the simplest cream really.

Girl It's unbelievable that –

Matchmaker Please, don't – it's me who is going to get embarrassed . . . So (*looking through in her book*), this man here will be your partner. (*Takes out his picture and shows it.*)

Girl This one?

Matchmaker You don't like him?

Girl Yes, I do, a lot. But isn't he married yet? He doesn't have a wife?

Matchmaker He did have a relationship, but it didn't work out.

Girl Any kids?

Matchmaker None. I told you I will not drag you into something that you don't want. I know my clients . . .

Girl I can barely believe that a man like that is single. He must have some flaws. Does he drink?

Matchmaker Of course not.

Girl Take drugs?

Matchmaker What are you thinking? I told you if they have problems, they don't even make the list.

Girl But isn't he – So, isn't it because he is . . .

Matchmaker He isn't gay, if that's what you are thinking.

Girl Gosh, I was getting worried.

Matchmaker And he isn't bisexual either.

Girl So what could be wrong with him then?

Matchmaker With this client everything is absolutely fine.

Girl Are you sure? Not even something small? Everybody has got something wrong with them.

Matchmaker Well . . .

Girl I knew there must be something.

Matchmaker Well, to be honest, there is a tiny thing, but it's not really that relevant . . .

Girl Still, what is it?

Matchmaker He . . . He is not very good with money, and he doesn't know how to sell himself in the work environment . . . He doesn't know the modern way of presenting himself at interviews . . .

Girl It's just that? Wow, what a huge weight off my shoulders.

Matchmaker I can see that. (*Laughs.*) So money seems to slip through his fingers. Money just slips through his fingers.

Girl The past is the past. I will teach him.

Matchmaker I like a determined person.

Girl If someone is without goals, they shouldn't expect anything from life.

Matchmaker You are absolutely right; you can meet each other on Saturday night at our club then.

Girl What club?

Matchmaker Well, it's actually like a pub.

Girl A pub?

Matchmaker Yes, but you can also have tea, and there is music and the staff are very discreet.

Girl Can anyone go in, then?

Matchmaker Anyone, yes, but mainly the ones I send there because I have a close – more like an exclusive – relationship with the owner.

Girl But isn't there the risk of . . .

Matchmaker No, of course not; this is a discreet place. And I want to share something with you.

Girl What?

Matchmaker This is how the owner found himself a partner.

Girl Through a dating agency?

Matchmaker Yes, but back then this club and this office didn't exist.

Girl Then how?

Matchmaker At my flat, actually. That's what I used then – well, one of the rooms.

Girl And you found him the right person?

Matchmaker For him and for someone else too –

Girl I am assuming for a lady too.

Matchmaker You could say that.

Girl I don't understand.

Matchmaker Well, for myself too.

Girl So this means that . . .

Matchmaker That's right. We have been together ever since. That was my first job and it worked out straightaway. Your future marriage is built on this success.

Girl It's reassuring to see a positive example.

Matchmaker And this one is a positive one. You can bet on it.

Girl   I shouldn't bet on anything, don't you think?

Matchmaker   It's just a saying.

Girl   I know, but in my situation, you see, things could very well not work out. I am superstitious.

Matchmaker   You are different. You are strong. Have faith in yourself. On Saturday everything will sort itself out if you want it to.

Girl   I want it to.

Scene Eight

Little boy arrives at his grandparents'. A few years have gone by since the first scene. Doorbell rings.

Mother   He is here.

Father   I can hear it. I am on my way.

Kid   Good afternoon, Grandad.

Father   Oh good, we were starting to get worried.

Kid   Good afternoon, Grandma. School just finished, I came right away.

Mother   Come on, quick, your lunch will get cold.

*The **Kid** throws his stuff down, enters the room, and sits in the chair that **Uncle Laci** will later sit on.*

Father   Are you sitting comfortably?

Kid   Yes, I am.

Father   That is the best seat.

Kid   Why?

Father   From there you get a good view of the window, the whole table, and even the TV.

Mother   All the seats are good.

Kid   The TV isn't even on.

Father   It's not on because we are eating.

Kid   It doesn't matter then.

Father   What?

Kid   That you can see it from here.

Father   Doesn't matter now.

Mother   How was school?

Kid   We had five lessons.

Mother   Isn't that a lot?

Kid   Six would be a lot.

Father   Do you like your teacher?

Mother   Women again?

Father   What women?

Kid   The teacher.

Mother   The boy knows this stuff already. He is no different, will turn out just like you.

Father   He is old enough to differentiate between a man and a woman.

Mother   I am not talking about that.

Kid   Yes, I like her.

Mother   Who do you like?

Kid   The teacher lady.

Mother   Oh, yes of course. Do you have friends?

Kid   Yes, I do.

Father   How many?

Kid   A lot.

Mother   Are they good students?

Kid   They are.

Mother   It's important to befriend those.

Father   Why only those? He can be friends with anyone he likes.

Mother   Better not with anyone else.

Father   Actually I used to have gypsy friends.

Mother   Let's leave this gypsy thing in front of the boy.

Father   Why?

Mother   I don't want him to talk about gypsies at school, and for the school to think that he heard it from us when we are not prejudiced like that.

Father   I wasn't being derogatory.

Kid   Dad took me to the pool on Sunday.

Father   You can swim? You didn't say.

Kid   I can.

Father   And where did Mum take you?

Kid   When?

Mother   Sunday.

Kid   On Sundays I am with Dad.

Mother   Oh yes, of course. It escaped my mind.

Father   Do you like the soup?

Kid   It's nice. What kind is it?

Mother   Parsnip cream soup.

Kid   From a packet?

Mother   Isn't it good from a packet?

Kid   It is. The packet one is my favourite. I saw the ad on TV. Looked really good.

Mother   Doesn't this look good, too?

Kid   This looks really good too, but I meant that did, too.

Mother   Well, that's okay. Grandad is bringing the meat in soon.

Kid   I don't want any meat.

Mother   How come you don't want any?

Kid   I am not hungry.

Mother   You are probably not eating properly at home, and your stomach must have shrunk.

Kid   No, it's just I also ate at school.

Mother   At the school too?

Kid   Yes, because I am on school dinners.

Mother   Why am I cooking then?

Father   We eat at home too.

Mother   I wouldn't bother for my sake. A little bread and ham is plenty for me.

Father   I like it if there is some hot food.

Kid   You are cooking so that there will be some left for the days I don't eat here.

Mother   Yes, sure. I didn't think of that.

Father   I didn't think so.

Mother   What?

Father   That you didn't think of me.

Mother   So what about you?

Father   That I also eat at home.

Scene Nine

The dating agency's club. A bit bare. Semi darkness. Oldies playing. Chatting couples obviously at different stages of relationships. A **Man**, *alone, is waiting at the table.*

The **Girl** *arrives.*

Girl Hi.

Second Man Hi. Did you recognize me straight away?

Girl The picture helped.

Second Man I recognized you too.

Girl Well – and you are the only one by yourself, apart from the waiter.

Second Man Do you want a drink?

Girl Something not too fancy.

Second Man What do you have in mind?

Girl The Hawaiian cocktail in this picture. (*Showing him the drinks menu.*)

Second Man Is that not too fancy?

Girl Well, it's possible that I used the wrong word. I meant something not too strong.

Second Man No, you didn't use the right word.

Girl Does it matter that I didn't?

Second Man No, no, just the precise type. Engineering degree. And I'm into computing. You can't be vague.

Girl That's good then. Precise people are reliable.

Second Man Yes, they are.

Girl And that is exactly the type I need.

Second Man What type?

Girl The reliable partner type.

Second Man Me too.

Girl Then, we have a lot in common.

Second Man In what?

Girl In that we both want reliable partners.

Second Man That's right, we are the same in that. Shall we dance?

Girl I don't know, isn't that too soon?

Second Man I have been looking for a year.

Girl Actually me too, more like for three years, really. But you see, because of the kid it can't be just anyone.

Second Man I know, the agency told me.

Girl But it's not a problem, is it?

Second Man Of course not, we will become mates. Does he like . . .?

Girl What?

Second Man Does he like boys' stuff?

Girl He does. Droids and GI Joes.

Second Man What?

Girl They're the boy toys nowadays, not soldiers.

Second Man Pity, because I am really good at playing soldiers. I wanted to become one when I was a kid.

Girl Aren't you disappointed you didn't become one?

Second Man Life comes with disappointments. What's important is that you know how to deal with them.

Girl And do you know how?

Second Man If I didn't I wouldn't be here.

Girl What do you mean? I am part of the therapy?

Second Man No, of course not, it's only like that with people who can't handle these things. And you wouldn't give them the time of day anyway, as they would be psychopaths or addicts.

Girl But not you?

Second Man Of course not. Do you want to dance?

Girl This slow one is good.

They dance.

Scene Ten

Sunday lunch at the parents'. **Father** *and* **Mother** *are peeking through the window.*

Mother They are coming.

Father It's about time. (*He gets closer to the window.*)

Mother He doesn't look bad at all.

Father Why would he look bad?

Mother   I didn't think that a woman with a kid had any chances.

Father   Why wouldn't she?

Mother   I wouldn't have had any when I was that age.

Father   No, you wouldn't have.

Mother   Why do you have to say that now?

Father   Others would have had chances.

Mother   No, they wouldn't have. They were different times. Women didn't have these opportunities. He is not even shorter than her.

Father   No. Because he is taller.

Mother   And isn't fat.

Father   No, he isn't.

Doorbell rings

Father (*opening the door*)   Come on in.

Second Man   Good afternoon. Here I am, sir.

Father   Please, formalities are not for me. Keep those for the mother.

Second Man   Thank you – from now on then. I was ready to be formal. Sorry if I messed up.

Father   You will get used to it. Formalities don't matter with us. We are not like that.

Second Man   Good afternoon, ma'am.

Mother   Good afternoon. I am glad to finally meet you. I have heard a lot about you.

Father   The kid?

Girl   With his father, Sundays are his.

Mother   It slipped my mind.

Girl   Could we go in instead of crowding in the hall here?

Father   Of course, come on in, come on in, you must be hungry.

Awkwardness in the hall, bumping into each other, they don't know how to get around each other.

Girl   Listen, we simply can't all fit here.

Father   Yeah, that's right. I'll go first then, and really – apologies for this narrow hall. Please take a seat.

Mother   I am bringing the soup.

Mother *brings the soup out.*

Girl   What kind of soup is it?

Mother   Cream of parsnip.

Girl   From a packet?

Mother   But I added sour cream.

Girl   Why do we have to eat such artificial stuff on Sundays?

Mother   That's all I've got energy for. I am doing it all alone. You know your father isn't –

Father   I set the table. You didn't have to do that.

Mother   Compared to cooking, it's nothing.

Second Man   I like it.

Mother   Yes, it's not so bad, is it?

Father   What do you do?

Mother   We know he is an engineer.

Father   Oh, yes we do. Where do you live?

Girl   What is all this cross-examining about?

Father   I am just showing interest.

Second Man   It's not a problem at all. Really. I have a bachelor's flat in the outskirts of Pest. That's where I live.

Mother   Don't you need a bigger place? How old are you?

Second Man   It didn't matter till now, but it will be different from now on.

Father   So you are serious about this?

Second Man   Yes, it's time to take these things seriously.

Girl   Especially now.

Mother   Why especially now?

Girl   Now that I am pregnant.

Second Man   You are pregnant? You didn't say anything.

Girl   I thought it would be a surprise. And I wasn't completely sure.

Second Man   We should have discussed this beforehand . . .

Girl   You are the one who said not to use contraceptives.

Second Man   But this is so sudden.

Mother   Another kid?

Girl   That is how we can become a family.

Father I am a little surprised myself.

Girl You will have another grandchild.

Father Okay, but still – it's a little unexpected.

Mother Another kid in that small flat?

Girl We will move by then.

Father When?

Girl By the time the kid arrives.

Second Man A kid and moving, it's all going a little too fast for me.

Girl (*stroking him*) It will be good, believe me. We wanted a kid, and now we have one.

Second Man I thought you needed more time to think about things like that. And that after you decided such things, it would take a little while after that. And I also thought that I would be the one to hear about it first.

Girl I did want to tell you first, but it just slipped out. But you are pleased, aren't you?

Second Man I am still in shock, so I can't just be yet – but I will be soon.

Father This gives meaning to a man's life. Otherwise we wouldn't do anything. If we didn't have to provide for our family, it would just be the pub and our mates. I actually have a theory that it is because of children that there is a European culture.

Second Man I thought it was because of the cold weather. Because you have to build houses and have heating, as opposed to where Blacks live, where they've got bananas hanging off trees and, no doubt, you don't even need to wear underpants, it's so hot.

Mother Well, family is the most important thing – that's how our society evolved. By the way, research proves that women who have brought up kids live longer than those who lived alone.

Second Man And the men?

Mother That, I don't know.

Father It may be better not to know.

Second Man We were going to go to Corfu. I have already paid for it.

Girl We can still go; it's only the third month. Doesn't even show yet. You can easily wear a swimsuit and do anything . . .

Mother You are going to Corfu?

Girl We need a shared experience.

Father What will happen to the kid?

Girl He is going to the lake with his father.

Mother Shouldn't you all go together?

Girl That's not what it's about now. It's about the two of us.

Mother He could stay with us.

Girl He can't now.

Mother Why not?

Girl He'll be with his father.

Mother I am getting the meat. You are not vegetarian, are you? Or some Asian type?

Second Man What do you mean, Asian?

Mother Like Krishna believers.

Second Man No, I am not religious.

Father We're not either.

Mother Only you aren't.

Father Well, are you?

Mother I have always been.

Father When did you last go to church?

Mother It has nothing to do with church. Besides, I wouldn't know which one to go to.

Girl To a Catholic one, where Grandma went too.

Mother But your grandad didn't go there.

Girl Of course not. Because he didn't go anywhere.

Father Only to Party meetings.

Mother Because he had to for his job. Anyway, he was a specialist in his field, wasn't into politics at all.

Father I know, I am just saying that he went there and not to church.

Mother Yes, but not in his childhood.

Father I think we should leave your father's childhood alone; there is no need to analyse everything.

Girl I am actually quite interested, since you started it.

Father Childhood is only of interest to psychologists so they can make the kids hate their parents.

Girl You don't need a psychologist for that.

A little silence.

Mother Only half, really.

Girl What is half?

Mother He was only half of what he was.

Girl Who?

Mother Your grandad, and I only a little, and you not at all.

Father Will you bring that meat in? I am starving!

Girl What am I not?

Mother I am coming.

Act Two: Eight to ten years later

Scene One

A street.

First Man   Hi. I haven't seen you for a while.

Girl   Me either. Actually, I saw you once.

First Man   Where?

Girl   I don't remember. Just from the bus. Are you all right?

First Man   I am.

Girl   And your daughter?

First Man   She is ten. And yours?

Girl   Ten and eight.

First Man   You've got two now.

Girl   Yes, two. And your wife?

First Man   She isn't anymore.

Girl   How come?

First Man   Just like you. She left and took the kid.

Girl   I am sorry to hear that.

First Man   I only married her because you had found someone new. If you hadn't, I wouldn't have started all over again. I wouldn't have burdened myself with a long term project.

Girl   So, it's still my fault, is it? You are still pointing at me when things go wrong?

First Man   Not anymore. But when I married her I still did. And the kid came along for that reason too. In a way it's lucky I am only just finding out you have got two.

Girl   How about work?

First Man   I went bankrupt.

Girl   So you are unemployed?

First Man   Yeah.

Girl   Since when?

First Man   It's been six months.

Girl   What do you live on?

First Man   Off the benefits for awhile, and nowadays I am working for a mate of mine.

Girl   Doing what?

First Man   He does flat renovations, and I take care of the plumbing and electrics.

Girl   So, you do have a job then.

First Man   Mostly in the spring. And the kid?

Girl   What about him?

First Man   Do you know how he is?

Girl   We talk on the phone sometimes. Don't you?

First Man   He doesn't call me.

Girl   You can call him too.

First Man   I don't have any credit on my phone.

Girl   He is well. A bit provincial.

First Man   You wanted that.

Girl   You too.

First Man   Not me, no. I just didn't dare say anything in case you'd think that I didn't mean well.

Girl   If he hadn't gone to boarding school, what do you think he would have been like at home? He was friends with some terrible kids, none had proper parents. Mothers and fathers all over the place.

First Man   Same with our kid.

Girl   We were well organized, though.

First Man   He is still the kid of divorced parents.

Girl   We are all better for it – and that it happened early enough. It would have been much worse to go through years of fighting.

First Man   Maybe, but I didn't want him to be sent away.

Girl   His teacher said he wouldn't pass that year unless I sent him away.

First Man   But he didn't have to go so far away.

Girl   The teachers there were priests. At least they've got some morality left.

First Man   Right, they abuse kids . . .

Girl   These weren't like that. I struggled with him at home. And he didn't have a father.

First Man   What do you mean he didn't have one?

Girl Only the weekends. All he saw was that you haven't made a success of yourself. A new kid, another divorce, you were too busy with yourself. You were not able to be like a real father to him, someone he could look up to.

First Man Look, you had something to do with this as well.

Girl No. That was simply your doing. And you were not a role model for him. Worse, you were a negative role model, and that is why he went to the boarding school. And he is alright at the university in Pécs. It's a lovely town.

First Man But I never see him.

Girl He is an adult.

First Man Does he ever visit?

Girl Rarely.

First Man He isn't happy anywhere.

Girl But he is.

First Man Where?

Girl Where he is now. Are you growing a beard?

First Man No, I just didn't shave.

Girl Why not?

First Man I didn't think I'd meet anyone today.

Girl Sorry, I have to go. I am meeting someone.

First Man Are things okay with you at home?

Girl Every woman wants this. Two kids, a husband, and a family home in Buda's leafy suburbs.

First Man Really?

Girl Yes, from selling my grandmother's flat and my husband's bachelor pad.

First Man You told me that you are only willing to live in Buda proper.

Girl As a matter of fact, it is Buda. Hardly any difference. And it's good for the kids to have a garden, and we are friendly with the neighbours. And you are still outside Pest?

First Man In a Buda suburb now.

Girl Of course – I am being stupid. I don't even know why I said that . . .

First Man Well, as it happens, I do live on the outskirts of town now.

Girl Why? Is it any good there?

First Man I didn't have much choice. When my parents died we sold the house in the suburbs.

Girl That wasn't a bad house, really.

First Man No, it wasn't. My old man built it. It had a few issues, but basically it was good – expandable, even. But my wife didn't like it.

Girl No, I didn't like it at all.

First Man I meant my second wife.

Girl Oh, I thought I was the only one who didn't like it – didn't realise she didn't either.

First Man No, she didn't. We bought another one; they live there now.

Girl Who?

First Man My ex-wife and my daughter. I believe someone else has moved in.

Girl I get it. Sorry, I really have to get going.

First Man If he calls you, tell him to call me.

Girl Who?

First Man The kid.

Girl Ah, of course I will.

Scene Two

A café. The **Girl** *walks in, two other women –* **Aniko** *and* **Kati** *– are already there.*

Kati We thought you weren't going to show up.

Girl I ran into my ex-husband.

Kati Ran into him? Don't you keep in touch?

Girl There is no need anymore.

Aniko How come?

Girl There is no need for the kid's sake. And there wouldn't be any other reason. I haven't seen him for ten years.

Aniko So what was he like?

Girl You only have to look at him to know that to divorce him was the best decision ever. He is now divorced from his second wife too. He lives in poverty in a studio flat in the fucking outskirts somewhere, no credit on his phone, and – I almost forgot – he is unemployed.

Aniko Poor guy.

Girl Don't feel sorry for him. He doesn't deserve it.

Kati You did leave him, after all.

Girl When was that? Fifteen years ago? What, he can't sort himself out in all that time? I hope you are not about to tell me I am responsible for his fucked up life. Look at me. I had a few shit years, but I fixed everything.

Aniko It doesn't work out for everyone. To some people a blow like a divorce is enough to knock them back – enough so they can't start over again. They get stuck with the idea that nothing will ever work out for them.

Kati Are you dating another loser again?

Aniko Not at all! I am just able to understand those who run out of luck. It's not their fault. One bad move . . . Let's say that he married you and then got divorced and that's it . . .

Girl You can only divorce people like him.

Aniko You don't know what could have happened if things turned out differently in his life.

Girl You have only got this one life. There isn't another one, and it wouldn't be possible.

Aniko You are too harsh.

Girl With myself too, though. Generally, I only say things about people I would say about myself. He, by the way, had his parents, who helped a lot. There was something to build on. I had no one, you see – did everything with my own hands.

Kati You did inherit your grandma's flat, didn't you?

Girl I had to fight for that . . .

Aniko It's easier to fight than to earn the twenty million that it cost.

Girl Since then I tripled its value.

Kati But not with your salary.

Girl That's in it too. And it's work to be able to deal with money. It's not enough to earn it. Do you know how much I made on it by the time we moved out?

Kati How much? Actually I know, you already said.

Girl It's gone up since then, property prices here are skyrocketing. I knew about the location.

Kati Does it matter what it's worth? If it were cheaper you would still be living in it just the same.

Girl It matters to me. I am happier if I know it's worth more.

Kati What, so you are sitting in your armchair and feeling that this place has got some value?

Girl Yes, I do, that this is not some shitsville dump where you don't know if you'll get through the night, or whether your neighbour is going to break through the wall and rob you.

Aniko Let's move on from this nonsense. Who is interested in property prices anyway?

Girl I am.

Aniko But I am not.

Girl You two started it, I really only wanted to talk about how you all are.

Aniko Same here. But it's hard to start when we see each other so rarely. It was easier at work when we saw each other every day. How do I start to say that I am feeling really shit actually, because I am thirty-nine years old and completely alone, and that every two years I date worse guys?

Girl But I thought you were dating the guy of your dreams recently . . .

Aniko He went back to his wife – said he could not imagine starting the same stuff all over again.

Kati I knew this would happen.

Girl How could you?

Kati Life experience.

Aniko When did you have life experience like that?

Kati My husband, too, always comes back. At first I was scared that he had a lover and that she'd pull him away and that he'd leave and have a new family, new kids, and end up ignoring the old ones. But he always comes back. He doesn't dare give up the hot meals. He doesn't know what's in store for him in a new relationship, so he stays.

Girl Isn't it crap for you when he has a girlfriend?

Kati I got used to it. It was shit at the beginning. Then I got bored of it. I don't ask him where he is going or when he is coming back, who he gets texts from. He does what he wants. There are, of course, some rules though. If he doesn't break those, I don't give a shit. I don't love him anymore – just got used to us being here together. A family. For the kids.

Girl Do they still live at home?

Kati The eldest isn't anymore, and the youngest wants to move out soon.

Girl It won't be easy when he's gone too.

Kati I can't quite imagine it yet. Until now, it was all about the kids.

Girl Is it not about them?

Kati I don't know, now they'll soon be gone. The question is: What next? I can't believe how quickly it has all gone.

Aniko No. No. It hasn't gone. It will be different, that's all. I, for example, get along really well with my parents. We go on holidays together. I don't resent them.

Kati It's because you don't have a husband and kids. If you had, you wouldn't be with your parents.

Aniko Ouch! Not sure that was necessary.

Kati Why not? It's the truth. Only single people hang out with their parents.

Girl But you will have grandkids.

Kati Those won't be mine. It could be good if one of them divorced and moved in with me, with the kid . . .

Aniko But then your daughter's life would be all screwed up.

Kati Not necessarily. She might be better off with me than with her husband.

Girl That is such bullshit.

Kati You are lucky that you could start all over again.

Girl You do feel younger this way. All the women I hang out with are ten years younger than me. I don't feel it at all. It's like we were the same age. It's the kids' ages that determine how old you feel.

Aniko I don't have any.

Girl You could still have them.

Aniko Last minute.

Kati Try it on your own. Lots of women do it. It's not the way it used to be – people pointing fingers, gossiping behind your back about who the father could be, and calling you a slut.

Aniko I have thought of that too. I am a member of every single dating website so that I could get pregnant by someone, disappear, and have it by myself, but you can't believe the losers. I can't lower my standards to that degree.

Kati All you need is sperm.

Aniko But it still can't be from just anyone. And you have to sleep with them at least once.

Girl But after it's been too long, don't you just go for anyone, when everything reminds you of it, even a cucumber?

Aniko Yes, cucumbers have started to do that. The men worth checking out, anyway, they lie about absolutely everything on the Net. Then you meet them and your jaw drops because they look nothing like what they said. They are ten years older, or have three kids and they need someone because they lost their wife to cancer last year. I went to someone's flat once and found a notebook with a list of how many women he'd slept with.

Kati But not with you?

Aniko Well, to be honest . . .

Girl   After you realized that you would end up on the list?

Aniko   Well, at least he reached the cucumber standard.

They laugh.

Kati   How are things with you?

Girl   Everything is fine.

Aniko   Don't you ever think that you made the wrong decision, maybe?

Girl   Days go by so quickly. A mother of two doesn't have time to think. Ferrying the kids around. School, swimming, private English lessons, Corfu in the summer, and stuff like that . . .

Aniko   Two?

Girl   What do you mean two?

Aniko   Well, two kids?

Girl   Yes. Even two is too many sometimes.

Kati   But it's been a while since you worked.

Girl   Don't you think that it's work to keep that fucking big house tidy?

Kati   But if you had a job on top of it, then it would –

Girl   This is my job.

Aniko   I couldn't bear being kept by a man.

Girl   Especially since you don't have anyone who could keep you. If you had one you would change your mind.

Aniko   No, I wouldn't.

Girl   You don't know that.

Aniko   You couldn't even divorce, even if you wanted to.

Girl   But I don't want to.

Scene Three

At home. It's the evening. The **Man** *arrives home.*

Second Man   The kids?

Girl   They are already asleep.

Second Man   They are always asleep when I get home.

Girl   Because you come home when they are already asleep. If you came home when they weren't asleep, they would be awake.

Second Man I work shit hard.

Girl Others too; they still manage to come home on time.

Second Man I always hurry, but can't leave earlier. It's company policy. I am the first to leave anyway.

Girl 'Cause they don't have anyone to go back to. And sure won't, working this way.

Second Man No, it's because it's an American company. When it's evening here for us, everybody is still working in New York. They need to order stuff for the manufacturing. These software programs become obsolete in five minutes, and it's a rush against time, or someone else comes up with it.

Girl To tell you the truth, I am not an environmentalist. I can't look at my life from a globalisation point of view. I can't think how world events impact my everyday life. Do you get it? I can't accept that I don't have a husband and the kids don't have a father because of a company's policy.

Second Man This is the only way. The ones who don't do it like this are completely broke. I am sure that you wouldn't want that. I don't think you could give up the car, the holidays, and the house, which we owe shit loads on.

Girl We made a joint decision to have these things.

Second Man I didn't have a choice when the kids came along. We had the house, then you. Well, not in that order, but it ended up all shit.

Girl Don't blame the family. You are doing it because you like to.

Second Man No. I hate it.

Girl It's not true. I can see it on you that you enjoy going to work.

Second Man I might as well try to do it with a positive attitude if I have to do it anyway.

Girl You can't talk yourself into it that much. Admit you are happy when you leave home.

Second Man If you didn't fucking nag me all the time, I would be happy to be at home.

Girl I am nagging you because work is more important to you then we are.

Second Man The nagging came first.

Girl I know exactly what came first, because I remember everything. You don't know anything about what goes on at home because you are never at home. You don't even know what my problem is because you are not at home – so how would you know what my problem is, if my problem is that you are not home?

Second Man Let's go to bed. I need to sleep. I put in twelve hours a day; I can't deal with these big arguments at night.

Girl We never discuss anything.

Second Man I have to go to work tomorrow. If you are bored, get yourself signed up for some classes – drama therapy or yoga – but do not nag me every night. I am under such pressure. These kids who were born into programming, they are nipping at my heels. Do you get it? They grew up binary. They will fucking walk all over me, the fuckers, and then it's kiss good-bye to this lifestyle.

Girl I don't care about money.

Second Man If you didn't have it, it's all you'd care about. The reason other things matter more is because we have some. A housewife in India would not have a leg to stand on with this argument.

Girl But we are not in India. If we were there, we would compare it to other things; but we can only compare things to what we've got over here.

Second Man I am sure all this crap won't last long anyway. The Arabs or the Chinese will blow it all up. Everything will collapse. There will be no more traveller's checks and Adriatic beach holidays. It will be the Middle Ages, get it? Then you'll be happy if you can scavenge something to eat and not freeze in the winter.

Girl I don't give a shit about what will happen, because it's not what we have now. I want to live now – the way a family should live. Like my parents who deserve respect for standing by and helping each other.

Second Man You've been saying that their marriage is worth fuck all, and the only reason they didn't divorce was because of you. They actually should have *because* of you.

Girl They still have other values in their lives.

Second Man Like what?

Girl They hold the family together.

Second Man With force.

Girl But we are still together. At least on Sundays. But – you hate them.

Second Man No. I don't hate them. We do get along.

Girl Then it's me who you don't love.

Second Man I do love you. I love you the way I love you. It looked like it was going to work out between us when we first met. And I didn't want it to be the way it was with Gabi when she left one morning and never came back – didn't pick up the phone and I never found out why. She never said she wasn't happy with me, or what I did wrong. She never said, Look Adam, we need to discuss things, and I didn't notice anything apart from it was lovely and good for me. It was bad when she left. I came back from work and there was nothing there. Not even a note saying goodbye. Only empty drawers. I then decided that this wouldn't happen again. I can only love this much. Not more.

Girl You should love me more, same as you loved Gabi.

Scene Four

Flat doorbell rings. The four of them are standing there: the **Girl***, the* **Man** *and the two* **Kids***. The* **Father** *lets them in. We have jumped forward approximately six years.*

Father Only the four of you?

Girl Four, yes.

Mother How many did you expect?

Eldest Kid Hello, Grandad!

Youngest Kid Hello!

Father I was just asking, that's all. Hello everyone.

Mother You are late.

Eldest Kid Hello, Grandma!

Youngest Kid Hello.

Girl Getting the kids ready, you know. And it's quite a distance from the suburbs.

Mother Why on earth did you have to move so far out? If you were here, we could see you more . . .

Girl It's better, trust me. It's a house with a garden.

Eldest Kid We have our own swing.

Youngest Kid And our sandpit.

Mother I have already reheated it twice.

Father It doesn't matter with soup.

Mother But the meat dries out if you reheat it twice.

Second Man Nice food is still nice food, even if it's heated twice.

Mother It is nice, alright, because I can only cook nice food. It's from the best meat. I know the butcher.

Girl If you've got the money, you will get quality anyway. You don't have to know them anymore.

Mother It's still better to know them.

They enter the room; they sit down.

Girl It's packet again?

Mother Isn't it nice?

Girl It is, but it's full of E numbers.

Kid What are E numbers?

Girl Poison.

Father Everything is full of poison. If your body doesn't get used to it, you are finished. Those who can adapt will survive. Those who don't will die out. Basically it's survival of the fittest.

Second Man There are too many of us anyway. Seven billion people. Simply from a logical point of view, a few billion need to die.

Girl I wouldn't like it, from a logical point of view, if it were my descendants who would have to die out. So, it's better to be careful and not overwhelm the system with all kinds of crap, especially not the kids'.

Eldest Kid I like it.

Youngest Kid Me too.

Girl It's full of flavour enhancers. It's got a stronger flavour than the original.

Mother Why can't you be pleased that you didn't have to cook and that we are all together?

Girl I am pleased.

Father How are things at school, kids?

Youngest Kid Everything is fine.

Girl They are studying, what else?

Father Alright, I just wanted to ask them something.

Girl They hate to talk about school.

Mother Do they have friends?

Girl Yes, they do.

Mother Nice ones?

Girl Yes, nice ones.

Father Have you heard yet?

Girl No.

Second Man What has happened?

Girl To who?

Mother With him?

Father Yes, with him. You wouldn't have thought so, right?

Girl No.

Second Man This is delicious. It really came out well.

Girl I told them on the phone that you don't give a shit about what goes on at home.

Second Man Why did you have to do that? It's our business, no one else's.

Girl But I did tell them – they are my parents, after all. Who could I talk to if not to them? So don't you try to sweet-talk everyone, because they know what you are like at home.

Mother His thing is work.

Girl Don't defend him.

Mother I am not, but I do know what they have to do.

Girl It's not compulsory to sit there until nine at night and mess around on the Internet.

Second Man That's when I finally get some work done, because it's so busy during the day I fall behind . . .

Father I know all about that too. When I was working, I also had to . . .

Girl You do it instead of having to come home. I know that's the reason.

Mother At least it's not women.

Girl Who knows? . . . I don't investigate. It's good news if I don't. Actually, can I take a look at your phone? I don't even know the code for it . . .

Second Man A phone is private. There are no secrets in it, but it's still mine. Just like underwear, we don't wear each other's.

Girl But I am allowed to wash them, right?

Father No, really – there are boundaries that need to be respected. It's embarrassing.

Mother You know this all too well. If I hadn't opened that letter . . .

Girl What letter?

Father It doesn't matter; it was a long time ago.

Mother It does matter. You, of course, didn't say a word, and waited in silence for our marriage to fall apart by itself. You didn't want to improve it or for me to change things, but I was able to.

Father It's true. You were able to change. And this is what it has changed into.

Mother Meaning?

Father This is as good as it gets.

Second Man This meat is really excellent, and the mash is –

Girl I can't cope by myself.

Father That house is far too big. Why have so many rooms and a garden on top of it?

Girl We weren't able to stay in Grandma's flat with the kids. No way. We had outgrown it.

Father Yes, but there is a compromise.

Girl But we got it at a good price.

Mother I have also always wanted a house with a garden, but your father wouldn't hear of doing anything about it. He was scared of everything, even of the little loan we'd need for it.

Father I'd like to know how I would have paid it back. You worked part-time. It wasn't feasible.

Mother I worked part-time because I was a housewife too, and I had to iron your shirts.

Girl Did you only work part-time? I never noticed.

Mother Part-time, yes. Couldn't have coped with more.

Girl Why did I always have to go to Grandma's then?

Mother You liked it there and they liked to see you.

Girl I preferred home.

Mother But I needed time to clear up.

Girl Only part-time?

Second Man But you don't even work part-time . . .

Girl No, because a mother of two has more duties, and I was always at Grandma's anyway.

Father A mother of two?

Mother Two.

Girl Where is Uncle Laci?

Father Abroad.

Girl Again?

Father He invested his money in himself, not kids.

Girl But he hasn't got anyone.

Mother Only us.

Father And the occasional tourist guide.

Mother Don't envy him.

Father I don't. He doesn't have a kid. Mind you, no wife either.

Scene Five

The house in a leafy suburb. Gate bell rings. The **Girl** *picks up the receiver. We can see both inside and outside events.*

Girl Who on earth would come at a time like this? No, we don't want to buy anything.

Kati It's me.

Girl Kati? What are you doing here?

Kati Will you let me in? Or should I stand here and freeze?

The **Girl** *opens the door.* **Kati** *walks up from the street side towards the main entrance.*

Girl You said you wouldn't come out here because it's too far out.

Kati I've got to talk to someone.

Girl What's happened?

Kati Do you want the short or long version?

Girl Your choice. Short.

Kati I am getting a divorce.

Girl What do you mean?

Kati I am getting a divorce.

Girl I can't believe it. Now?

Kati Now.

Girl But you've been with him all your life.

Kati Better late than never.

Girl Why?

Kati My youngest daughter has moved out. It's just the two of us. Two of us, you know what I mean? It's unbearable.

Girl What is?

Kati He comes home, doesn't say a word, has been speaking all day apparently. He drinks and farts and stinks. I recently started to notice that he stinks. I don't want to smell this stench. I don't want to live in this stinky atmosphere.

Girl What about the girls?

Kati They don't matter.

Girl They don't?

Kati It made sense to stay together when they were little. It was easier too, because there was someone at home who loved me. But not anymore. They don't want me anymore. They show up sometimes, but can't wait to leave. They pack up some old clothes, eat something. That's it. Even on the phone I can tell that they can't stand speaking to me. Why am I so nosy? They don't care that I show interest in what they've been up to and with whom. They say that I wouldn't know them or the places they've been anyway. I don't matter to them anymore. It truly is just the two of us. My parents are not alive anymore. If they were, at least I could go and see them sometimes. But I can't.

Girl You weren't too keen when they were around.

Kati I always delayed visiting for when I'd be less busy. When I finally had time, they weren't alive anymore.

Girl Are you seeing someone?

Kati Of course not. I didn't go for it when I could have. I didn't want to be doing what everybody else was doing. I thought you could do it differently. Well, you can – but this is how it ends. I prefer to be alone. Alright, I am not saying that if someone lands in my arms I would say no, but I won't be looking. I am happy to be independent. No one will be telling me that I am living off him, and when it's time to do the dishes. I will support myself – won't be much, but I will turn on the washing machine when I please. I won't have to listen to someone else's breathing, to their nightly fogging up the room, and put up with breathing in the air he breathes out.

Girl It's ecological.

They laugh.

Kati Silly cow.

Girl I thought it was alright for you.

Kati Hell, no. It's not alright for anyone.

Girl Yes. For some.

Kati Who?

Girl For your daughters.

Kati Only until they find out how it all ends. That you'll end up hating your husband, that you'll lose your kids. Nobody loves you and you are not able to love anyone else.

Girl When, then?

Kati I will do the Christmas thing. I don't want to divorce around a family celebration.

Girl How is your husband going to take it?

Kati I don't know. If I don't tell him, it's possible that he may not notice for two weeks, when he runs out of clean boxers.

Scene Six

Doorbell ringing. The door opens.

Father Is it the four of you?

Girl Us four, yes.

Eldest Kid Hello, Grandad.

Youngest Kid Hello.

Father Hang your coats up quickly then.

Girl Is Uncle Laci already here?

Father He's been here for half an hour. We've been waiting for you.

Mother *arrives.*

Eldest Kid Hello, Grandma.

Youngest Kid Hello.

Mother Hello. Come in quickly, I am sure the table is set.

Father As in, I set it.

Mother You know you can't cook and set a table at the same time.

In the room

Second Man Hello, Uncle Laci.

Uncle Laci Hello boys.

Kids Hello, Uncle Laci.

Father Sit down now, because it will get cold.

Uncle Laci Well, that's true, cold parsnip soup isn't very nice.

Girl We are having parsnip soup?

Mother We always do.

Girl I know.

They serve and eat.

Second Man It's nice.

Girl Don't bother. It won't change anything.

Mother Let's leave that now. Every Sunday. It's soon Christmas.

Father Right, and we've got to talk about it. Everything needs to be discussed in a family – like Christmas lunch, for example.

Girl Yes. We do.

Uncle Laci It's strange that when I am over here for lunch, the third kid is never here.

Father What do you mean by over here?

Uncle Laci I mean that he is not here.

Mother You have lunch here every Sunday, so there is nothing strange in that . . .

Uncle Laci So he doesn't come on Sundays?

Second Man He would get bored. At his age, they prefer Oscar-winning films and nightclubs. He wouldn't enjoy it here, not like us, me appreciating Mother's soup.

Girl They know what you are like, so it's better if you stop this right now!

Mother It's nice to be complimented sometimes.

Uncle Laci He could show up occasionally.

Girl I would appreciate it if you didn't make it your business what he does. He lives in the country. Doesn't come to Budapest very often, and is quite busy when he does.

Mother What matters is that he is a good student.

Uncle Laci But he is still a family member.

Girl Alright, he'll come next time.

Uncle Laci At least for Christmas.

Girl Christmas it is.

Uncle Laci I am curious about how he turned out.

Girl He is bigger.

Uncle Laci I gathered that, but want to know what he is like.

Father Are you bringing the meat out?

Mother I am.

Father By the way, have you heard of the massive sales on at the moment?

Second Man Products have lost their value now.

Uncle Laci Because they are from India, made by children. They don't even feed them. If one of them dies of hunger, there is another to take its place. Families sell their kids because they have so many. Eight – even ten.

Girl I don't believe that a parent could give up their child.

Uncle Laci From where we're standing, we can't possibly imagine the things that happen in the world. But I have been there. I saw them.

Mother You've been everywhere. Haven't you?

Father It's worth nothing if you can't share it with anyone.

Uncle Laci I can. With you.

Father It's not the same.

Uncle Laci What do you mean it's not the same?

Father That it's different.

Scene Seven

The house in suburbia. Ironing room. The radio is on.

Radio At Christmas, let us think of Jesus not as a Saviour, but as a small child. What does the Holy Family teach us, after all, if not to remind us that we too live in a family, that every person is someone's child, that everybody has got a mother and a father? And let us not forget, especially at this time of year, our loved ones, so that at least everyone will receive once a year the warmth that they craved all year long, as the scriptures remind us. For life becomes harder now for those who are lonely. It is hard to be alone. The lonely person who sees all the warmth on TV, for example, will feel the coldness and emptiness of their lives even more. The suicide rate amongst the lonely increases during the holidays. This is what we should aim to prevent with our love. For Christmas is love.

The radio voice fades and the **Girl** *goes to the phone.*

Girl Hi.
Are you well?
It's soon Christmas.
It's going to be at Grandma's.
Could you come?
Why not?
I didn't know that you had a girlfriend.
Oh, yeah. The one that I saw you with when we bumped into each other. Of course I remember.
So you are going to hers? They invited you?
To the country?
I will really miss you.
At least on Boxing Day.
Yes, I know that it's far, but still if –
Bye.

The end of a lyrical piece of a song. The **Girl** *is tearing up. The door opens. The* **Husband** *comes in.*

Second Man Hi.

Girl No one works this late.

Second Man It was the Christmas do. You can't not show up.

Girl What is it for?

Second Man   Nothing. Drinking and eating and laughing at the boss's jokes.

Girl   Office Christmas. Christmas is for families.

Second Man   Why are your eyes watery?

Girl   It doesn't matter. It's nothing.

Second Man   It's conjunctivitis, isn't it? I told you not to watch too much TV.

Girl   I don't watch it – it hasn't been working for six months.

Second Man   Not working? We even watched it yesterday.

Girl   That's the one that is in the living room. I said before it needs to be fixed because it is so bloody boring to iron without it.

Second Man   Start the eye drops, or it will get completely infected by Christmas.

Girl   Is your attentiveness linked to Christmas?

Second Man   I am always like this.

Girl   That's right. You always know what's going on with me.

Second Man   Not everything, only stuff I can see. Like now with your eyes.

Scene Eight

*Leafy suburbs, the **Girl**'s street. A relatively well-dressed **Man** is just about to close a wheelie bin. We are not entirely sure whether he is saying the truth or not, but the **Girl** believes him.*

Girl   Hi, I barely recognized you. What are you doing here, doing the bins?

First Man   Yeah, just getting rid of a banana skin. I didn't want to litter. And you? What are you doing here?

Girl   I live here, in that house over there – and you?

First Man   Doing quite a big job here. A complete renovation. We are doing it all.

Girl   Can you carry mortar in this outfit?

First Man   Oh, I don't do that anymore.

Girl   How come? What do you do then?

First Man   My mate has given me the business.

Girl   What do you mean given?

First Man   Yes, for me to run it.

Girl   Just like that?

First Man He's got another that keeps him really busy, getting reorders in. So, he said I should run this one.

Girl For free?

First Man He is only asking for the bank's borrowing rate, I can keep the rest. He is not bothered, long as he doesn't lose money.

Girl So what is your role exactly?

First Man Business manager but I also own a bit of it. So this is where you live, then?

Girl So this is what you do, then?

First Man I'm telling you, I am. We are running out of time, and I promised they could be here for Christmas – so we have to work day and night.

Girl Right, so Christmas is important for you too.

First Man To me and my clients too. Just the last touches and they can move in.

Girl Isn't it crap for you to be alone?

Second Man What do you mean alone?

Girl At Christmas?

First Man Oh, at Christmas! I won't be alone now.

Girl How come?

Second Man Didn't the kid tell you?

Girl What?

First Man That his girlfriend's parents have invited me over for the twenty-fifth.

Girl What? They invited you?

First Man Yes. They did.

Girl But you don't even know them.

First Man That's the kind of people they are. They found out that I would by myself, and they suggested it right away. 'There is always room for an extra plate on the table' type of thing.

Girl They've found out and are just adding an extra plate?

First Man Yes. I was pleased not to be alone. I better go, sorry; I need to buy another switch. I miscalculated – it happens sometimes on big jobs. This is where you all live, then? And what about you? At your parents' again?

Girl What at my parents'?

First Man Christmas at theirs?

Girl Like always, yes. Nice car.

First Man   Not mine.

Girl   I didn't think so.

First Man   Well, kind of mine, you know . . . on credit.

Girl   So, you will be with him?

First Man   With who?

Girl   With the kid?

First Man   Yes. I will. He was pleased too. I am his father, after all.

The **Man** *disappears and the* **Girl** *stands there, lost.*

Scene Nine

Doorbell rings. Door opens.

Father   Four of you?

Girl   Yes.

Father   You said he would be coming too.

Girl   He wasn't able to.

Kids   Hello, Grandad!

Coats off, then toward the room.

Mother   Come in then, come in quickly, the table is ready.

Second Man   We are coming, Mum. Just putting the coats away.

Youngest Kid   When do we get the presents?

Second Man   After dinner.

Eldest Kid   Why not before?

Second Man   Because that's how it is.

Mother   The four of you?

Girl   Yes.

Kids   Hello, Grandma! Hello, Uncle Laci!

Uncle Laci   I thought he'd come.

Second Man   Hello, Uncle Laci.

Uncle Laci   Hello, guys.

Girl   He wasn't able to make it. He is in the country.

Father   Where?

Girl   He is at his girlfriend's house.

Mother It's that serious? You never said.

Girl I didn't know either, just found out.

Father Well, it doesn't matter – it would have been a squeeze anyway. You can't just fit an infinite number of plates here, not even on a round table like this. And actually this table fits the most.

Girl What wouldn't fit?

Father The extra plate.

Girl You mean that it wouldn't have fit here?

Father It would have been possible, but not easy as there is so little space.

Second Man We barely managed to fit the seven of us, so eight would really be –

Father I'll take it down, actually, so it doesn't get knocked down.

Girl So there wouldn't have been a place for him . . .

Father I am not saying that it would have been impossible, because I did manage to squeeze it in there. But it was a challenge, and it wouldn't have been comfortable, since you four are here and us two, and Uncle Laci is here because where else would he be at Christmas?

Mother It's seven of us, counting Uncle Laci.

Girl Counting Uncle Laci?

Father Yes, counting Uncle Laci.

Girl Whose place is Uncle Laci sitting at?

Mother His own usual one.

Girl But really, whose place is Uncle Laci's place?

Mother Uncle Laci's place is Uncle Laci's place.

Girl But whose place did it used to be?

Father In our house, we don't have your seat or my seat. Anyone can sit wherever they please. Uncle Laci usually sits there, me here, and Mum –

Girl Uncle Laci is sitting in my son's place.

Uncle Laci I am only sitting on a chair.

Girl Uncle Laci sat down where my child should have sat.

Uncle Laci The kid is never here when I am here. I said that he should be.

Girl Uncle Laci, did you push out my son?

Uncle Laci I never pushed out anyone. Never needed to do that. I was talented enough not to have to push anyone to the side, because without me they couldn't get their bigger investments, they couldn't do without my expertise. I didn't need the flat, either. I gave it to you because I had another one.

Mother Alright, that was a long time ago. There is no need to bring it up.

Uncle Laci I didn't want to bring it up, but I did give it away.

Girl Why did you, Uncle Laci? It was worth a lot – nobody else would have given it up, that's for sure . . . Not all that money . . .

Father I have been asking the same thing, but your mother never told me.

Uncle Laci I didn't ask for anything. It was free to you.

Girl What was its real price, Mum? What did Uncle Laci want? Tell me what.

Mother Just to be there for him as his family, because he is lonely.

Girl What? Tell me what. My son's place? Did he want that?

Mother He didn't ask for anything. I am the one who invited him for lunch.

Girl You gave it to him?

Mother I didn't give anything, and he never asked for anything.

Uncle Laci I was the one always saying that you should tell him to come.

Girl You did it because of your guilty conscience. Just like murderers who go back to the crime scene.

Mother You are speaking utter nonsense. Everybody wanted what's best for you. That was the problem – that all our lives we wanted to do what was best for you.

Girl Uncle Laci pushed out my son. (*Crying.*)

Uncle Laci I never did anything of the kind and never needed to –

Girl And did you two help him?

Father I don't know anything. Your mother –

Girl You're involved, too, because you let it happen.

Father I had no idea.

Girl You think if you are not doing it personally, that you are not involved. But you are in on it, because you didn't say anything and you just let it happen.

Father I did try to force a place for the plate and an extra chair. But there is such little space.

Girl I can't stay here a minute longer. What kind of parents are you?

She jumps up and runs away.

Mother And you – what kind of a kid?

Girl (*answers back*) You have more responsibilities as adults.

Mother You are not a child anymore.

Girl A child is a child as long as their parents are alive.

Door slamming, silence.

Eldest Kid Where did Mum go?

Second Man Out, onto the street.

Youngest Kid When is she coming back?

Second Man When she gets cold. It's winter.

Mother You think it's that simple?

Second Man Yes, it is.

Mother Don't you think that she would actually rather freeze? Shouldn't you go out after her?

Second Man No.

Mother My husband would have come out after me, wouldn't he?

Father Well . . .

Second Man I develop software and when you first look at it, it seems that it's full of peculiarities, but there is a logical system behind it all. Emotional worlds are the same. It's all spectacle. Inside, it's pure logic.

Father But the computer could freeze.

Second Man Yes, some malfunctioning can happen; but otherwise, only hackers could screw it up. They're the equivalent to shrinks in psychology. They disturb the system.

Uncle Laci Well, there was a man in the company, who by the way was perfectly alright, apart from being a little anxious. He went to see a shrink who then proved it to him that in his childhood he wanted to kill his parents. He laughed it off at first, thinking what nonsense, but the shrink insisted to such a degree that he ended up believing that he had killed his parents.

Father Why? Were they murdered by someone?

Uncle Laci No. They were simply old, had cancer, and died.

Father How could he have thought that he did it then?

Uncle Laci He believed he caused it by transfer because he had wished it. Needless to say that the therapy resulted in job loss, hospital, everything.

Father It's because of Christmas.

Mother What?

Father It's Christmas that has upset her.

Uncle Laci What do you mean it's because of Christmas?

Father Christmas makes people crazy.

Uncle Laci Well, that's true, the whole of December is a crowd of bloody people, consumerism, pushing.

Father And having to be together from morning till night.

Uncle Laci It was fun when we were kids.

Second Man Everything was good when we were kids.

Eldest Kid Isn't it good now, Dad?

Second Man Yes, it's good now too.

Eldest Kid Yes, it is good!

Second Man It's very good. Just different.

The End

The Dead Man
By János Háy (2016)

Translated from the Hungarian by Szilvi Naray

Translator and English producer's notes

Multi role-ing is recommended. The children in the early scenes (Boy, Little Girl, Girl 2) and the neighbours and women villagers can be played by the same actors. The Dead Man can also play the Boy, as well as the Priest and Barman and villager in Scene Six. The use of Brechtian scenic devices is recommended. It is also possible to have a small band on stage and have the musicians play some of the small roles such as Postmaster, Village Man 1, Village Man 2.

With multi role-ing, the play can be produced with a cast of 5.

Cast

Mother, *woman in her early thirties*
Man, *around forty or older*
Little Girl, *between six and ten years old*
Woman next door, *thirties*
The other male roles are played by one or two actors
Postmaster, *elderly man*
Neighbouring man, *around forty*
Men in the pub, *the generation back from the war (Village Man 1, Village Man 2)*
Women (villagers, neighbours)
Barman, *old man*
Priest, *ageing man*
Children, *six to twelve years*
Boy
Girl 1
Girl 2

Premiere, October 2017, Szkéné Theater, Budapest

Author's note

There is no set; a woman in her early thirties sits on a chair facing the audience (not necessarily centrally). The scenes take place between her and the back of the stage, which is covered by a black screen or drapery. When performing she stands up and enters the scene, then sits back down.

The scenes frame a story, a cycle of thought or emotion. They are not identical in size, and they also differ from the previous or next scenes.

Changes and pauses should be scenically dealt with by the use of music and lighting.

Two timelines appear in the play, the narrative in the present and the narratives of the past(s) The separation between the two can be shown by doubling the actors with puppets. An actor can move several puppets, it is the director's and actor's choice to what extent this is used. But the use of all other scenic devices is possible, for example, for certain scenes (distribution of letters, funeral, arrival of the man) a moving image, video can be used or in case no other actors are cast, one actor can act as the narrator who can act out all the other characters except The Man's.

In several places in the text, I indicate (and in many places I leave it in the narrative space) when the other character speaks. It is the director's decision how many times and when they let another character speak (this may require minor textual changes). The less you allow other characters to speak, the stronger the utterances, and of course the less they speak the higher the stakes when they do speak.

The Little Girl: she can be an actual little girl, but she can also be a puppet, moved by the mother who then steps out into the little girl, as if stepping in into her self-reflection of herself. In fact, these two people represent the two different ways of relating to the events, this duality can be how a person is able to think differently in such a case.

Time and place: The fact that the action takes place during the Second World War can be indicated but the *mise-en-scène* should nevertheless strive, as the text does, to communicate that the theme is war in general. The specific details need to be credible as to preserve the reality of wars that are in time and in space close to us.

The setting is a rural village, but the costumes should not be archaic or convey the kind of sentimental village ideal that people in Budapest would have in mind. The setting should follow the language and the props the set, and costume alike should aim to make the story relatable and tangible for today's audience. This is not a rural story; the rural setting is merely the necessary basis for the realia element.

When I was writing, I thought of all the grief that comes from when a woman loses the person, she had planned her life with because he either abandons her, comes home every six months or because he dies, and she has to adapt to the absence, and I thought of all the men who wanted to return from this abandonment and return to past reality as if no time had elapsed. I have thought of all the men and women who think they can just seamlessly reenter another person's present and, like pigs before Christmas fasting, they will most likely be slaughtered down, unnoticed. The story is both realistic and symbolic and no stranger to big dramatic expressions.

The director is given wide freedom in how to stage the work, but as the author I would still ask for them to prioritize people and text, and to keep other scenic tools to a minimum.

Translation notes

Kocsma is a quasi-silent, no-frills drinking place mostly frequented by men, perhaps a boozer describes it best. It is impossible to faithfully render it into English, so I kept the Hungarian as a foreignization translation strategy tool. The same goes for *Palinka*. I kept the Hungarian drink intact. It is a very strong alcohol that is often home made from the distillation of various fruits. It is unique to Hungary.

Scene One

Children *wait outside the post office; the* **Mother** *sits in the front of the stage.*

Boy   I can't wait.

Little Girl   He's inside the post office now.

Boy   I know that if we wait for him, he will come.

Girl 2   Everybody knows that, but you still get sick on the side of the road.

Boy   Did you throw up?

Girl 2   Of course, I did, didn't you?

Boy   I didn't, no. I did last year, yes, but not this year.

Little Girl   Next year I won't either, but I'm only in year three.

Mother   They were waiting there, like they were always waiting. I knew where the place was as I had often walked her there so that she'd know where to go when I was unable to. I was often busy with the animals and the land and sometimes the letters only arrived in the afternoon because they were sent late from the capital. They would sit down on the riverbank and talk. Naturally they couldn't keep quiet while waiting for the postmaster to open the door and deliver the letters. They just couldn't be silent, they had to talk, and they always talked about what they always talked about.

Boy   When is he bringing them?

Mother   When is he bringing them? Asks one of the children. What else could they say when they were there for the letters?

Little Girl   You might not get one.

Mother   The other one said, as they believed that if a letter didn't arrive for one of them then at least it will arrive for someone else. They believed this without daring to say it, that if the other's father died then theirs would still be alive. They didn't think that both could die, or both could live, they could only think that if one died then the other would escape.

Boy   And what if you don't get one?

Little Girl   I will get one because I didn't get one yesterday.

Boy   I get one every day.

Mother   Some of the children received a letter every day or they thought they did because they didn't count the days when they didn't get one, but in reality, nobody could get one every day. *I get one every day*, one of them would say, I knew whose son it was, and they would end up talking and wondering what it must be like over there. They didn't know.

Girl 2   What's it like over there?

Little Girl   I don't know.

Boy Do they kill people?

Girl 2 No, definitely not, that's not allowed.

Boy Then why do so many people die?

Girl 2 From the war, 'coz there is a war.

Boy War can't kill people, only people can.

Little Girl You are allowed to kill the enemy.

Boy What if he dies?

Little Girl Then he dies, it's his fault for being the enemy.

Boy He's coming. The door is opening.

Girl 2 This is stupid.

Little Girl What?

Girl 2 That enemy thing.

Little Girl Why would it be stupid?

Girl 2 Because Daddy doesn't even know him, how can he be Daddy's enemy?

Little Girl It's because they are the bad guys, bad guys exist.

Girl 2 They have children too you know.

Little Girl Mummy said they only went there because they would have been shot if they didn't go, because it was compulsory, at least that's why Daddy went.

Girl 2 Compulsory?

Girl 1 Yes, you are not allowed to say that you don't want to go.

Girl 2 How can it be compulsory?

Boy It's either you or them. If you don't fight, they win, like football, you know, it's like a big . . .

Girl 1 Stop it with this stupid football thing, football has goals, not dead people.

Boy But it's similar because . . .

Little Girl I've told you to shut up with your football.

Boy My father is a hero; he is there because he is a real hero. He protects us.

Little Girl Yeah, I agree.

Girl 2 I hate war.

Little Girl Me too.

Boy He is coming.

The door opens, the **Postmaster** *steps out with the letters.*

Mother And then the postmaster came out, as he always did, and he started handing them out. He knew everybody, he knew where each kid belonged.

Postmaster You got one. You got one too. You didn't get one this time.

Little Girl And me?

Mother That's what she asked, frightened, because the postmaster, I think he made a sport of purposely missing out a kid even if he had a letter for them. He was like that. He wasn't malicious as such, he just wanted to make them happier by pretending *oh no I've almost forgotten*, and then the most anxious of them all would hear their name called out and burst into tears, but this time they would be shedding tears of joy.

Postmaster Wait a minute, yes, you too.

Little Girl I knew he would write. I knew it because yesterday he didn't write, I knew.

Mother She was always happy in the same way. In a way that only a little girl can be. She took in bits of air – took three breaths, and her face was bright. As if the sun reflected it from the envelope.

The **Little Girl** *moves downstage centre, sits in front, cross-legged*

Mother I knew how she'd be on her way home. I knew she would stop at the creek bridge – she would be by herself, and I knew she was reading it. She'd be wiping her eyes – sometimes struggling with the illegible writing. In pencil. In very small letters, or because of what was written in the letter.

Everyone is running home. The **Little Girl** *stops at the stream bridge, reading:*

Little Girl *reads, stuttering, repeating sentences and words:*

Little Girl My dear wife, my little sweetheart Anna. I'm well, fed well, my comrades are good people, we help each other. I hope that you too are well, that you are coping with the domestic chores, with the land, with the animals, and that you are not in danger. I miss you very much! Happy birthday, little Anna, I'm sorry I couldn't be there for your birthday, but I'll be there next time for sure. Sending you thousand kisses Daddy

Mother (*changing tone, showing the reality of war and how soldiers were manipulated by guards*) All the letters were the same, because these men were not used to expressing how they were feeling in writing. They were used to other people noticing what was going on with them. But this time, nobody could see them because they were so far away.

Every letter was the same.

If they had been different, the camp mail correspondence censors would have given it back and asked them to write another one – the same as everyone else wrote, and they would have kept on giving the letter back until it with the same as everyone else's the same as they had written until they had to give back.

She looked at the letter some more, read it again, maybe said it out loud that he was alive or just thought that he was, and ran.

Little Girl Yes! He is well, he's alive!

Mother He's alive, she said running home to tell her mum that he's alive. And she was running but I couldn't see her yet because she was running from where I couldn't see. I was in the yard, not far from the gate and then suddenly I saw her happily running in, squeezing the letter in her hand.

Scene Two

Mother When she arrived, she told me, holding the letter up to my face, that he was alive,

Little Girl Mum, he is alive!

Mother And I told her he was no more. (*Light changes.*)

Little Girl What is no more?

Mother She asked, her eyes staring at me. They were like her father's I thought, and then I thought no – they were only partly like his, because they were partly like mine as well – and I began thinking that they were like mine.

Little Girl Mum, what is no more?

Mother I told her that that man is no more.

Little Girl Who? What man?

Mother The one we've been waiting so long for.

Little Girl You're talking about Dad.

Mother Yes, I said. I sounded like I was saying a number, one or two.

Little Girl I just received a letter; I've already read it. It says he is fine.

Mother That letter is an older one, it happened while the letter was getting here.

Little Girl What happened in that time? I don't understand. What?

Mother It happened that he died. I told her that he died. While she was bringing the letter and while she stopped at the bridge to read it. And who knows how many times she must have read it.

Many times,

because she couldn't read it in one go due to her father's writing and also because of tearful eyes, she couldn't see the letter properly.

And, during that time, someone came out from the post office with a telegram.

The man who delivered the telegram looked at me and then at the letter. As if he were looking for something on me. Or something on the letter or in the air between us.

Little Girl How could he die in such a short time?

Scene Three

Mother How could he die in such a short time she asked and kept saying but

Little Girl Mum – he wrote. Here is the letter, here! He wrote that he was well and that he was sorry he couldn't be here for my birthday.

Mother She was saying what she had read in the letter. And I told her or maybe just thought it, that maybe it isn't so bad for him now.

Little Girl Why is it not bad?

Mother Why is it not bad? She asked and I said it's because nothing is bad for him anymore. It can only be bad for us because he doesn't exist anymore. My voice hadn't changed, it sounded like pass me the salt.

Little Girl How can it be that he doesn't exist anymore?

Mother How can that be that he doesn't exist she asked, and I said that the truth is not what was in that letter, that it's not true that he is alive and thinking of us, but something else is true.

The telegram is the truth about the time that happened after because that's the way the post works.

The telegram can arrive before the letter, and it says that he died a heroic death and he's not thinking about anything anymore, not even us.

I told her that before she managed to ask whether he was thinking of us still.

She didn't ask about the heroic death.

How could a death be of any specific kind?

A death is just that: death.

There once was a man, then . . . there isn't one anymore.

And this death is not like old age death, but it's like being plucked unripe from the fruit tree.

Yes, people were ripped from their lives unripe and pushed into the pits that the soldiers made the villagers dig out. Just like the Russians in this village, we didn't know who these enemies were.

What is the enemy?

They lived in our houses, they were tired, hungry, exhausted, and the next day they went to the river – where the battle took place – and they brought back the bodies on carts, then threw into a big pit in front of the church.

Some were still moaning; some were saying names.

Whose names?

The names of people they loved but no one would hear as the names meant nothing to them.

They died and their last words were not heard by anyone who could have understood those words.

Died as a hero and they will arrange for his repatriation – that was in the telegram – and he got the small silver medal for dying.

Mother He's not dead.

Little Girl Mum, he's not dead!

Here's the letter and I think that is the truth,

it's just a mistake – we shouldn't have received that telegram, we shouldn't have.

They put Dad's name on it by mistake, that it was him. I am sure that there – in the war – everything gets mixed up. Mum! Someone else died.

I know it can't be Dad.

Mother I told her that they don't make mistakes like this – not with death. They can only speak the language of death which is the language of running out of things, ammunition, and people. Everybody there speaks this language, whether they are German or Russian, they fight each other, but they understand each other, because they have long forgotten their own language, and they now have this common language. He died, and now we must live without him. It will just be the two of us going to the fields, to church and to visit our relatives who will be larger families than us. And we cannot miss him because we need to get on without him.

Little Girl He is not dead to me!

Mother He's not dead to her, the child kept saying to me he is alive. I let him be alive for her. I didn't want her to feel pain. She didn't really have a father anyway because as soon as she was born, he was conscripted. Then after the occasional home visits he was taken to the front. She didn't have a real father rather than an idea of one –

and it was this idea that she expected back-not the real one, because she never really had a real one.

I was wondering what it would be like to see everyone happily welcoming their men back home with me not expecting anyone. A coffin arrives, free of charge, because the state will take care of the transportation cost, the funeral and everything. This is payment for a heroic death.

Scene Four

Mother Everyone in the village found out, and they felt sorry for me, because they had to feel sorry for someone like me, but deep down they were happy that it wasn't their husband or son who died a heroic death.

Neighbour When will they bring him home?

Mother Wednesday. I told them when they asked.

Neighbour That's quick.

Mother Yes.

Neighbour How will you cope?

Mother I don't know. I have the child. I still have her, I said.

Neighbour It's good, that.

Mother Yes, it is. But she's a child after all, and when she stops being a child, I won't have one. I'm on my own really. That's what you have to get used to – to being alone – I said, because that's what I was thinking at nights when I wasn't asleep, that I really ended up alone, and that the child was only going to be around for a short while, and that my duty was to bring her up and send her away from me. This is what needs to be done to be finally alone for good –

Neighbour Everyone is alone.

Mother I know, I said, but it's good to have someone else there when you're alone.

Scene Five

Mother Then they brought the coffin.

The coffin was small, even though my husband was a big man.

They said you weren't allowed to see him because he was so dismembered by the explosion – by some kind of land mine the platoon walked on – because they didn't know it was there, and everybody was blown up.

They had to pick up the body parts and match them with their owners – wrote a surviving comrade, who by pure accident was left behind the others. Maybe because he was vomiting with fear, and only remembers the part where his comrades' body pieces were flying about.

He wrote that just moments before the explosion he was laughing and talking and reminiscing about home and the wives' delicious chicken paprikash, then the next moment these same comrades' bodies were flying in pieces mixed with blood and earth. And that since then, of course, he can't return home, but is in a hospital, where he is given medicine to fade this image in his head, but it won't fade, it just keeps playing faster and faster.

The medication is useless, the doctors think that if he falls asleep, the treatment has been successful, but in his sleep, he sees nothing but that image and wakes up drenched in sweat, only to see the same thing when he wakes up. How small he is, the women said. How did that big man become so small? I heard what they were saying, because I heard them saying it, everywhere near me and behind me. They came, because they had to come and experience someone else's loss as their husbands lived, still.

Scene Six

Cemetery.

Neighbour 2 He is so small.

Mother I've heard them say that.

Neighbour 1 How could that massive man become this small?

Mother I heard that one too, no one could be far away enough from me.

Neighbour 2 It smells.

Mother I heard that and smelled it.

Neighbour 1 Who knows how long he's been dead. In this heat.

Mother I knew how long it's been, but I couldn't remember or calculate how many days have gone by.

Neighbour 2 It would have been better not bringing him home but bury him over there.

Neighbour 1 Maybe, but then you wouldn't know if he was really dead if you didn't see it.

Mother She was right, it's good that they brought him home, if they hadn't, I would have still believed that he is alive.

Scene Seven

Mother It had a smell. Everybody smelled it. Was the moisture leaking out? It was wrapped up with tarpaulin which didn't let the moisture through –

But the smell.

It was horrible.

That stench that was my husband.

I couldn't wait for the priest to speak faster. And for the uniformed man not to say anything on behalf of the army.

But he did. In the bad smell

And then finally he went into the ground – and they sang that the pain had begun, that he has arrived at his grave. They were singing with such might as if they wanted to bring him back with their voices to call others to the grave, his relatives, and that is when the tightness cutting into my chest began to loosen.

It was over.

He was out of my life.

He was put into another world where I was not.

He's gone. He doesn't exist for me anymore, I thought as they were putting the earth above him.

It was strange at first, but I was strong – and I wasn't terrified that there would be an emptiness in the space he used to be.

No emptiness remained – because I never looked in that place in my heart where he used to be.

It's not him! – the child said, when the cross was placed on the pile.

Child   That's not him!

Mother   His name was there with the dates from when and to.

It was short –

That time in between was short.

Very short.

This can't be, the child said.

Scene Eight

Mother   Why are you looking out the window? I asked the child who was looking out the window. I was in the kitchen too and she was sitting by the window on the bench.

Little Girl   I can see Daddy.

Mother   See said she could see him.

You can't see him, I said.

Little Girl   Who do I see then?

Mother   Nothing and nobody I said, because he can't be seen anymore. There is only his memory, and that memory must be forgotten because it only brings bad things. Memories push you back to what was long ago, to when there was life that is no more.

He's gone, I said. The point of his death is that he has died -that he is no more but that we are still here. From now on we must bury the place that was him in the same way that earth was thrown on the coffin, as the clods fell on that stinking smell.

For me he is alive. He will always be.

Mother   She said that – and – every day she would look out of the window where she could see anything except her father walking on that road except that she didn't.

Scene Nine

Mother There is such a thing as no fathers – because they either vanish, die, or just don't come home,

or go somewhere and are expected home in vain.

Maybe the odd promising letter from abroad about saying that when he earns enough, you'll be able to join him.

But no more letters arrived because that money was needed for other things, for other people, for other children. And then you just carry on without him. Carry on alone with the child and there's no one else, not even his memory.

No, I didn't want to replace him.

I could have – as there were the willing men on their trip back from the kocsma. Everyone who was still alive came back thin, grey, with shoebox like skin, and then – they turned back into *recognisable* people.

On the outside at least, because no one knew what they had brought back from war and captivity.

On their way from the kocsma they'd ask to be let in – apparently, we would both benefit as we were sharing the same problem.

They don't get *any* from their missus apart from excuses on why not – even though the truth is that they have been away from men for too long.

It's not as good as you may think to have your husband back. At the beginning it was good, but these, but these men who have been in war and gone so long were different now to how they were in their wives' minds.

And it would be no use if the men explained what it was like over there and that is why they were the way they were – as no one could imagine but only those who were there.

Nobody talks about it just in the same way the wives don't talk about what it was like when the men weren't home.

They'd yell for my attention on their way back from the kocsma as they didn't get any from their missus.

Apparently, I'd enjoy it with them as I miss the same things they miss.

But I wouldn't let them in,

No.

Their drunken breath in my bed – lingering until the next day was the last thing the child and I wanted. I certainly did not need the child to wake up and ask me what Uncle Laci or Uncle Imre was doing here. I didn't need a scene in which she'd run screaming after seeing a man in my bed. *I told you that Daddy is coming home and* running to the bed only to find her mother cuddled up with a man not her father, but the father of one of her classmates from down the street.

No, it was a no – no matter how they bragged about their big cocks or grabbed their crotches in front of the gate.

They did and said those things because they wanted it to become reality, but it never became it. The men and their wives thought that because my husband never returned home, I wasn't given the chance to end up hating him and that I would want the sex that was offered.

They gossiped about how the men must surely visit Annuska. A few got so drunk that they believed it themselves and bragged about their night with me which never happened. Then the other men got jealous of the successful one. Even the priest would ask me at confession whether I told him everything.

Yes, I told you all. I said.

That's not much, the priest said.

What else could I say?

What possible crime could I have committed? I asked him.

Priest   But you must have something else to tell me.

Mother   What? I asked, because I didn't know what he meant, and then he named a man who of course confessed to something he hadn't done – because he didn't remember not having done it – but the priest was convinced and was waiting for me to confess, and he also said he would come and see how I was getting on, like a family visit of sorts, a broken family visit he added. And he laughed at the word broken.

When he came, he asked the child if she was still waiting for her father, and the child said yes, because she knew he would come home, she prayed for him.

The priest said that I shouldn't say such things to the child because then she won't believe in God, and that God is omnipotent, that he can do anything.

And I said that praying doesn't work at all – and certainly not in this situation. could undo the fact that he destroyed that.

But it does work.

Oh right, so he can?

Yes, he could.

Then he is not omnipotent if what he does is not eternal, I told the priest, and he didn't understand what I meant by it, and then I ended up not knowing myself either, because I just felt angry at someone who created such a world in which people are destroyed like that.

Why should I hallow his name?

Why should his kingdom come? What kingdom is that? Why should his be done? What will is that?

What nonsense it all is, I thought to myself that I will never say this prayer again because I want nothing from such a god, and I want him to have nothing to do with me either.

I don't want us to know each other anymore.

I don't want him to occupy the space where he used to be.

Priest   Isn't it time for the child to go to bed?

Mother   He asked whether the child should go to bed, yes, I said, you should go, my girl.

Little Girl   I don't want to yet.

Mother   Why don't you want to?

Child   Maybe father will tell us stories about where Dad is.

Mother   He doesn't tell stories anymore, I told you.

Priest   I don't know where he is.

Mother   The priest said that he didn't know. The child didn't ask more questions because it was painful to hear that the priest didn't even know as much as she did, even though he practically lived in the church, in the house next door. She went to her room.

When the child had closed the door, he asked if there was any *palinka* left from last year's batch. I told him I had all of it because I didn't want to sell any as I didn't want the men to see it as an invitation, and I don't drink it.

Would I mind pouring him a glass, he said, as he would enjoy a drink this evening as there was only the evening prayer and a little Bible reading left to do.

Of course, I told him, and I took out the bottle from the cupboard to give to him.

As I handed him the glass, he reached for it with his right hand and then with the other hand, he grabbed me from behind, pressing my skirt to my body with his palm.

What can one do in this situation?

I didn't know what to do, my face got quite red, and then I just said, 'You can't do that, Reverend, it's not allowed by law, it's never allowed for a priest.

But, he is allowed – he said because he will confess it later, to his friend who is his confessor, he will tell him and he will absolve him, they do it to each other, they have an agreement.

'But, Reverend', I said, and by then I was pushing his hand away, though the touch made me feel warm inside.

No.

Do you get it?

I said no.

'Why are you saying no?' the little girl ran out, and the priest blushed. It's the *palinka*, he was stuttering, the *palinka* went to my head.

Priest   The *palinka*, the *palinka* did it.

Mother   He said it was the *palinka*'s fault.

Why are you saying no? the little girl asked, but the priest said nothing, except good night and that he would come back to visit the family, but he never did and even turned his head away in the street.

Then the others thought that he was turning away because he knew of my sins, even though he was the guilty one.

But who could believe that the priest was the guilty one?

I did and maybe those whom he also tried it on with.

But it was no use,

Because

I could not be right, because everyone else thought I was someone different from who I was.

Scene Ten

Goodbye party, dancing.

Mother   He said he loved me,

There was a goodbye party in the village, everyone in the main square. People were drinking and shouting. The music was playing at the merry-go-round, that's when he came over.

Man   Come on!

Mother   Where?

Man   Well, to the merry-go-round!

Mother   I'm scared, I said, but I wasn't scared, I just didn't want to go with him because I wanted to go with someone else.

Man   Come on!

Mother   He was pulling me to go and then I couldn't do anything else but go. I was swinging round and round and higher and higher and he grabbed my swinging seat. No, he was already holding it, as he was meant to, the two seats were together, like we were a couple, even though we weren't.

Man   I'll push you.

Mother   I'll push you, he said, and he pushed me, and I flew out from under him, and then swung back to him. He laughed. He grabbed and pushed the seat again.

Man Aren't you scared?

Mother No, I said, and I was laughing by now. I felt lightheaded and didn't mind being here with him anymore.

Man Will you come dancing tonight?

Mother Are you coming? He asked, we had got off the merry-go-round – and I almost fell over from vertigo, it was like nothing I had ever felt before. The sun above me stayed in my eyes but not whole, but broken, as if bits of light had been scattered into my eyes. I will I said, and I was there that night.

He said, I should go dancing now.

He took my hand.

And

I went with him.

He is not the one I had wanted to go with but the one I wanted had already chosen someone else. He did a year ago. And had a baby too. His wife was at home with the baby, and he was here, spinning the girls, because he was like that. He didn't stay home, which is where he should have stayed.

Man Dance, Annushka, come on, dance!

Mother I'm tired, I said.

Man Dance, come on, dance!

Mother I'm tired.

Man What are you looking at?

Mother Nothing.

Man I see what you're looking at. No use looking now. You can see what he is like, his wife at home with the baby and he's here. You wouldn't have wanted that.

Mother I'm tired.

Man Dance, come on – dance!

Mother I saw him spin the girls one after the other, a different one for each dance. He would have taken me too, if the one who took me hadn't taken me. Yes, me too. I didn't care what he was doing, who was waiting for him at home, or that he shouldn't have been here, that he should be at home. I didn't care, except that if he hadn't taken me dancing, I would have waited all night for him to take me, but not now.

We went home after the dance. The evening was chilly, I was drenched in sweat and cold as the air slipped under my clothes.

Man Are you cold?

Mother He asked me if I was cold, I said yes. Then he said he loved me and hugged my wet dress and pressed it against my skin.

Man   I love you.

Mother   Me too, I said, when the cold dress touched my skin and it started to warm through, because that's what you're supposed to say, and I was at the age where you're supposed to say that to someone and that's how we got married and had the baby. We didn't have time to get used to each other, because we had a child, then war came, then the army. At first it was just months at the time, no going to the front yet, he had a child, so he wasn't called up but then later they took everyone, or not everyone, they only took the kids later. But everyone apart from the kids were called up.

Mother   Do you love me? He asked when he left.

Man   Do you love me?

Mother   Of course, I love you, I'm your wife.

Man   But would you if you weren't my wife?

Mother   But I am your wife, I said. So that's how he left knowing that he will come back alive because I loved him.

I wasn't surprised that he came back dead but then I didn't love him that much.

I didn't love him enough for him to survive.

Scene Eleven

Mother   It wasn't bad with him.

I had kept an eye on my first choice, and he was worse, he became a worse person than the one I was with. Of course, who knows what kind of person he would have become if I had been with him. Maybe he turned out that way because he didn't choose me, he chose someone he shouldn't have. But it was alright for me.

He didn't drink, he was so big. Every part of him was huge but still no angry word came out of him. He loves me so much, he used to say that every day he'd fall asleep thinking and feeling how good it is that I am with him.

I remember thinking how good it must be to feel that.

He wasn't soldier material, in size yes, but not otherwise. He wasn't a fighter but a doer, doing what he was expected to be doing. He'd be pushing the roof tiles back to avoid leaks.

It turned out alright for me with him, and nobody could wish for more.

A man by my side to have a baby with, and someone to move the wheat bag if it was in the way, someone to lean against if you got dizzy. Never having to ask for help from others because he did it all. At most, you'd needed the neighbour to help you with holding down the pig while he pierced his throat. Fetch the bowl, he shouted.

Man   Get the bowl, come on, hurry up.

Mother And I ran to catch the blood.

Man Stir it, it's going to curdle.

Mother It was cold, he was shouting, because it cooled down quickly. The pig's warm blood felt good on my hands. The animal was still rattling through the hole, rattling through the blood when it pushed the air out, the blood jet suddenly intensified, breathing its blood into the bowl I thought. I looked into his eyes, they had stiffened, no longer looking at this world. Then, I made the blood onions for breakfast and called for them when they were done. The pig was in the back kitchen in a tub, that big animal was cut up in pieces, luckily every year it was a big and fat one that fit in the tub. I would only sometimes remember that it wasn't him I wanted. Then I forgot about it again, why think about the things that you don't have when you can think about the things that you do have.

Scene Twelve

Mother When they brought him home – I was sad – the way you should be sad when your husband is brought home like that.

I put on the black dress that I had put out in case someone died and I'd have something to wear to the funeral.

I would've have thought at the time that it would be his funeral I would have to go to.

I put it on and the dress itself made me look sad. I went out into the street and a neighbour said, 'I see you're in a lot of pain'.

Neighbour Woman You are wearing black, Annuska.

Mother I must, I said.

Neighbour Woman Are you finding it difficult, love?

Mother It is never going to be easy, I said.

Neighbour Woman How will you cope?

Mother Just like before, when he was not around.

Neighbour Woman But then you were able to wait for him.

Mother I won't anymore, and I went on my way. I had removed him from inside myself – removed the man I had married, the one who told me he loved me, even when he shouldn't have, because why say it when you're married. But he said it and he wanted me to say it. He asked why I didn't say it, but I was unable to and all I could manage is *of course I love you too.*

Bad teachers came to the school because during the war the good teachers had left or died. These teachers didn't know how to deal with this post-war situation, where many were left fatherless, or if not they had to tip-toe around sick, wounded and mute fathers who sit all day long, listening to the world that they were once part of.

They didn't know what it was like for the children to have waited years for their father to return only to be circling their father's chair in the kitchen. One teacher even asked for a homework essay called *My daddy*.

I have no idea how she came up with it because she insisted on it even if you didn't have a father saying that if you don't have one you still had one and if there is no other replacement dad then you needed to write about your memory of your dad.

They should never have set homework like that.

I was chopping wood in the garden but through the open window I could only hear her writing the essay about her dad.

Child My dad is a war hero, fought against the enemy because the enemy wanted to invade our country. If they invade our country, we won't have a place to live as we won't have a country. That's why my father went to war and died a heroic death, and that's why he received a medal, which he couldn't receive, of course, because he was not alive anymore. My daddy protected us from the enemy because he was a very strong man. He was brought home to be buried so that he would be in his own country, where his relatives are and not in foreign soil but I know he is still alive because my dad would never have died without telling me.

Mother I was listening to her as she was chewing over the sentences. I knew that only one sentence mattered, and she wanted to make it believable – so that it could be believed that he was alive, even though he had died.

Scene Thirteen

Mother I didn't have anyone to talk to about what I was going through. The ones I asked couldn't talk to their husbands either – even though their men were physically back – they weren't the same men. They would be standing in the same place, doing the same things they did before they left, looking the same, even wearing the same clothes, but they were not the same. Something inside became different.

And the men didn't talk to each other either.

They just sat in the *kocsma* and drank.

Sometimes the barman would ask them.

Barman What was it like?

Village Man Where?

Barman At the front line.

Village Man It was front line stuff.

Barman What happened?

Village Man 2 What had to happen happened.

Barman You mean killing?

Village Man No.

Barman What about when you got captured?

Village man 1 What about it?

Mother Their issue, the barman explained is that they were unable to tell us what had happened, – that there were no words to describe what happened, so it was better for them to keep quiet about it.

Anyway, those things didn't live inside them in words but in images. It was as if someone had painted them into their brain and that, anything they looked at they saw through those images.

The barman said that one of the men had broken the silence by saying this once.

They were silent in the *kocsma* and they were silent at home.

And then –

as time went on,

they started getting used to

one another,

to their wives,

and

you could talk about the things that happened,

but things like

where did you put such and such and whether you'd done a task or not, and where the child was.

They ended up rubbing along together-

just like I did with loss – with the fact that he was gone.

Scene Fourteen

Mother By not having a husband, everything became mine. I didn't have to share anything with anybody. I didn't have to half this bread or that soup nor did I have to think that the child was mine but a little bit somebody else's too.

No. I didn't have to share.

Then autumn passed, winter passed, spring passed, and summer came again, and I learned what to do in each season.

Because everything was mine, I didn't actually need to know what to do because the animals told me and the weather told me, the plants told me and the tools told me, everything spoke around me and we understood each other.

And the child went to school as she was supposed to. And when she came home, she helped me because I had told her that things don't get done by themselves and they only get done if we do them.

She added that other things will get done by Daddy when he comes home.

What? I asked because I wasn't paying attention.

Often when you're alone, you focus inwards, and you just do things like a robot, inattentively, you can't see what's out there with your eyes and your ears can't hear either. It's as if your hearing and sight have fallen deep into your body.

Mother   What? I asked.

Little Girl   I said that other things will get done by Daddy when he comes home.

Mother   Yes, those things too. I said.

Little Girl   The pig pens for example, look at the state of them, the pigs are nearly falling out of them.

Mother   They're still perfectly fine. They are just as pig pens should be. The planks are wearing out because the massive beasts are leaning on them, nailing them back together won't do much.

Little Girl   Daddy can hammer in a giant nail so that it stays there.

Mother   The child talked about the nail, so I went into the pantry and started looking for those big nails the child was talking about. I found them. I went back to the pens and took the big nail and the hammer and hammered it in because I can do that too I told her. I hammered and hammered, and she watched the nail go in a third of the way only to bend because the pen was made of hardwood. You couldn't have built it out of soft wood because the piss would rot it.

Scene Fifteen

Mother   I was alone, and it suited me.

Sometimes in my dreams there was something there because a body cannot be a non-body.

If you don't do it, you get out of practice, and I think it would hurt if you did it. But then at night this feeling gets out and it's there screaming wanting this thing.

Then in my dream I'd let the men in – the ones shouting at me on their way home from the *kocsma*, and they'd come and do their business.

I was done with the sixth one, but I felt that I hadn't had enough yet and that I needed the seventh and the eighth. I needed the whole village, I even needed the priest, who repulsed me, but now I needed him, and he too did his business. I was soaking wet when I woke up, and disgusted with myself mostly because the last one was the priest, and I was shaking from shame but still I had that feeling inside of me. I reached into that feeling and put my hand there. It felt good that time and I couldn't stop. I slid my finger up and then there was something inside of me, I moved it a little and it felt good. It felt good to feel something there, even though I knew it was my hand, then I fell asleep. The next day I didn't need it, it was like every other day again and I didn't need it. The child and the fields were enough for me. When I thought back to that night, I got a bit red in the face as if windblown. But I didn't owe any explanation to anybody about what had happened to me, because no one could tell me how to be because I became who I wanted to become. The child was not awake at night when it happened.

Scene Sixteen

Mother What else could I have done but to think that this was how I was going to spend the rest of my life?

I told myself that I didn't even love him. I wanted to convince myself that it was reality.

Everybody wants their bit of self-delusion, to think that their situation isn't so bad after all as nobody would want to live with knowing that what they have is bad.

And why would it have been bad?

I had a child, it's bad for those who didn't have one.

The other women working next to me wondered how hard it must be for me to be on my own – it's only difficult sometimes I said.

When it was winter, the man next door offered to come over to chop the wood for me. His wife was stood there behind him threatening to beat him to death with a grape pick if he went over, '*As I am sure that it's not because of the wood you want to go but because of that woman who wants everything for herself. If you go over, I'll cut it off while you are asleep*'. At least I think that's what she said or something like that.

But the man didn't hear it because he was focused on me, and kept repeating, Annushka, I'd be happy to do it.

You don't have to, I told him, because I must do these things myself.

You won't always be here to do it for me.

But I will always be here or in the *kocsma* the neighbour said. I heard his wife going on about really cutting it off and I said thank you.

I heard his wife shouting at him as he shut the door.

In the winter everything is shut in and you'd think that nothing leaves the house except smoke but there are pictures and vague, faint sounds, but still – you know what kind of pictures and what sounds they are.

Scene Seventeen

Mother I worked alone the way other women worked alone, because the men were working away in factories or building roads.

They earned more money there, and money was needed because everything was expensive in the shops – and houses soon became cramped as more kids came along and they didn't want to share a bedroom anymore.

Maybe people built their extensions just to show how well off they were. They wanted to show off to one another, they couldn't show it with anything else but their houses as only the houses were visible.

'I want another room,' the wife said to the husband who then went out to earn and, in the evening, dug the foundations for the new room.

Later, in bed – hoping for intimacy from the person he was lying next to, he'd be told that clearly, he must not be tired enough and must not have worked hard enough.

She then wanted another concrete walkway and another pantry. And the man fell asleep wanting to come over to my house, because he felt I was closer to him, to his heart at least.

Still his body wanted me the way he wanted the woman lying next to him.

All the men in the village were dreaming about how much better it would be with me, because then they wouldn't have to build new rooms and kitchens, because my house hadn't been extended. They would yearn for me or that is what they said when they passed the gate and called for me. *Annuska, it would be so nice to have you – what a pity for you that your man didn't return.* It is a pity and it's bad for me too that it turned out like this, but I didn't know, and I could not have known whether I would have become like those women who wanted a new room, a new kitchen, a new pantry and a new pavement in the yard. I didn't know when it was time to make love whether I would just ask if such an extension was finished or not. I don't know, I thought that I wouldn't have done it at the time.

Scene Eighteen

Mother We were working alone, but we were together, and we chatted to each other '*how about sitting down for a while*' and we sat down, under a walnut tree, and the women said things that made us laugh. Old stories about people who were no longer alive and sometimes about people who were. Remember the one who was not drafted because he had one leg shorter than the other? *Well. . . his duck feet didn't stop him from becoming the stud when the real men went away.* There is no such thing as the objectively real man, it's' all relative.

If he is the only one around then it doesn't matter what he is like, he then becomes the man.

Well, this one was in heaven now as he was certainly punching above his weight with the pretty women who now made do with him.

The women then listed a whole lot of women who made do with him – they never mentioned their own name of course as they would never . . .

We went back to work and were just laughing at something; we must have remembered the duck feet man again who became the village stud for a few years. One woman was very funny and only took one of us to say that word and her laughter would make the others laugh too. By then we didn't know what was funny anymore, we were laughing at laughter itself maybe. It was then that somebody said, look *there's a man walking on the A road.* We could see onto the A road from where we were.

Where? Asked one.

Woman 1 There, can't you see?

Woman 2 Can't see the church tower either.

Mother Another said, and they laughed wondering who that person could be.

Woman 1 He's a massive beast of a man.

Woman 2 How can you tell that he is massive when he is so far away that everything is so small.

Woman 1 I just can. If he was smaller, then he would seem smaller too.

Woman 3 What is going on?

Mother What is going on? asked another woman.

Woman 1 Anyway, you wouldn't understand.

Woman 3 But I understand, why wouldn't I understand? I'm not stupid.

Mother We laughed at her saying stupid then we watched the man again, walking down the motorway with a makeshift bag on a stick, as alone as a thrown away corncob in a corner. What is it doing there when the rest are all there together packed in the garbage bin? How did this one end up in the corner of the kitchen floor? And this man, as he got nearer, he did really get bigger. I could see him well, only the old ones couldn't see him well but those who were my age could see him coming, when one of them said, 'Anna love, is this man not your husband?'

Woman 1 Anna really, isn't he your husband? Can you hear me?

Mother She asked me that, and I told her not to talk nonsense, you know exactly where mine is. But she said it again.

Woman 1 That man is just like your husband.

Mother He could be like him yes – but can't be him. He can appear to be like him but cannot be him I said. And then the man came closer and closer, and I saw it only a little bit at first but then a lot, that this man was really my husband. I was joyful and dropped the hoe, it really was my husband, I said, and I did not hear the other woman say, who then is in the coffin?

It is my husband, yes and I rejoiced, as one should rejoice at such times, but not with a pure heart, for my pure heart was empty, it was not filled with the man who had come as the man who had been in it long ago could no longer come. I acted the way I was expected to.

I ran up to him and asked Janos is that really you? And then I said the things that you are meant to say at such times: Is that you? The others ran up to me the way it was expected. Is that you Janos, are you him?

Man I am, Annuska. I'm here, I'm back.

Mother Are you alive? I asked him, because I had to ask him if he was alive, because he wasn't alive to me, he was dead to me, as he was dead to everyone who knew him.

Man I am alive, Annuska.

Mother He said he was alive. You thought I wasn't? He asked. I thought you weren't because they sent you home in a coffin. What? He asked. They wrote that you were dead, and we buried you. He didn't understand what I was going on about and kept asking what, how? Who? And I explained what had happened and he kept laughing and how strange it must be then that he was here now. Strange it was, as it's not an everyday event for someone who is no longer alive to be here.

Man The little girl?

Mother In school, I said.

Man Shall we go and get her?

Mother I talked about the ploughing that needed doing. I don't know why I talked about ploughing, maybe because I wanted to say something that was real , and ploughing was that.

Man Tomorrow then.

Mother He said tomorrow.

You've lost weight, I said.

They didn't feed me, he said.

Scene Nineteen

Mother I went into the classroom and told the teacher I had to take the child out. It was packed in there; it was hard to comprehend why there were so many children after a war – why would people want more children when they know what fate awaits them?

Maybe they purposely want more people around who can then go through the same suffering that the parents had to go through. This may minimize their burden to think that their children will suffer just the same as they did. The teacher wanted to know why and I told him without the child hearing that her father came back.

He came back? The teacher kept asking – he couldn't keep his voice down, the old teachers were like this . . Isn't he dead? he asked.

Apparently not, I said to the teacher.

Who has come? The child then asked. Come, I said. Come, you'll see.

Little Girl   I know who has come, I know it.

Mother   She said as he didn't say goodbye to her.

Little Girl   I know that daddy has come, where's Daddy, where's Daddy?

Mother   He is waiting outside in the schoolyard. The little girl then started running and running out of the school saying Daddy, Daddy, I knew you'd come, Daddy, Daddy, Daddy and tears were streaming down her face and then onto the schoolyard and then onto her father. My dear Little Anna her father said and picked her up, I'm here, you see, I'm here. I knew it, said the little girl, I knew it, I knew it wasn't you in the graveyard, because that man couldn't have been you. He had a smell that couldn't be my daddy's smell. I never forgot what you smelled like, never, my nose can remember. Then this man kisses her tear-stained cheek, and the little girl kisses his tear-stained cheeks as by now tears are flowing from my husband's eyes.

Man   Come over here, let's just be the three of us again.

Mother   I did go over there because you have to go over when you hear this. He didn't notice how difficult it was for me. It was because he no longer existed for me and if somebody has left, you can't pretend that they haven't and can't pretend that they reappear. If I had known that he was alive somewhere I'd have just waited knowing that he is alive and you then don't erase his memory. But I had to erase it, because the telegram had said he had died a heroic death and then the corpse came, and then he was gone for me. And then I had to figure out how to carry on with life, and the only way I knew how to do that was to erase him from my mind and my heart, and now this dead man shows up, someone who doesn't exist. I was supposed to embrace his living presence, but he was completely dead to me. A stranger with whom I had to act as if he wasn't a stranger, but he was; his hands, his face, the rest of his body, even though I could recognize that he had once been my husband, this man could no longer be him because my husband had died and we had buried him and I had built my life around me and I was unable to give a part of that to this man.

Scene Twenty

Neighbour Man   So are you happy he's home then?

Mother   That's what the man next door asked, and people popped over as people pop over when this kind of thing happens. I am – I said. They'll be someone doing the chores now. That's what I said, because that's what I was expected to say. Then my husband went over next door too, but the neighbours didn't say anything bad about me. They told him that I had done everything myself, so that everything would all be in good order for when he came home. But the truth was that since we buried him, I had done nothing for anybody else apart from me and the child. Someone in the *kocsma* told the neighbour that a few men were sniffing around me, wanting to come in. To be fair we weren't to know that you were alive, and he poked my husband's shoulder.

Man And did they come in?

Barman No.

Mother No, they didn't – another said or at least that's what my husband told me at home. It's good that they didn't say anything about what didn't happen, because some believed that it did happen.

The child went to bed, and he pulled me towards him, started stroking me at the right place and I told him that I was not used to this kind of thing anymore and that when you stop doing it makes that feeling disappear. *Same for me* he said, and *we must do it as I got out of practice and that we need to make up for the lost time that I wasn't here*. But it will hurt me, I said.

Man I'll be careful.

Mother He said he'd be careful, and he was actually careful. He took our clothes off, pulled me onto the bed and I went with him, because it was my duty to go with him. And he said that just the thought of it made him go almost crazy he wanted it so much, and then he put his huge body on me, like he used to, but his weight was very heavy now, it was the weight of a dead man, because he was dead to me. And he did it, and sometimes I would forget that he was doing it and then it felt quite good for a bit, but as soon as it felt good, I remembered that it was him doing it, this huge weight, the weight of his lifeless body was pressing down on me again.

Scene Twenty-One

Mother Don't you want to talk about it? I asked him, hoping that talking about it may change something in me, but I knew it wouldn't. You don't want to talk about it?

Male No.

Mother He said no. Why? I asked.

Man You can't explain so you better off keeping quiet about it.

Mother There are no words that can explain what happened, he said, just like the others said the same to the barman in the *kocsma*. He did tell the child about the German officer who wiped his nose and that it was so cold the nose ended up in the handkerchief because it was frozen and had broken off. And the child said it wasn't true, Daddy.

Man But it's true.

Mother He said that it was true, but the child didn't believe it.

Little Girl And did you laugh at it?

Mother She asked if they laughed at him. We laughed, her father said, because it was fun to laugh, but the German, he didn't laugh because he was missing his nose.

The child was laughing too at what a German officer would look like without a nose. She had seen German officers, because when the Russians came, the Germans had passed through the village before them. They retreated, thinking that they would not strike here, but further in a more favourable place from a military point of view. But they went there in vain, because even at this more favourable place, which was specifically at the river, they lost the battle and had to continue towards their own homeland, which was by then finally occupied by the enemy, that is, the enemy soldiers who were enemies to them and who were still alive and not thrown into ditches dug out by the villagers for the dead soldiers to prevent infection.

The child laughed and cuddled up to her father, and he said, 'Go to bed, little Anna, you have to go to sleep, it's a school night'. I want to stay up a little longer, the little girl said, because she wanted to be with her father so much, but her father said no – because he was already thinking about going to bed with me.

It was like that every night and even when I was bleeding, it didn't bother him – that blood was nothing compared to what he had seen in war.

There was no time to waste for him.

Man It doesn't hurt, does it?

Mother No, I said no, because I knew that it's what he expected me to say even though it hurt, because I didn't want to, because it was like a dead man's weight pressing me down, and I could feel his cold hands and feet. His blood circulation had changed in captivity, because of the cold. I didn't not want to because of that but because he was dead, he didn't exist for me.

Scene Twenty-Two

Mother Go to bed, he said, and the child said *not again*. Every night you must go to bed, he said, and I knew that after bedtime, I would have to do the thing I didn't want to do again. I didn't dare say that I didn't want to do it as you are supposed to want these things. And he did the same thing again. He took our clothes off and took me to bed. He was very strong by now having rebuilt himself on the home cooking. I was light, because I was just losing weight, unable to eat because of what was happening. He stroked me where he always did, his hand was cold. I could feel the cold hand of this dead hand, and then he flipped me sideways and used his hand to put it inside me. He penetrated me, and it wasn't wet, because it couldn't get wet. He just went in, skin to raw skin and with every dry thrust I was in agony, but I didn't want to show it because you don't show that kind of thing. He talked a lot throughout about how good it was for him to be inside me, how many times he had thought of doing this when he wasn't home yet, when he didn't know if he would ever return. He'd talk about when he was away as prisoner of war in a foreign country, and they weren't even allowed to send a postcard home if nothing else to let us know he was alive and that one day he would be back home to experience what he is experiencing with me now. He spoke about how they were starving and cold because there was no food and no heating in the barracks and they huddled together like animals to keep each other warm, and if someone was no longer warm, they were dead and they would be kicked out onto the ground once the body was completely cold. He said this as he put himself inside me, finally being able to warm himself up with my delicious body, he said that I was delicious and soft, even though every muscle in my body was tensed so that I could bear the dead man's weight, but for him, compared to what was there, in that other country, everything was soft and delicious.

Then he stopped talking because he was so into doing it. I knew how long it would take. The first few days it took less than a minute to orgasm, but he started again and he could do it a second time. This time it took longer. It took as long as before he left, no shorter actually – because the dry vagina was holding his body better, so then he needed less time to climax, to finish. I knew which phase he was in.

His eyes were popping, he was so in the moment, saliva was starting to trickle down a little from the corner of his mouth and the muscles in cheeks were relaxing when I reached from under the pillow. I had put it there the day before. We used to use it for pig slaughtering, it was very pointy, like a military foil. When he was just about to climax, I stabbed him with the full force of my body.

I don't know where I got the strength from, as I had hardly eaten for months, but there is such a thing as this inner will power giving you the strength, a kind of force that is not really in you, that comes from outside of you. I stabbed from behind, first through the skin, then the back muscles, the lungs, and the heart, something crackled, maybe I reached a bone. His eyes stayed frozen, his saliva kept dribbling, he stopped moving, he didn't understand what was happening, he didn't feel me stabbing him because he was focused on that other feeling.

His body fell on me, that great weight that was his weight, and I had lost that strength that was in me in that moment, he squeezed the air out of me, like when you squeeze a cream out of a tube, and I lay lifeless under him. I woke up to her tugging at my hand 'Mummy, Mummy, what happened to Daddy, what happened?

Little Girl Mum! Mummy!

Mother She was screaming and looking at the bloody body and the bloody bedding and then she ran out of the house and the neighbour came over and he rolled the now cold body off me. I was naked, the neighbour covered me up. He couldn't say anything, he just looked at me, looked at me the way you look at a stranger, I was no longer his neighbour. He couldn't say what had happened. Mum, Mum, the child just cried, but I didn't say anything. What happened to Dad, she asked? He came home, I said, to say goodbye to you. And what about now, she asked.

Little Girl And what is happening now?

Mother He has gone back now, I said.

The woman stands up, the drapery covering the back of the stage comes down. There is a jury in a courtroom behind the drapes, the light highlights them and the woman. The woman turns around, the light goes off her, we stay with this a few seconds.

Curtain.

The Bat
By Krisztina Tóth (2020)

Translated from the Hungarian by Szilvi Naray

There is a large screen in the middle of the stage. It is sometimes a TV screen, sometimes a Skype screen, sometimes with the nursery as background, and sometimes other backgrounds, billboards. CS there is a bench, the door is SR.

Cast

Nursery Teacher
Mother
Psychologist
Father
Policeman
Voice
The Policeman and Father are played by the same actor
The Nursery Teacher, Mother and Psychologist are played by the same actor

Premiere, online during Hungary's lockdown in 2021

Scene One

Mother *enters through the door from Stage Right. She is on the phone to someone. Backstage on the screen we see a gym hall with children lining up. A whistle is blown and the children's clamour dies down.*

Mother Hi. No, he's already in his gym class. He'll need new trainers as he's been complaining about his feet lately. I'll buy them, okay? Listen, you won't believe it. Bobby the bat has gone missing. You know, the little black rubber thing. He is really upset about it.

. . .

It won't be, it disappeared yesterday afternoon.

. . .

He says he had it at nap time.

. . .

But I'm sure someone took it home.

. . .

What do you mean who'd want it? Anyone who took a liking to it the same way he did. Remember how he pounced on it in the shop? He took it right off the shelf, didn't he?

. . .

Do not bring the 10 euros into it. I am telling you he is completely freaking out.

. . .

If my kid were to bring an unknown toy back home – and by the way, it has happened – he once brought home this little thingy (*she gesticulates above her forehead*) this rhinoceros

Unicorn, yes that's it – okay, what, are you being difficult again? You know exactly what I'm talking about!

. . .

Of course, he 'll remember, Jesus. He's *a child*, not a nutter!

. . .

We need to get him another one somehow.

. . .

I didn't tell you to go to the aquarium in Genoa.

. . .

I'm not making a big deal.

. . .

Are you in a witness meeting now? At this time? In the afternoon?

. . .

Okay, we'll talk later then. Don't forget to pick him up tomorrow. Oh, and Friday is fruit day.

. . .

Bye.

She hangs up.

(*To herself*) Insensitive prick.

She calls again.

Hi. Is this a bad time?

. . .

I'll keep it short then. You know what – he's such a jerk, he really is an insensitive prick.

. . .

You won't believe it, Bobby the bat got lost at nursery school, and he then starts with this. . . . It's like a black rubber bat.

. . .

No, we bought it together, back in the summer when we were in Italy.

. . .

Of course, you know we were still on holiday together. In July. That's when we fought so hard that he threw the GPS out the window. You know, I told you . . .

. . .

Yes.

. . .

No, it was his idea. It was Lalika who wanted to buy it.

. . .

Well. . . he liked it.

. . .

It's not disgusting, it's cute, like a little black bat.

. . .

Don't be silly – of course they don't suck blood – that's the South American species. Stop messing around! They don't suck, that's only true for Latin American species.

Listen to me please. Bloody hell – we are talking about a rubber bat, okay? Actually, I had a real live one fly into my old flat once. A real live one, remember? In the attic. It was flapping about knocking into things then it hid somewhere. There were these two jugs, on the shelf and crawled between them.

She goes quiet, ponders for a few seconds.

Have you noticed that for some reason you can no longer say that it crawled between a pair of jugs. That's a bit weird, isn't it? So, it got between a. . . a. . . a. . . a jug. No! No, I reached behind one of the *jugs*, and there it was, in the dark, and as I touched it, as I touched it, I could feel its little heart beating in my palm . . . It was so scared, poor thing!

. . .

Of course, I didn't kill it? Are you nuts?! I wrapped it in a scarf and set it free.

. . .

But I wasn't going to say this. I meant to say that Bobby . . .

. . .

Well, it's Bobby the Bat!

. . .

Yes, that he got lost in the nursery school, and then this insensitive arse tells me that it's okay, that at least the child will learn not to take all sorts of crap with him.

. . .

I promise you. That's what he said.

. . .

Like this, word for word.

. . .

That was all he could say.

. . .

He is bonkers right? The kid is sobbing here, you know, that they took his stuff, his little bat, and he is like, 'Never mind, son, at least you will have learned a good lesson. You'll learn not to take stuff into nursery school'.

. . .

Your private student?

. . .

You still teach at home?

. . .

Yeah, sure, no worries. I'll ring you after two. Bye.

(*To herself*) Blood sucker! What a stupid thing to say! The rubbish in people's heads, seriously.

She calls again.

Mother Hi, Mum. Bobby has disappeared.

. . .

What do you mean which Bobby? Bobby the bat.

. . .

No, in the nursery school. Someone took him home.

. . .

Yes, I am telling you.

. . .

A poster?

. . .

And what should I write on it?

. . .

Wanted? Are you actually kidding?

. . .

No, I don't have a photo of it. Why would I have?

. . .

Nor do I have one with him holding it. No!

. . .

But I can't draw a bat!

. . .

Print from where?

. . .

No, I can't do a stylized one either.

. . .

Right, I'm not sure how well it would go down. They don't usually do posters.

. . .

But there is a notice board.

. . .

Listen, Mum, why don't *you* draw it? When Zoli brings Lalika home on Saturday, he could pop in for it by car. Should he bring you something?

. . .

Ah! (*Laughs.*) He won't know that.

. . .

There is absolutely no way that he could recognize a celeriac. No way.

. . .

How could I explain?!

. . .

Are you serious? Send him a picture of a celeriac to his phone to say – this is what a celeriac looks like? Once, he called me from the shops asking me to explain what an aubergine looks like.

. . .

Okay, if you are sure, I'll tell him.

. . .

Ah. He won't.

. . .

Mum, you have no idea *how* stupid he is.

. . .

Okay, okay, maybe he is good at that, but he can't do everyday things.

. . .

What multiple paragraphs? Why, you don't think I can't memorize fifty pages of text? Do you think I'm stupid?

. . .

Yes. I do like celeriac salad.

She walks out nervously.

Scene Two

Father *comes in. His phone rings. He answers it.*

Father   I can.

. . .

I'm not, I just don't see it as such a tragedy.

...

We'll leave that for now, can we?

...

I'll ask, of course. But they'll let us know anyway if they find it.

...

What kind of fruit? What's wrong with apples?

...

Celeriac? Your mother? What does that. . . look like?

...

I'm not being difficult; I just really don't know. I haven't the faintest idea.

...

A poster? Isn't that a bit much? And what should I put it up with?

...

I don't know if I have cello tape. Why would I have any?

...

I'm not asking the nursery school teacher, you put it up!

...

One extra day won't make a difference.

...

I reckon around four o'clock. I need to put the phone down. I am about to go pick up Lalika.

...

I will not forget.

He knocks on a door. **Nursery Teacher** *looks out from behind the door.*

Nursery Teacher Well, well. They're here for Lalika. Here's sweet, kind Daddy for Lalika. Lalikaaaaaa! Daddy, Lalika didn't sleep today.

Father Never mind, he'll just go to bed early.

Nursery Teacher He was entertaining the others throughout the whole of nap time.

Father Did the bat show up?

Nursery Teacher No, it has not been found. But we gave him Robbie the puppy, he used to sleep with it.

His ears are hanging loose, Mum needs to know so she can get on sewing them back up.

Father (*handing it over*)   They're not hanging, they're torn off.

Nursery Teacher   Lalika pulled them off because they were hanging loose. His behaviour has been aggressive lately. He had to go on the naughty step again.

Father   For that? I will discuss it with him.

Nursery Teacher   He was chasing Sandika around the room with the ears.

Father   With what ears?

Nursery Teacher   With these. With Robbie Puppy's ears. (. . .) Did Mum buy him the bat?

Father   No, he chose it for himself.

Nursery Teacher   He chose it?!

Father   Yes. He liked it.

Nursery Teacher   But it's a bloodsucker. Bats are vampires.

Father   Not this type. My wife says that it's only the South American breeds that feed on blood. The ones over here only feed on insects and plants.

Nursery Teacher   Well. . . Mum must know what she is talking about. I certainly wouldn't buy him a bat, though.

Father   But it's a rubber bat.

Nursery Teacher   I wouldn't buy a rubber one either.

She shouts in a drawn-out voice.

Lalikaaa, you're coming, aren't you? Daddy is being boiled alive in his coat. Put the Lego away, Lalika, not there, in the box, nicely. We don't throw it, we put it in its box. (*To* **Father**.) It's fruit day on Friday. I've already told Mum, but I know how busy she is.

Father   I'll be bringing Lalika tomorrow.

Nursery Teacher   Mum won't have time?

Father   No. She won't.

Nursery Teacher   Well, in that case. . . I prefer to keep Robbie Puppy's ears. They would only get lost.

Father   Ah, I'm happy to take them home.

Nursery Teacher   It can wait. Come on Lalika. There are some left over there. There on the carpet. No, Georgie – No climbing up in the basket. I said, no climbing!

Father   I'd like to put up a poster please.

Nursery Teacher   A poster?

Father   Yes, on the notice board about the lost Bobby the bat.

Nursery Teacher   I would not buy the kid a bat.

Father   It wouldn't be Miss Magda who put it away, would it?

Nursery Teacher   Me?! I wouldn't go near it, not even with a bargepole.

Father   I was only joking. I thought it was disgusting too.

Nursery Teacher   And where does Dad want to put that . . . poster then?

Father   Here, on the notice board.

Nursery Teacher   I will still have to discuss it with the management.

Father   It's an A4 sheet.

Nursery Teacher   Whether it is allowed to put up an A4 sheet of paper.

Father   Of course.

Nursery Teacher   Because then everyone will start posting whatever they lost and totally cover the notice board.

Father   Well, I agree that it is a bit much, but my wife insists. Lalika, are you coming, sweetie?

Nursery Teacher   I don't want to interfere. But . . .

Father   Will apples do?

Nursery Teacher   We will appreciate whatever you bring. We need vitamins. To be honest, the apples from last time were sour.

Father   We didn't bring those. Our fruit day is now.

Nursery Teacher   There is still a chance it might turn up. It might be in one of these baskets.

Father   Maybe.

Nursery Teacher   I need to ask about the poster. It is not so simple, you know. But I will let Daddy know.

Father   Goodbye. Come on, Lalika.

Scene Three

*On the screen, we see the **Nursery Teacher**'s giant face in full view, from a low angle, as if seen by a child. Background noise. Children's feet tapping, shouting, doors closing. General nursery school sounds.*

Nursery Teacher Lalika, if you refuse to sleep, I'll move your bed apart.

. . .

Then close your eyes and be quiet.

. . .

Here is Robbie Puppy. I won't give you his ears because you tore them off. It must have hurt him. He's crying now. Poor Robbie Puppy dog.

. . .

You need to make him feel better.

. . .

Come on, go to sleep!

. . .

I don't know.

. . .

Listen, Lalika, I've had enough of this! Look, everyone is asleep.

. . .

You are not letting the others rest.

. . .

No, it's not there, Miss Kati has already checked.

. . .

You are not allowed to bring toys into the nursery school, you know that. You deserved to lose it. At least you'll learn that you're not allowed to bring anything in.

. . .

It is not alone; someone must have taken it home.

. . .

Of course it's not going to fly back, Lalika. It's a rubber bat. Toy bats don't fly about.

. . .

Come out here into the corridor, I've had enough of you. There, you stand here. I won't give you Robbie Puppy. He is for nap time, and you are not sleeping.

. . .

Don't you move, go and stand in the corner and shut your mouth. I won't let you mess with me.

. . .

Did Mum tell you? Did she really? (*Raises her eyebrows.*) No Lalika, this is a toy bat. They don't fly about. The real ones live in dark caves and feed on blood because they are vampire bats. And if you get your blood sucked out you die. Do you understand?

. . .

Yes, because they suck it out and they go into people's hair as well and then their heads need to be shaved bald

. . .

The screen goes black for a few seconds, and all we can hear is desperate weeping

The **Nursery Teacher**'s *face reappears.*

Well, I am back. I hope you've come to your senses.

. . .

No, I won't give it to you. Of course not. I have zero intention to give it back to you.

. . .

Oh, dear God, what on earth is that? What are you up to? What on earth do you think you are doing?

. . .

Answer me properly, I don't understand! We'll take this off now.

. . .

You can't say you need to go? But how old are you, Lalika? It's only the playgroup children who wee themselves!

You can tell by her face that she is busy with her arms as she tries to undress the child.

. . .

I will tell everybody, and they will all laugh at you that you still do things like that. Please get out of this, will you? Come on, hurry. This left one, then the other one. Done. I don't believe it!

Oh no, it can't be. Of course, there are no spare pants, why would there be? (*Glances sideways as if searching.*) Everything is more important to your mother.

. . .

No, this is Georgie's. Stop crying and put them on. I can't believe it, really, Lalika.

. . .

Scene Four

*The **Father** is sitting on the bench and looks at his watch. The bench is a bus stop, the projection on the screen alternates between various billboard posters. In the background, street noise. The **Mother** arrives.*

Mother Hi, sorry. The bus didn't come. Did everything go okay?

Father Yes. I brought in apples on Friday.

Mother Did you drop off the celeriac at Mum's?

Father You know what? This celeriac is such an interesting vegetable. I went to Tesco, and there was this nice lady in a red T-shirt who helped me. It's like a human brain! It really looks like someone's brain. I put two human brains in the basket, they looked really weird. Do they really cook them?

Mother I'm glad that at your age you have finally discovered celeriacs. Seriously now.

Father What's your problem now? I do anything you ask of me. I will go and visit your mother. It's not my responsibility anymore.

Mother Did you bring the poster?

Father Listen, I don't think it's a good idea to put it up . . .

Mother Don't start that now!

Father It's totally unnecessary. He will have forgotten all about it in a few days.

Mother Would it be so hard for you to stand up for your child?

Father It's not a matter of standing up. . . Why make such a big deal out of it?

Mother Just think about it for a second! Some little guy took it home, and back home Mummy or Daddy would have said: 'That's my boy, well done son. You are a ballsy kid, you! It doesn't matter that it doesn't belong to you. This is life! You need to grab what you like. That's how things work in this rotten country.' You realize that this is what goes on in the nursery school. Are you telling me that you want to contribute to this? Because I don't know how else I can explain it. You are complicit by not doing anything while this arsehole chav is having a laugh.

Father Hold on now. That is an exaggeration. I don't want to blow it out of proportion. There's no need to create such a drama. Lalika is about to go to school.

Mother I don't want drama, I just want to awaken the conscience of the bastard parent who lets their child steal from others. Do you realise the enormity of that? They are raising kids to pocket things. When they come in in the morning and look at the poster, they'll be ashamed.

Father So according to you they will bring it back, will they? They will walk home ashamed and blushing, and the next day they will bring it back saying 'sorry, it was me.' You think they will rat themselves out?

Mother I don't know. But they will have a shitty day, that's for sure. Do you have the poster on you?

Father I do.

Mother Jesus! You folded it. You should have rolled it up.

She unfolds it.

Meanwhile, the hand-drawn poster appears on the screen. A bat with WANTED written underneath it and a request to bring it back to the Kitten Group.

Father You want to put it up?

Mother You put it up! They won't have a problem with you. You are Miss Magda's favourite, sweet, sweet daddy.

Father Put it up yourself . . .

Mother No. If you're able to buy two celeriacs, you are more than capable of pinning up an A4 sheet. I feel it, deep down, that you will succeed.

Father It was your idea, you put it up!

. . .

Lalika wet himself on Friday.

Mother No way. At nap time?

Father No. Apparently, he didn't sleep at all.

Mother Well, how come he wet himself then? He hasn't done it in years. Something isn't right. Did they have spare clothes for him?

Father No, they gave him Georgie's. I washed them. They are in the bag.

Mother But I have spares in the cupboard – in the top bit. I always do.

Father Yes, but on Thursday they were out in the playground, and he got all muddy, so I took him home in the spare ones.

Mother And you didn't replace the spares.

Father No. Your mother made a ton of celeriac salad. . .

Mother Can't you take them?

Father To the trial? These? No, I can't.

He bends down, smells the bag.

It stinks.

Mother You used to like celeriac salad.

Father I still like it. You, this. . . this celeriac, it's like a human brain. They look like calcified brains.

Mother   Alright, I will take them.

Are these Georgie's trousers?

Father   And here is the poster.

Mother   I'll put it up this afternoon if you won't.

Father   Ask Miss Magda for Robbie Puppy's ears. She's got them.

Mother   Did they fall off?

Father   Apparently, Lalika ripped them off.

Mother   Lalika? I know he didn't rip them off. It's a lie. Aunt Magda ripped them off, and you know we should be pleased that it's not Lalika's ears she pulled off. She's fully capable of doing that. That woman is not right in the head. I'm not joking. Have you not noticed how she stares at me?

Father   No. Does she?

Mother   Like this. Well, of course she doesn't look at you like this. She's a sadist. She hates kids.

Father   You are exaggerating.

Mother   I am not. We should have taken Lalika out of there a long time ago. They steal. The children wee themselves. They cripple them. And the nursery teacher is a sadist.

Father   Don't take this out of proportion, it's only a few months away.

Mother   Oh yes – a few months. Lalika wees himself; no doubt will poo himself, and by the time he goes to school he will have forgotten to speak because they mutilated Robbie Puppy in front of him.

Father   Don't work yourself up with this.

Mother   Why shouldn't I? Are you nuts or what? Your six-year-old wets himself, the nursery school is a mafia hideout, the teacher is a full-blown psychopath, and all you have to say is don't work yourself up? Plus, you can't even put up a freaking poster because allegedly you don't have cello tape. Miss Magda this, this Magda that. I just don't know why you'd be licking her arse when you can see how two faced, she is. We will not bring any more gifts. Oh no – not for Easter either – no more moisturizer, scented candles. Where are Robbie Puppy's ears?

Father   She has them. She said it's not a good idea to buy him a bat.

Mother   Who does she think she is?

Father   Because they are vampires.

Mother *bounces up.*

Mother   Not true! There are no vampire bats in Europe. They are a strictly vegetarian and insect eating species. They only have the vampire subspecies in South America and they only feed on cattle. On cattle, do you get it?

Father You explain this to Miss Magda then!

Mother You explain it! You're the chief explainer, aren't you?! She thinks I'm a complete idiot. An actress, now that's stupid. She probably gets up at noon, does nothing and ignores her kid. There, that's what's in your Miss Magda's stupid head. But Margit. . . on the other hand. You mean you didn't take your new girl with you? Miss Magda would dig her. I think she's probably even older than she is. . . All would work out well, wouldn't it? Here's a new, reliable mummy . . .

Father Why are you shouting? Have you lost your mind? Everybody is staring at us. And how did you cook up something this crazy? Margit has never even met Lalika. She is actually really. . .

Mother Yes, please do tell me what she is like. I am so interested. I really would like to know more about how she is – about her hair colour and I could send her recipes and tell her what to expect – shall I?

Father Stop shouting!

Mother I am not shouting. Can't you see that Miss Magda is a cretin. I can't believe that you don't see it or maybe secretly you agree with her? You are pleased that Bobby the Bat got lost. You and Miss Magda are singing from the same sheet.

Father Of course, you are shouting, you are shouting right now. No wonder the kid wees himself.

Mother Don't you start that alright? I really wouldn't start on that. It is not me who threw out the GPS of the car in the summer. Throw it out for Margit. I am sure she will get out and pick it up, or does she have sciatica perhaps?

Father You're not in a good state.

Mother You want to be a shit then? Do you want me to be a shit too? Shall I start ?

Father Me? I don't want that at all. I spent three days looking after the kid. I even went and got fruit. I brought celeriac for your mother; I picked up that sodding poster from hers and all you do is fucking tell me off. Oh and I washed Georgie's trousers!

Mother I am so impressed! No, you didn't look after the kid – you had him for the duration of time that we had agreed. So, don't you play the martyr for me please. If you are busy, then call Margit to step in as a replacement grandma.

Father Okay then. I have to go.

Mother It's funny that – whenever we need to discuss something you always have to go.

Father I really have to go, I have a meeting . . .

Mother Okay, I'll call you. And I'll talk to Miss Magda and ask why on earth is the kid weeing himself at six years old.

Scene Five

On the screen is **Mother**'s *face. She's Skyping with her own mother, but we only see her in full. The sound is a bit crackly.*

Mother Hi, Mum. Can you see me alright? I can't see you. Turn on the camera. It's there at the bottom.

Voice I can't turn it on, but I can still hear you. I've plugged something in the wrong place.

Mother Listen, Mum, the whole point of this is that it's not a phone. The point being that we can get to see each other. There is this button, there's a camera on it.

Voice I see no such thing. There is something . . . but what is it? It's like. . . it's got the shape of a Christmas tree sweet.

Mother Yes, that's the one, down there, click on it!

Voice I don't know what click on means. I can't see the Christmas sweet now. It's fine like this too. Tell me, darling, did you enjoy the celeriac salad?

Mother It's the Christmas sweet type but looks like half of a sweet. It's got this twisted bit.

Voice Have you finished eating the celeriac salad?

Mother It was delicious.

Voice When is opening night?

Mother In February.

Voice You must be very busy then.

Mother Yes, pretty much. Guess what? Lalika wet himself at the nursery school.

Voice At nap time? These things can happen.

Mother No, not a nap time. I think there is something not right, something is bothering him.

Voice Did you put up the poster?

Mother I did but I don't think it will turn up you know. What is that noise?

Voice Nothing. The oven clock. It might still turn up. Remember the teddy bear we left in the department store? In the furniture section? You remember, don't you?

Mother Yes, it got lost and we had no luck going back. Then one morning it just decided to walk back home.

Voice It had a cup of tea next to it, like it had just finished his tea.

Mother He was such a cute teddy. . . Had a red nose. . . I think we should try and find another bat. The same one, poor little darling.

Voice He'll come around. He needs to toughen up. Sometimes things get lost. I made some apple pie.

Mother But it didn't get lost. If it had gotten lost it would have been bad, but this was stolen, do you understand? Somebody took it and it messes with my sense of justice. Do you see that? I wouldn't rule out that it's Miss Magda who took it.

Voice I doubt she'd do that.

Mother That one? She is a lunatic.

Voice She's always been very nice to me.

Mother Listen, Mum, you see her twice a month. Believe me, she's not nice

Voice I just said she was nice to me.

Mother You are all the same. Why can't anyone take my side and show a bit of solidarity you come up with this. Lalika wees himself.

Voice You should take him to see a psychologist.

Mother Really? You believe a stranger can just take a good look at him, chat a bit and then give out some expert wisdom?

Voice Well, I don't know. The woman we saw last year in the parental guidance services she seemed. . . she seemed pretty sympathetic.

Mother Once you take him, you run the risk that they will find something that is wrong with him, and they might not let him go to a normal school.

Voice Don't over think this darling. For now, just focus on the opening night, you can take him after. Ask for an appointment then take him.

Mother (*in a more peaceful tone*)   The poster turned out really cute. Thanks.

Voice You're welcome. I had a lot of fun with it. I haven't drawn in so long.

Mother You should do more of it.

Voice Well, I wouldn't start on my own, unless something needs doing.

You look so tired.

Mother I am. Slept four hours.

Voice Oh, darling girl, I am so concerned about you – Maybe you shouldn't have rushed into this separation, your father and I. . .

Mother Please don't start, don't try to make me feel guilty, okay? I've got enough problems without this.

Voice I don't want to make you feel guilty at all. It's just that Lalika is in the picture, you are telling me now he wees himself. You will take him to the psychologist, won't you?

Mother Fine, I'll take him. You keep referring to this psychologist as if you needed to take the car in for a service. They'll tinker with it a bit, adjust the ignition, and then it'll be fine. What do you think that woman knows about our lives? I've got to go. Miss Magda makes comments if I arrive late.

Scene Six

Father *arrives at the Nursery school. He knocks on the door. The screen shows the children playing inside in the nursery classroom. Little chairs, toys on the floor. The teacher opens the door of the classroom.*

Nursery Teacher Sweet sweet daddy! He came for Lalika. Mummy? She must be doing her theatre things.

Father She is *at work*. But she sent something.

Nursery Teacher You forgot to pay for the gym classes. The cut off was Tuesday.

Father No, my wife . . . well . . Lalika's mum sent me a . . . (*He rummages.*) She sent a poem.

Nursery Teacher A poem?!

Father Yes. As we have enjoyed reading these lovely poems on the door. She thought she'd send one in too.

Nursery Teacher Well, that's very kind but we have our own.

Father I'd like to give it to you anyway.

Nursery Teacher Now?

Father Yes. It isn't long.

The **Teacher** *starts reading.*

Nursery Teacher Oh, you poor maiden / what is that in your braid / don't be afraid of it / it's just a bat shaped hair clip. / Bats don't go into hair you see/ as it would get him into trouble maybe / it flies above our houses / and flees from under roofs. / It can navigate by ultrasound . . . navi

She struggles to read, squints.

Navigates with ultrasound and his nocturnal non-stop activity is allowed . . .

What kind of poem is this, Dad?!

Father My wife found it in the *Rainbow Slide* poetry anthology.

Nursery Teacher *Rainbow Slide*? We don't post poems like that.

Father Like what?

Nursery Teacher Well, like these modern ones. They need to be beautiful with a moral message. And they need to rhyme.

Father This one does.

Nursery Teacher Does it? Well, I am not sure. I need to discuss it with the management. They decide what we put out. We do not usually put modern ones out but mainly old classics that the parents are familiar with as well.

Father And what is the selection criteria?

Nursery Teacher (*pondering it*) Well, it needs to be a pretty poem without unintelligible words and without connective pronouns, and nothing that may be scary and nothing with aggressive content either.

Father Bats shouldn't be feared.

Nursery Teacher I'm sorry, Daddy, but I'd rather not go into this now.

Father Fine. I've passed the poem on. Lalika really likes the Rainbow Slide.

Nursery Teacher We are not familiar with it, but we do sometimes read modern ones. The baby chestnut one is lovely and touching too. Lalika, Dad is about to melt into his coat. Please come out now, Come on pet. Here is Daddy.

Father I'd like to put this up on the notice board.

Nursery Teacher Wow! Did Dad draw this?!

Father No, my mother-in-law did. My ex-mother-in-law. She used to be an art teacher . . .

Nursery Teacher And for how long will it stay up, Daddy? I did ask and you are allowed to put it up after all. There is no legislation against it, but for how long?

Father I don't know . . . for a few days. Until the bat reappears.

Nursery Teacher Doesn't bother me, you know best. Lalika would forget about it by himself, but this will now bring attention to it, they will point at it, everyone will ask him if it was found or not.

Father But the children can't read.

Nursery Teacher They can't know but the parents will read it and talk about it. They will point at Lalika and say: 'This is the kid who lost his bat.' I won't get involved, me. Dad knows best.

Father I'll put it up anyway.

Nursery Teacher Pins are forbidden. They are not allowed in the whole building – not just here. They can pop out of the wood and the little ones could step on them. It'd pierce through their little feet.

Father I brought cello tape. Come on, Lalika. You too can help. We'll put it up on the board.

Nursery Teacher   It's all the same to me. Please make sure to cut Lalika's nails so that he won't injure someone when he fights.

Father   Why? Did he fight?

Nursery Teacher   No, but he has very long nails. It's a health and safety issue.

Scene Seven

On the screen we see **Mother**'s *face. She is Skyping.*

Mother   Hi, no, I'm here. I can't see you again. Press that button and the image will come up. You know, the Christmas tree sweet.

Voice   I pressed it.

Mother   But I can't see you. It's just like we're on the phone.

Voice   Does it matter?

Mother   Look, I thought of this Skype thing so we could at least see each other.

Voice   You can visit anytime, sweetie.

Mother   You know it's not about that. It's crazy how busy I am. But next month will be easier. We're preparing for next season. It will be *Three Sisters* and Sipos will be directing. We put the poster up.

Voice   Did anyone get in touch?

Mother   Not yet but quite a few people went to take a look and commented on how real it looked and that they were sorry. So, it created an impact.

Voice   And do you think it will turn up?

Mother   I haven't the faintest. People are bastards. I have a strange feeling. Not a suspicion, I wouldn't say that, more like a . . . gut instinct. There's a couple at the nursery, the guy always comes in an Audi. He's this . . . big, tattooed jerk. And his wife is this short, stocky little woman, wears a pink jacket. You might know them from the playground, their little boy is in Squirrel. They call the kid Kevin.

Voice   Gypsies?

Mother (*annoyed*)   Why should they be gypsies?!

Voice   Just because . . . of the name they give their child. Such a . . . different one.

Mother   Mum, stop being *so* racist! It's embarrassing.

Voice   I am not racist. You called me racist the other day too when we saw that cute little negro kid. If someone says negro, it does not make them racist.

Mother   Mum, nobody says 'coloured' anymore. We just say Black. Maybe they like *Home Alone* and that's why he's called Kevin.

Voice But he was a coloured baby, wasn't he?! That adorable baby in the pram was a coloured boy! Why can't I say so if he was!

Mother Never mind, let's move on. Kevin is not a gypsy. He's not Black. Okay? Let's leave it at that.

Voice What did you say they liked? Home what? I don't remember Kevin. What does he look like? Guess what, I moved the palm tree. I had to as it had no space for its roots.

Mother Never mind. It's a movie, it's not interesting. And Kevin . . . he goes to the middle group, they dress him in the coolest latest clothes, nothing special. He looks like his mother. She is always on her phone. She wears a pink hooded jacket on the playground.

Voice You've already said that. I don't know. I don't remember Kevin's mum.

Mother Anyway, that's not the point, the point is that yesterday I put out a poster and this morning, the dad, the Audi guy is walking down the stairs while staring at me. Do you get it? He is always staring at me, right into my face. Even his neck is covered in tattoos.

Voice So what? He must like you.

Mother Me? Come on. Mum . . . Don't you think that's . . . suspicious? That he looks at me in that way? I have always had a bad feeling around this guy. Especially nowadays. I wouldn't be at all surprised if it was them who took Bobby the Bat home. Kevin 'little sweet pea' may have just pocketed it even though he has buckets full of toys at home and wouldn't even notice if a new toy got mixed up in there. But now that I put the poster up, they will have realized that, oh yes . . . that little bat.

Voice Then they will bring it back. Keve will bring it back.

Mother You must be dreaming! Kevin. Not Keve. That name does exist but . . . .

Voice Why, are they gypsies?

Mother Jesus Christ, Mum, stop irritating me with this nonsense. I told you before that they are not gypsies, and by the way you are not meant to say gypsy – you have to say Roma. But they are not.

Voice But . . . then why wouldn't they bring it back?

Mother Mum, listen, can you for a moment imagine that this guy drops off Kevin with his colossal Audi, despite the fact that they live five-minutes away behind the shops, so I have no idea why they need the car but never mind. So, let's say he gets Kevin ready for his Squirrel group, he then straightens himself up, takes a deep breath and walks over to the Kitten group, stands in front of me and says: 'Hello, Lalika's mother. Yes, we took Bobby the bat and our conscience woke us up – the whole family's. So, here it is. We have brought it back. Tomorrow we are going to sell our Audi as it was bought with stolen money. From now on we will engage in good honest work. We will teach Kevin that too, because private property is sacrosanct and you can only truly appreciate the fruit of good honest labour, one that is built on sweat'.

Voice Darling, what is your actual problem here? I re-potted the palm tree.

Mother You want to know what my actual problem is? Some unscrupulous mafioso stole my kid's favourite toy, his silly kid stole it, and they are keeping it hostage, and while I am trying to look for it, get it back you know, he just shamelessly stares into my face thinking: 'Bad luck loser! You think you can get it back? Miss famous? Or mister barrister will have to step in, will he now?' Cynical pigs – that's who they are.

Voice I don't actually think he thinks that.

Mother Maybe not exactly this, no. Maybe he doesn't think anything at all as he may not even have a brain. He may not be able to read

Voice He will have seen the drawing though.

Mother This country is full of tough-guy arseholes speeding in their massive cars. Amoebas they are. They gave little Kevin a haircut that is very short on one side, almost fully shaved off, and long on the other. It's not actually the kid's fault that his parents have low standards. I can't get over why they would give the poor kid a haircut like that. He is not even in reception, and he already looks like a bouncer. I am convinced that it's them who took Bobby the Bat. I can feel it. I can feel it in my bones, right here. It's like a sixth sense.

Voice Have you called that psychologist yet?

Mother No, but I have her number on the table. But the one we had last year was awful. I remember she sat Lalika down to draw something and he started to colour in the whole page with black pen, all the way to the edge. He went through a phase like that, where he would colour everything in . . .

Voice I know, he did it at ours too.

Mother And when the psychologist asked him what it was, Lalika told her that it was the sea at night. Do you remember that?

Voice Of course, I do. Your father and I had a good giggle. Just call her anyway. I really wouldn't suspect that bloke, he might just fancy you. He would have seen you in the papers and recognized you, that's all.

Mother In a newspaper? This guy doesn't buy printed newspapers, he just plays on his phone. Of course, he didn't recognize me in jeans and without makeup. You should see the state of me in the mornings nowadays. Even if he did recognize me, he'd just hate me even more. His wife knows exactly who I am and hates me accordingly, that's for sure. She says hello in this affected way, but I can see in her eyes what she thinks of me exactly. I can tell she would drown me in a puddle if she could. Maybe they took Bobby the Bat as revenge.

Voice Darling, please, don't work yourself up like this. You need to save your energy for more important things. Calm down please. If you come over at the weekend I'll cook something nice for you. Pork stew maybe. Don't you want us to bring over the large evergreen, you know, to put it where the sofa used to be, that was taken by . . .

Mother I am very, very calm, really. Like a Buddhist, can't you tell? Anyway, I hated that sofa. Alright make some stew then but put some heart and offal in it too, but I can only stay until three as I've got rehearsals.

Voice Alright, we'll manage with Lalika. We'll watch movies, play cards.

Mother Bye, Mum, kiss, kiss.

Voice Look after yourself, sweetheart. And Lalika, too.

Scene Eight

Mother *comes in, makes a phone call. In the background, the screen shows a room with shelves and pictures.*

Mother Thank you very much, it's really nice of you.

. . .

Yes, please, put it next to his gym stuff – in the side pocket.

. . .

What? I'll sew it back on.

. . .

No, it won't fall out, put in next to his gym pass.

. . .

No, it won't if you stick it deep down . . . What did Miss Magda say about the poem? Did you give it to her?

. . .

I thought so. I swear, I knew it.

. . .

What do you mean by those types?

. . .

I don't believe it, really. That was already crap back then, in my childhood Donka Kotaszy, sweet lord. They have been repeating the same thing for forty years. . . .

Rainbow Slide. (*Laughs.*) No, you really told her that? Shit, what she must have been thinking! Poor Miss Magda must have been shit scared, that it belonged to some foundation thing, some obscure publication, probably full of gay authors, you know, why else would it be a rainbow otherwise? And a slide, a downhill slide, it's already a slope downhill from there, straight to hell.

. . .

I bet you, that's what she would have thought. I know her. Sure, I'm sure that's what he had in mind. I know him. You know, like the joke: Oh well dear Miss Magda, if everything makes you think of that. (*Laughs*.)

. . .

I actually think that she didn't put it out because she shat herself out of fear because it's me who sent it . . . You should have said that you chose a gorgeous little poem, yes, a magyar folkloric gem it is. She would have put it out for sure. The barrister is *so* trustworthy. She hated me from the get-go. I reckon she hates Lalika too because he looks like me. Of course, he looks like you too. I didn't mean it like that. I just mean that I must come to mind when she looks at him.

. . .

What are you getting your knickers in a twist about now? Of course, he looks like you too. And . . . looks a little like Margit too.

. . .

You can be so childish sometimes. It's you who should be in the reception class. Seriously though, it's lunch time for Daddy, should we open the little bed? Come on, it's sleepy time. Everyone would be better off . . .

. . .

Do you think it will have an effect?

. . .

But now it's a long weekend.

. . .

Okay, I'll figure it out. Did you send the red hat back?

. . .

Thanks. Hey, listen, what happened to that bloke who sued his employer?

. . .

No, really?

. . .

And now he is allowed to bring his dog in?

. . .

But if it's like that for him . . . so a therapy dog is okay too?

. . .

What specific training? Who can tell me what makes my cog therapeutic?

. . .

Oh, I see. Guess what, *Three Sisters* will be in the next season! Sipos is directing. Yes, yes! I know. Everybody knows.

. . .

He was but has now recovered apparently and is back at work. Do you remember Szilvi Kardos? You know the blonde one with big tits?

. . .

Yes you do. You were there. We saw her on a recording, you know when your ankle . . . yeah, when you had it in a splint . . .

. . .

Yes. Her, well. I'd be a way better Masha. Wouldn't I? A hundred per cent better.

. . .

Well, I think she was terrible. It was unbearable. The way she was whining and hamming it! *My head is all messed up*! She was dreadful that woman, always doing the same thing. She's got this distinctive movement, you know, the way she grabs her forehead. My God, I've seen it a thousand times. She doesn't understand anything, she is thick as a brick, and she just keeps pushing and pushing this throaty, whingy whine. And the audience falls for it. Well some do anyway . . .

. . .

Cheese festy, like she usually is

With great passion, she starts to read Masha's monologue:

Dear Sisters, I need to confess, my soul is heavy. I shall confess to you and never say a word of it again to anybody. I am saying it. It is my secret, but you must know it too.

. . .

Oh no. They haven't cast it yet.

. . .

Of course. Well, there aren't too many options. I don't think it is in doubt.

. . .

I have been waiting for this for so long! Oh my God. '*I can't keep quiet. . . I love, I love. . . I love this man. In a word. . . I love Versinyin. . .*'

Scene Nine

Father *arrives, looks around. The screen shows a long corridor with closed doors.*

Father   Good afternoon!

Scene Nine 239

There is no one in the corridor, no answer. He sits down. He waits, looks at his watch. His phone rings. He tries to speak quietly, half covering his mouth with his hand.

Father ...

No, I'm already here at the education and parenting services. No, inside, on the second's floor corridor. There is nobody here.

...

I've found it, but there is no name on the door.

...

Of course, I will tell her, but you already did.

...

Okay, I'll call you. I have to leave here at 2.30 anyway.

...

No, I won't mention it. It's not a secret. Is it?

...

Well, if she asks, I will tell her but why shouldn't i?

...

I think you're way too anxious about this. Why would she think of something bad?

...

That is Miss Magda, not everyone is like that. Why would I say that you are a voice tutor? Are you crazy? She may be a theatre goer and may know who you are.

...

Please don't start on this! Okay. I'll call you.

He finishes the call.

Father (*to himself*)   A voice tutor? Sweet Jesus. She has lost her remaining marbles. I don't even know what a voice tutor does. Tutor? Tutor who?

The door opens, and the **Psychologist** *looks out.*

Psychologist   Oh, Dad is here. Please come in.

They sit opposite each other on either side of the bench. On the screen is the **Psychologist***'s office. Sofa, paperwork, toys.*

Psychologist   Thank you, Dad, for having made the effort. Mum and I already talked about it a lot but I thought I should let you know as well.

Father   Yes, of course. Thank you.

Psychologist   I believe you are divorced.

Father Yes, well, I, I mean . . . we weren't even married. We are now living separately. But . . . we're fine.

Psychologist So, you can collaborate in regard to co-parenting your child.

Father Yes, we can. We discuss everything.

Psychologist I see. And . . . how long have you been separated?

Father It will be five months now.

Psychologist And this was . . . discussed with Lalika? Did you tell him that you had made the decision not to be a couple anymore?

Father Well, not in such concrete terms, no, just as we never told him that we were a couple either. He can see that we are living separately. We didn't make it into a big deal.

Psychologist And how does the child experience the fact that his father and mother are never together at the same time?

Father Look, even in the past it was rare for us to have done something all together. My wife works nights and I'm running around during the day, so we take turns looking after him. During the summer we'd sometimes go places, but not during the year. In the evenings my mother-in-law used to look after him because my wife is an actress and I . . .

Psychologist An actress?

Father Well, a tutor who acts sometimes, occasionally, I mean. She teaches singing. It's either that or that during the day. It varies in the evenings.

Psychologist I see.

Father So . . . in fact we spent little time together,

Psychologist And . . . may I please ask if there were more tensions, harder periods prior to the separation?

Father Do you mean if we argued? Things like that?

Psychologist Yes, I do.

Father Yes, we had arguments from time to time, like all families, but we don't argue nowadays. We argued more before. We kind of stopped arguing when we moved apart. I don't know, the whole thing calmed down really. We are not in conflict, there is no tension between us.

Psychologist I sense a lot of tension in the child. He's been here three times so far with mother, and all three times he's pretended that a volcano is erupting, and the lava is overflowing.

Father He loves volcanoes. He has a book on them, with pictures of different volcanoes. He has known the difference between the Stromboli type and the Hawaiian type since he was three years old. They erupt differently.

Psychologist He also pretended that a ship was sinking. And everyone fell into the water.

Father He loves submarines. We also have a Titanic picture book. The type you fold out.

Psychologist Does the child wet himself at nights?

Father Not at night, but during the day, yes. At his nursery school whilst he was awake.

Psychologist And a bladder infection was ruled out right? Meaning it can't be a medical issue?

Father He did not have an infection. And . . . personally I don't think we need to attribute much importance to this. It happened once. It was a one-off accident.

Psychologist He sucks his thumb a lot.

Father Yes, unfortunately he does. We tried to discourage it, but it didn't work. I told him that his teeth will be wonky, but he wasn't bothered.

Psychologist This is simply a symptom, Dad. It's one thing to suck your thumb, and have your teeth pushed forward and have a curved palate. These things can be corrected later with orthodontics. But as a consequence of thumb-sucking, the child will also develop mouth breathing, tongue induced swallowing, and night breathing problems. Respiratory apnoea, which can also cause blood flow problems to the brain. With thumb-sucking you are looking at underlying anxiety. You can't simply wean a child off finger sucking, because then they'll start to show symptoms, like, for example, chewing their fingernails to relieve the tension. We have to find out the root causes and find out what is causing the underlying tension in the child.

Father Well, let's start by the fact that he hates his nursery teacher.

Psychologist Do you mean to say that the child's relationship with one of his carers is not entirely harmonious?

Father Yes, I do. He hates Miss Magda because he feels she hates him, and there is truth to that.

Psychologist Regardless, does the child enjoy going to nursery school?

Father Regardless? He spends half his days with that woman, but yes he has many friends and he gets invited to birthday parties. He has playground-mates as well.

Psychologist I will hand you the result of the assessment. There are some issues within the personal responsibility area.

Father Well, I have those as well. No, just joking.

Psychologist What I would like is for you to bring Lalika at least once a week. I believe it's important to get to the bottom of what causes these anxieties for him. This child needs to relax.

Dad, could you make this happen?

Father   Of course, if you think we need to, we will . . . like now? on Wednesdays?

Psychologist   It might be better in the mornings.

Father   I don't think I can do that. I'm usually working, and my wife . . . she tutors.

Psychologist   Shall we make an appointment for the afternoon?

Father   Yes please, let's make it in the afternoon. Thank you for your flexibility.

Psychologist   Dad must work a lot. How about four o'clock on Thursday?

Father   I think it'll be fine, but I'll have to check with my wife . . . I mean . . . Lalika's mum.

Psychologist   And when can you do that, please?

Father   Anytime. I'll call her and then I will get back to you this afternoon.

Psychologist   Okay. I'll wait for your confirmation. You can always reach me here on this mobile number.

Father   Thank you very much. Goodbye.

Psychologist *leaves,* **Father** *stands in the corridor. On the screen we see the closed doors again.*

Scene Ten

Mother *and her mother are chatting.* **Mother***'s full face appears on the screen.*

Mother   Hi, how's your leg?

Voice   It's gone down. You look tired.

Mother   Yes. I'm upset and fed up. Guess what. I saw that little prick again in the staircase.

Voice   Who?

Mother   Little Kevin. Cheeky little prick. Wouldn't even look at me. I had already dropped off Lalika by then and I was on my way out when he was arriving with his dad. He is so two-faced, that one. Straight away he tells his kid off about not saying hello, kid didn't give it a shit of course.

Voice   Lalika never says hello either. I was so embarrassed the other day when he was last here. My neighbour, Gizike, came over, the one that lives on the left. She was so keen on meeting him so they could get to know each other a bit. Well, do you think he said hello? He just kept staring at the TV.

Mother   I told you not to let him watch it.

Voice But he wanted it so badly. In the evenings his animal cartoon programme is on, he loves it.

Mother It's mind-numbing nonsense that. There isn't a single human voice in it, just all kinds of noise. Don't let him watch that!

Voice You'd already said hello by this age.

Mother Oh yes, of course, and I was reading music and was also composing shorter pieces but maybe that was in year one actually.

Voice I was stricter with you.

Mother Oh, Mum, let's leave this alright. Anyway, we are talking about that Kevin kid now. The one that stole Bobby the Bat.

Voice This Kevin kid. Is he. . . a gypsy?

Mother Jesus Christ, Mum, it just drives me crazy how clueless you are. Clueless and insensitive, yes. I'm trying to tell you something important and you constantly interrupt, like always, you know? What happens is that I start on something and then you barge in with something stupid and I am unable to tell you what I wanted to.

Voice Tell me then. Don't work yourself up like this. I just wanted to say that Lalika doesn't say hello.

Mother Well if he doesn't, he doesn't. Who cares? He will at some stage but at least he doesn't steal. I cannot cope with how they cynically stare into my face.

Voice Did you see that psychologist?

Mother We did even though it makes zero sense apart from fucking up our Thursdays. She keeps saying: 'The child this, the child that'.

Voice Why? Doesn't she know Lalika's name?

Mother She does but just loves to say 'child'. Have you noticed that no one who has kids speaks like this? I bet this woman doesn't have them. It's only priests and government officials who say 'child' with that kind of emphasis and those who don't have any.

Voice Well, that doesn't sound like a huge issue, if she is a good psychologist otherwise.

Mother You never really get me. I think it's terrible. Sipos' wife said to me the other day . . .

Voice Who is this Sipos?

Mother Never mind. A director. An old one. We just worked with him. Some old cretin who used to fuck everyone he could, and his wife who is this insignificant little praying mantis used to come to the rehearsals and would do spirited blinking as if she had no idea what her husband was up to behind her back, that for years he fucked anything that moved.

Voice It is possible that she didn't know about it. That's very common.

Mother . . . anyway, that woman. We are standing by the snack bar area, and she starts asking me whether I cook or not. She gives me these meaningful looks because apparently that is the highest form of relationship between a man and a woman, the child and food. Crazy stuff. I almost gave her a piece of my mind, but I stopped myself .

Voice Poor thing, the nonsense she was trying to fill your head with. Did you tell her what a good cook you were?

Mother No, why bother? So, she tells me that we mustn't neglect cooking because it's a mystical bond between man, woman, and the child. Good timing, just as we are separating. Anyway, that psychologist, she also keeps saying the *child*. With, with that emphasis and tone Every time it makes my skin crawl.

Voice And what did you tell her?

Mother The psychologist?

Voice No, to the other one.

Mother Well, I pulled this godly face somehow and said that the only solution is to cook the child and that would certainly create a bond.

Voice Oh my God! You said that? Did she get it? Did she know you were joking?

Mother Of course she didn't, but at least she moved away and left me alone. I don't know why she is hanging around the theatre. There is no longer a need to spy on her husband, as apart from his libido they took all his bits out. Such an old, impotent fart. She comes to give him his medication.

Voice You said he is going to direct again.

Mother . . .

Voice Won't he?

Mother . . .

Mother *starts to tear up then bursts into tears –*

Voice What's wrong with you, darling girl?

Mother You know I wanted to be cast as Masha, and I'm not even Olga! Do you realize what this means? Do you know what on earth is happening? I am going to be playing the grandmother now!

Voice Don't get upset over this, darling. You are not eighteen anymore. You cannot expect to play teenagers at forty.

Mother (*shouting*) I am not forty, I am thirty-eight! I could have easily played Masha, and definitely Olga! And thirty-eight is not forty, it's thirty-eight. Klara Katai is exactly my age, and she doesn't look younger either. Her eyelid droops down like a spaniel's and she is fat on top of it all. She is fatter than me. There is no reason I can't be playing Masha. I know that Sipos is ignoring me because, ages ago, when he was pursuing me, I turned him away.

Voice Oh, darling, this theatre world is appalling but you mustn't get upset like this. It's not worth it. Why care so much? I am not surprised that Lalika has to see a psychologist now.

Mother So, you are saying that he needs to see a psychologist because of me, huh? You have to see a psychologist because of me, huh? It's because I'm a shitty, nervous wreck of a mother, right? Go on. Rub my face in it. And not because his nursery teacher is an arsehole and because they are thieving in the nursery. Oh no, nothing to do with that because I am a bad mother, and I am responsible for every single thing, right? And not his absent stupid father, and even when he is here, he just sits in front of a computer. Oh no, It's me – me – me.

Voice There's no need to work yourself up like this. All I said is that you're not eighteen anymore. You'll get another part.

Mother Yes. Sure. I will get cast as Blanche from *Streetcar*. Do you finally get it? That I couldn't even be Olga? Not even Olga?

Voice That is one of the three, right? I don't remember exactly who is who.

Mother Jesus, Mum, you really don't understand anything. Never mind. The point being, the precise point, is whether Lalika says hello whether or not he articulates it nicely. Really, let's focus on the important things in life. Next time, he will say hello. I will make sure of it.

Voice What about his little toy that got lost. Has it turned up?

Mother The bat? Of course it hasn't. The poster is up and people said that they saw it, and someone on the nursery Facebook page even commented on how cute the drawing was, but no, it's gone. I don't think it will turn up.

Voice I'm sorry. We can still have hope.

Mother Listen, Mum, I need to put the phone down as I have got an appointment at the beautician's. I'm going to get beautified. Maybe she will manage to make me look alright. Maybe in a few years' time I can audition for the granny roles. Age gracefully. Everybody just repeats this. That is all you hear in the idiotic TV ads. Wouldn't you age disgracefully rather

Voice You are not old yet. Don't forget to let me know about opening night. Forty isn't old.

Mother Thirty-eight . . . Only thirty-eight!

Scene Eleven

The nursery school's corridor. **Nursery Teacher** *and* **Policeman** *are talking. The screen in the middle shows a slightly blurry security camera image. The image shows*

*the **Mother** stepping out of the nursery gate holding the hand of her child Lalika. Both figures are blurred. The gate is half open, and another child is standing at the **Mother**'s feet.*

Nursery Teacher   Here now and at your disposal. You don't mind if I leave the door ajar. Don't want any trouble in there. I'm listening.

Policeman   Have you noticed anything unusual yesterday afternoon when the incident occurred?

Nursery Teacher   No. I mean . . . Lalika was very aggressive.

Policeman   Has he not been aggressive before?

Nursery Teacher   Yes, he has been. He fights. They don't tell him off at home. That little boy is allowed to do anything.

Policeman   Do you know anything about the circumstances surrounding the accident?

Nursery Teacher   Me? How could I? I was in the classroom. We only have pick up time from 4.30, until then everybody waits here where they are supposed to. Only little Vera got picked up at that time. Sweet pea.

She counts on her fingers

Wait a minute! And Balazs too because they take Balazs to football. But what happened? All I know is that poor little Kevin got hit by a car. And that he broke his back. Miss Gabi from Squirrel told me that he broke his back and his leg. Darling little pet, sweetheart. Everybody ran down, but I couldn't leave them, could I? All I knew is that there was the sound of a big screeching, then the ambulance came. Did Lalika push him on the road?

Policeman   We are not aware of anything of the sort. The parent stepped through the gate of the institution with the minor belonging to them and through the open gate another minor stepped out. We will need the security camera footage to get a clearer picture.

Nursery Teacher   You will need to ask the director. I don't have a say in it. It would not surprise me if it was Lalika who pushed my poor little one out. I bet his mother didn't even notice what was going on. She is like a sleepwalker. Well, she works nights when others are asleep. She always leaves the gate open. I am surprised that she doesn't forget to pick up her own kid. Odd woman, that's for sure. Artist type you see. I never know if she's listening. She seems so . . . confused.

Policeman   In any case, we must clarify how the little boy got out of the room.

Nursery Teacher   Kevin? He went out to pee.

Policeman   And you didn't notice that he hadn't been back for a while?

Nursery Teacher No. I thought he was pooing. I didn't go after him. We don't check whether the middle groups are wiping properly or not. I am by myself with sixteen kids.

Policeman Within the walls of the institution, the responsibility of the teacher can also be questioned.

Nursery Teacher I don't think he was hit within the walls of the institution. He went out with Lalika, but I have no idea why.

Policeman So you didn't allow him to leave with another parent?

Nursery Teacher How could I have? I can only do that if the parent in question brings a written request the day before signed by both parents.

Policeman So, this hasn't happened according to this.

Nursery Teacher No. That woman must have brought him out with her. I don't know. Kevin only went out to wee.

Policeman Did you notice anything unusual in their behaviour that day?

Nursery Teacher In Kevin Batha's behaviour?

Policeman No, in the other parent's behaviour. The one who left with the two children. In your opinion, did she consume any . . . alcohol or mind-altering drugs?

Nursery Teacher Well . . . I wouldn't know that, but it could be. You can't rule it out. She didn't seem to be under the influence but with the lifestyle these people lead. She must be used to it, used to these substances. How else could you survive nightlife sort of thing?

Policeman If necessary, could you offer an expert opinion on how the parents have looked after the child? Whether he was properly clothed, whether he was malnourished, whether he was picked up on time, that sort of thing. Could you please write it down in a few sentences?

Nursery Teacher Well, that lovely, sweet dad, he is always on duty, on time. But as far as I know, and it's none of my business, they don't even live together anymore. I'm sure that dad couldn't stand it, but no wonder. He's got a proper job to do. He's a barrister. He needs to get up in the mornings, get dressed and go to work, you know, like me or you.

Policeman Where can I find the director, please?

Nursery Teacher Her office is at the end of the corridor. It is the door with the turtle on it. It is because she carries it all, it's all on her shoulders. That is why it is a turtle. It is not a nursery group name no, it's what the parents always think. I will let her know.

Policeman Your collaboration will be needed when we're done.

Nursery Teacher Mine?

Policeman You will have to repeat what you said earlier. That the child went out to urinate. Are there cameras in the corridors?

Nursery Teacher You should discuss this with the director. Is it possible to know who hit Kevin?

Policeman The responsible was a man in his thirties. I can't mention any names. The father had parked on the other side of the road, the kid saw him and ran across towards him. He didn't look right or left. He ran straight into the Honda.

Nursery Teacher But we spent so much time covering road safety! This year we had a separate training track and used the little plastic bikes. But it seems it's not enough . . . Poor little mite, little Kevin, we hope he'll recover. Surgery's getting so advanced . . . they'll figure something out. This is the director's office, see, the turtle's here. But it's locked, the key's in it. Would you like some tuna sandwiches? Here is the snack trolley, please help yourself.

Policeman No, thank you.

Nursery Teacher Do have some please. They won't take them back. That's why they are on the trolley.

Policeman Really no, thank you. I have hated tuna sandwiches since nursery school. Funnily enough I haven't encountered any since. Maybe you only get them in nursery.

Nursery Teacher Do you not like fish either?

Policeman Me? Oh no. I like a good catfish stew or a chowder! Perch isn't bad either.

Nursery Teacher Carp in on top of my list. Say what you will. It's not true that it tastes like mud and that it is bony. You just have to be careful. The silver carp is the healthiest of them all.

Policeman The silver carp isn't bad. I like it too. But I wouldn't eat an eel though. Not for any money. It's like a snake. This bread is alright.

Nursery Teacher The children aren't keen on it but it's a school requirement that we have it because of the phosphorus in it.

Policeman Grey catfish, that's the best.

He takes another fish paste sandwich.

But we rarely buy seafood. My wife once saw a programme about how they produce it, or don't produce it, they farm them, right? It was how they farm pangasius, and she said we shouldn't buy pangasius because it's full of mercury. To be honest we never bought it before.

He takes another sandwich.

Nursery Teacher Everything is full of rubbish nowadays. How are you meant to know what to eat. I don't know. I mean, with the first kid I ate all sorts. The kid is absolutely fine. By the second kid I had read loads on everything and still, he ended up sick. I don't know if it's from that, but we found out early on when he was young, you could tell sadly.

Policeman (*stuffing himself*) What is wrong with him?

Nursery Teacher Oh, muscular dystrophy. He received treatment, but he has the type that progresses. He just gets worse. (*She gesticulates.*) Here, there isn't a lift at this bloody underground station. Now that my darling boy is forty kilos, I can't take him down with the wheelchair. He just turned twelve in October. We once asked the council to build a ramp, but they didn't do it. The mothers with pushchairs are also complaining. Do you know where they deal with hazard clearing?

Policeman Used to be the council. It's meant to be compulsory – it's EU legislation now. No. I forgot the pike. The pike is also very good. You just have to cook it right. So it's not greasy.

Nursery Teacher Take a napkin! Well, our Agnes is back. She's our turtle. Because she carries everything on her back.

Scene Twelve

The screen is showing the **Father***'s face in full. He is talking to* **Voice***, his mother-in-law.*

We see the man's face on the screen throughout.

Voice Well, I'm very sorry. I hope it gets sorted soon.

Father I doubt that it will be as quick as that. Would you be able to take Lalika to the family services counselling on Thursday?

Voice Can't we just skip it this once?

Father I don't think we should. Lalika is already very tense. He doesn't understand what is happening. If I could, I wouldn't even make him go to nursery, but I work every day. I'll explain how to turn the camera on, okay?

Voice Don't explain anything, son. I am fine with it as it is. Tomorrow, you can bring him over before noon, but Thursday isn't that good.

Father There at the bottom, if you look down, there's a sign like that, a camera. Can I ask where you are going?

Voice Nowhere . . . it's just . . . what do I say if they ask why it is me who brings him?

Father Say nothing. Only that his mother is busy and his father works. They both work.

Voice But if they ask specifically?

Father What for? Why would they ask? Thousands of children go there with grandparents, sometimes with aunts, no one gives a monkey's about who is bringing Lalika.

Voice Eva's such a poor little thing. I hope this will all be sorted soon. Have you spoken to the little boy's father?

Father I phoned him. I actually don't know what we need to discuss. I don't even understand our involvement with the accident. This poor, silly kid suddenly runs out into the road. Lalika would never do that. Poor kid. He may never walk again. Looks that way. What is he guilty of? He invented this story that Eva whispered into his ears that he was fine to go, this is the latest, that's why he crossed, ran across the road. It is mind boggling. He is obviously petrified by his father, scared that he is going to get blamed for it so he is trying to blame it on us. He is shitting himself, poor kid. He may get hit too. I wouldn't be surprised if that meathead tattooed arsehole hits him.

Voice What a nonsense accusation that she whispered such a thing! Come on! And what about the kid, what's his name, Keve . . .?

Father Kevin. His spine is broken.

Voice What does that mean? That's . . . big trouble, isn't it?

Father It is. He is paralysed. At least it seems to be the case for now anyway.

Voice Seems that way?

Father Yes. that's what doctors are saying that he will *probably* remain paralysed. That's what is driving the parents. They have taken it as a fact instead of pursuing it further, maybe get a second opinion. That's what they are saying.

Voice But how could he have run out? Could it have been that Evike didn't see the car?

Father His father had just got out of the Audi and the kid spotted him. The guy was about to head for the nursery gate, but Kevin, just like that, bolted across.

Voice Poor Lalika. You must have been shaken to have seen this, my little star. No wonder my little angel wets himself.

Father The wetting is from before all this, and he doesn't do it anymore. It wasn't because of this. Thanks for the chicken paprikash.

Voice Did you eat the mushrooms? Mushrooms don't keep for long.

Father I ate them. Lalika does not like mushrooms.

Voice Where you live now . . . do you have a stove or a microwave?

Father Yes, I have a stove and I am very capable of turning it on, moreover I sometimes heat things up without pretending that the activity fulfils me, but yes, I have a stove if you want to know. You make it sound like I'm some kind of wild beast that eats and sleeps on the ground, give me a break. I have everything here and I am able to look after myself. I was able to look after your darling daughter too if you want to go there.

Voice I didn't say that. It's just that up until now she did everything.

Father Well, maybe not *everything*. Dinner and lunch, yes. Sometimes. But I was earning the money, let's make that clear. I'd rather not go into it now, but I'm still making hundreds of thousands a month and it's costing me a small fortune that she is messing about playing pretend at the theatre.

Voice Excuse – me. She is not messing about and playing pretend!

Father Alright, I didn't mean it like that, she isn't playing, but we did not live on her income. I hope that you are aware of that. She may be an enormous artist, but you need to live off something somehow. And don't let me fall over with gratitude from the fact that, indeed, she sometimes cooked as well. It's shocking really, as she was at home way more.

Voice I didn't say that.

Father Well. I am glad to hear that you didn't say that, just very subtly dropped hints. That is very thoughtful. I fully furnished the house. Lalika has his own desk – it will be useful when he starts school.

Voice That's good. He will need that small lamp on it to see better. So, you will be alright for a few days, won't you? Look after Lalika, won't you? Things will sort themselves out.

Father Well, I do hope so . . . Why do you keep telling me to take care of Lalika? Eva is constantly saying that too. It is as if he was somebody else's sacred possession, I could borrow for a few days. Like this bloody expensive . . Herendi sugar bowl. I mustn't break it at any rate of course. I look after him, how could I not? Yesterday, Kevin and his father made their depositions.

Voice Kevin? But what can he say? If his little spine is broken . . . He must be better then, if he can speak. Is he better then?

Father Yes. He's doing great, just a tiny bit paralysed from the waist down . . . We wanted to go in to visit him, bring him a present, but his parents won't hear of it. I don't know what they're thinking, but they're very hostile. They're threatening to sue. Can you take Lalika on Thursday?

Voice My poor baby. But if he doesn't wee himself, why take him? He hasn't weed himself, has he?

Father It's not the weeing that's the main issue.

Voice But what is it then? What else is wrong?

Father It's complicated. I think he really would benefit from chatting to someone from time to time to ease his tension.

Voice What tension?

252   The Bat

Father Our lives are hard. Mine too. All of ours. Obviously, he will have a good dose of tension.

Voice I've made some strudel as I went to the market this morning and bought some pumpkin. Will you be able to heat it up?

Father Why do you keep talking to me like I'm some kind of imbecile?

Voice Oh, don't be offended, for heaven's sake. You're too sensitive, son, and so irritable too, my boy, I don't understand. I was simply asking because I will then bring some pumpkin poppy seed dumplings over Lalika loves it. And the strudel too!

Father So, it's all good for Thursday, right?

Voice Yes, it is. of course. Poor Eva love, poor Lalika too. My poor darling. She was so distraught about that part she didn't get. Awful that. I remember she completely lost it at the school carnival once. It was in year two, she dressed up as a leek but there was this other vegetable. I can't remember, maybe a celeriac. She was a fat little girl, called Anita. See, I remember her name, yes she was called Anita. She cried because of her. Went out to the bathroom and just sobbed with green makeup dripping down off her face.

Father A leek?

Voice Yes, she loved leeks, so we wrapped her in green crepe paper, and we put this green ribbon around her head. But maybe it wasn't just the celeriac that upset her but someone asked her if she was a spring fairy. How that poor darling cried, she sobbed. Should I give her a call tonight?

Father Please don't call tonight, better tomorrow after eleven.

Voice Look after Lalika, and please eat.

Scene Thirteen

Father *arrives with a bag.* **Mother** *is sitting on the bench. On the screen we see inside the flat.* **Father** *rings the doorbell.* **Mother** *answers the door.*

Mother I just got in.

Father Gosh, this plant has grown big. It never used to be here.

Mother Listen, did you ask?

Father Let me wash my hands and have a wee.

He steps behind the screen. Sound of water splashing.

Mother Did you ask?

Father I'll tell you in a minute.

He flushes the toilet; we can hear it.

Mother Because at the police station they said that . . .

Father I took all the paperwork, and I went through it with a colleague, because I'm not so savvy with criminal law.

Mother And? What did he say?

Father *sits down next to her, takes out a pile of papers.*

Father Premeditated murder attempt.

Mother What?!

Father It's only an attempt because Kevin didn't die.

Mother But nobody wanted to kill him! It was an accident.

Father Well, that's what you say.

Mother Why, who says otherwise?

Father Kevin's parents.

Mother Parents? His mother wasn't even there. Why is she getting involved in this?

Father Things are not looking good. The responsibility of the nursery teacher also comes into play. Reckless endangerment in the course of duty of care.

Mother Well, interesting that Miss Magda is stained too. Oops.

Father But she testified that she only allowed the child out to use the toilet and that he went out of the building with you both.

Mother I wasn't paying attention. I only noticed when we were at the gate.

Father Why didn't you send him back?

Mother Because . . . because I saw his father coming. I thought . . . they'd go in together to get their stuff.

Father But hers is still only a negligence charge. Yours is potentially a premeditated attempted murder one.

Mother Potentially?

Father Behaviour where the accused saw the possible consequences of their actions and resigned themselves to them.

Mother What?! How would I see that a Honda was going to come and run him over?

Father Luckily though it is not a direct intention, that you intended it to happen. That's more serious.

Mother What do you mean?

Father You could be convicted. Five to ten years.

Mother *jumps up, starts pacing.*

Mother This can't be true. It simply cannot be true. We need to talk to them. I am sure they want money from us, those low lives.

Father They could only claim that in a civil action. Even with the best-case scenario it's gross negligence. It means that the individual in question failed to exercise due care or diligence.

Mother This can't be true. Find me a good lawyer!

Father I don't know anyone better than this one. He is the best. Attempted murder of a juvenile.

Mother I don't understand a word you're saying. Couldn't you for once in your life put it in terms that others could understand? Just once in this fucking life!

Father It's a shitty case. They are claiming that you pushed him onto the road.

Mother It is not TRUE! I told him to wait for his daddy, he'll be here soon, so you stay nicely here until then.

Father You said that.

Mother I did!

The screen shows a black and white image from the nursery security camera. The image shows the figures of **Mother** *and Lalika from slightly above and behind, as they exit the gate, he is next to his* **Mother**. *Then, as the gate opens, another child appears next to the* **Mother**. *The* **Mother** *opens the gate and leans down for a moment, placing her hand on his back. The child then suddenly runs down onto the road. The shot starts again and repeats continuously.*

Father According to the footage you just bent down next to the kid.

Mother To tell him to wait.

Father But it was only a second!

Mother And?

Father You couldn't have said what you just said to me in a second!

Mother I may not have said it like that.

Father But how?

Mother I don't remember. Just differently.

Father I think you need to come up with something, a . . . a two-word sentence that you could have said in that time.

He starts to gather paperwork.

Mother What do you mean, come up with something? You don't believe me? Seriously, do you really think that I . . . that I . . . that I could . . . that I . . . that I would . . . that I would be capable, that I wanted to . . . This can't be happening. I don't believe it.

Father   Look, it will depend on the judge. It's an evidence-based procedure. The court can use any means they want. There are witness interviews, forensic evidence, causation evidence, viewing recordings, a whole lot of things can come up.

He puts everything away, closes his bag.

Mother   I don't understand a word you're saying. I never have. In fact, I never understood a word you said.

Father   I am telling you now. A lot depends on the judge, but it's not looking rosy.

Mother   What should I do? I need to talk to them.

Father   It'll be useless. This is a criminal investigation.

Mother *sits motionless.*

Father   I have to leave soon. What time is your mother bringing Lalika?

Mother   At five. She took him to gym class.

Mother   Lord. Oh my God. Fucking hell. Even this.

She hits herself in the head.

Father   You mustn't despair like this.

Mother   I forgot that the carnival is tomorrow.

Father   So what?

Mother   Lalika. God, I am such a shitty mother! I am! A shitty mother. I completely forgot that it's tomorrow and he doesn't have a costume!

Father   Come up with something easy. He could be . . . a pirate.

Mother   Great that. Kevin's spine is broken, and I bring my kid in with one eye? Are you serious?

Father   Oh yes, sure. So . . . how about. a clown!

Mother   No, he can't. He wants to be a *bat*.

Father *rolls his eyes.*

Father   A bat?!

Mother   He's been saying it for weeks. And I . . . I forgot. Didn't I ? I did that. I forgot. It just slipped my mind. Oh, dear God.

Father   Just give him something black to wear or talk him out of it. Say that they *won't like it.*

Mother *stares angrily.*

Father   That it's not a good time to be a bat . . . He could be Batman!

Mother   But he doesn't want to be Batman. Can you get it through your head that he wants to be a proper, real bat like his lost toy. It's not the same.

Father It's almost the same. Give him a big black jumper.

Mother I don't have a black jumper.

Father Or a coat.

Mother A coat? An adult coat? I don't have a black coat either. Oh yes, I do . . . but it's got these red patterns on it.

Father Do you have a . . . black tablecloth?

Mother No. I don't. This is not a funeral home. Grieving is in the air, yes, and there are candles, but it's not a funeral home. I might be going to prison but I'm not dead yet.

Father Tell them he's got a fever! You could both do with a day off.

Mother But he is looking forward to it! He wants to get dressed up and I have a rehearsal. Wait . . . I've got it.

Father What?

Mother You know that black thingy . . . that you lawyers wear sometimes, you know that . . .

Father What black thingy?!

Mother Yes! You know! The one you had custom-made because the one that was given by the court was polyester and it made you stink.

Father I didn't stink. It's called a robe.

Mother That, yes! Do you have it on you?

Father I am not giving you the robe!

Mother Only for a second! At least let me have a look.

Father Only to look at. I'm not giving it to you! It's only for inspiration.

Mother *immediately grabs it and puts it on.*

Mother And then he opens his arms . . .

Father . . . and will look like a flasher.

Mother You could cut out the sides to make wings.

Father Are you stupid? This is not a toy! Give it back!

Mother It looks really worn out anyway . . .

She is inspecting it.

Father For ten years I have won all my cases in this. Have you lost your mind? It's a . . . it's a work tool! A . . . symbol! A symbol of justice! You are insulting my vocation, you . . . you . . . do you actually want to dissect the truth?

Mother (*sneering*)   You want to dissect the truth? You are insulting my vocation . . . If you could only see yourself sweetheart. And anyway, you said you could rent it at the Bar Association. You once told me.

Father   Did I say that? The things you remember.

Mother   That's exactly what you said. It's a photographic memory. When you once left it at home. We fucked in the morning. We had a massive fuck. And then I called you to say you left it at home.

Father   You need to come up with a short sentence.

Mother *walks up and down wearing the robe.*

She stands behind **Father**. *She raises her hands.*

Father   And it will need two big ears. That can be made of socks.

Mother   Wow! Really. That's very clever that. You clever you, you. From black socks.

Here, two big bat ears. They need to be sewn on somehow.

Father *picks up the robe,* **Mother** *stands behind him. She takes the black socks off her feet and puts them on the* **Father***'s head.*

Mother   Wait here.

Father   Wait for what? You want to take a picture?

Mother   Wait here.

Father   What are you getting ready for? Your mother will soon get here with the kid.

The security camera footage projection is now replaced by the shadow of a running child dressed as a bat. He flies across the road.

Mother (*whispering*)   Wait here.

She stands up on the bench and leans down to the bat.

Wait here.

Father   Shall I close my eyes? Or should I just wait?

Mother   Wait here. This is it. This is short enough. I'm going to tell them this.

The End